FREE Test Taking Tips DVD Offer

To help us better serve you, we have developed a Test Taking Tips DVD that we would like to give you for FREE. **This DVD covers world-class test taking tips that you can use to be even more successful when you are taking your test.**

All that we ask is that you email us your feedback about your study guide. Please let us know what you thought about it – whether that is good, bad or indifferent.

To get your **FREE Test Taking Tips DVD**, email freedvd@studyguideteam.com with "FREE DVD" in the subject line and the following information in the body of the email:

a. The title of your study guide.

b. Your product rating on a scale of 1-5, with 5 being the highest rating.

c. Your feedback about the study guide. What did you think of it?

d. Your full name and shipping address to send your free DVD.

If you have any questions or concerns, please don't hesitate to contact us at freedvd@studyguideteam.com.

Thanks again!

FTCE General Knowledge Test Prep

FTCE Test Prep Team

Table of Contents

Quick Overview

As you draw closer to taking your exam, effective preparation becomes more and more important. Thankfully, you have this study guide to help you get ready. Use this guide to help keep your studying on track and refer to it often.

This study guide contains several key sections that will help you be successful on your exam. The guide contains tips for what you should do the night before and the day of the test. Also included are test-taking tips. Knowing the right information is not always enough. Many well-prepared test takers struggle with exams. These tips will help equip you to accurately read, assess, and answer test questions.

A large part of the guide is devoted to showing you what content to expect on the exam and to helping you better understand that content. Near the end of this guide is a practice test so that you can see how well you have grasped the content. Then, answer explanations are provided so that you can understand why you missed certain questions.

Don't try to cram the night before you take your exam. This is not a wise strategy for a few reasons. First, your retention of the information will be low. Your time would be better used by reviewing information you already know rather than trying to learn a lot of new information. Second, you will likely become stressed as you try to gain a large amount of knowledge in a short amount of time. Third, you will be depriving yourself of sleep. So be sure to go to bed at a reasonable time the night before. Being well-rested helps you focus and remain calm.

Be sure to eat a substantial breakfast the morning of the exam. If you are taking the exam in the afternoon, be sure to have a good lunch as well. Being hungry is distracting and can make it difficult to focus. You have hopefully spent lots of time preparing for the exam. Don't let an empty stomach get in the way of success!

When travelling to the testing center, leave earlier than needed. That way, you have a buffer in case you experience any delays. This will help you remain calm and will keep you from missing your appointment time at the testing center.

Be sure to pace yourself during the exam. Don't try to rush through the exam. There is no need to risk performing poorly on the exam just so you can leave the testing center early. Allow yourself to use all of the allotted time if needed.

Remain positive while taking the exam even if you feel like you are performing poorly. Thinking about the content you should have mastered will not help you perform better on the exam.

Once the exam is complete, take some time to relax. Even if you feel that you need to take the exam again, you will be well served by some down time before you begin studying again. It's often easier to convince yourself to study if you know that it will come with a reward!

Test-Taking Strategies

1. Predicting the Answer

When you feel confident in your preparation for a multiple-choice test, try predicting the answer before reading the answer choices. This is especially useful on questions that test objective factual knowledge or that ask you to fill in a blank. By predicting the answer before reading the available choices, you eliminate the possibility that you will be distracted or led astray by an incorrect answer choice. You will feel more confident in your selection if you read the question, predict the answer, and then find your prediction among the answer choices. After using this strategy, be sure to still read all of the answer choices carefully and completely. If you feel unprepared, you should not attempt to predict the answers. This would be a waste of time and an opportunity for your mind to wander in the wrong direction.

2. Reading the Whole Question

Too often, test takers scan a multiple-choice question, recognize a few familiar words, and immediately jump to the answer choices. Test authors are aware of this common impatience, and they will sometimes prey upon it. For instance, a test author might subtly turn the question into a negative, or he or she might redirect the focus of the question right at the end. The only way to avoid falling into these traps is to read the entirety of the question carefully before reading the answer choices.

3. Looking for Wrong Answers

Long and complicated multiple-choice questions can be intimidating. One way to simplify a difficult multiple-choice question is to eliminate all of the answer choices that are clearly wrong. In most sets of answers, there will be at least one selection that can be dismissed right away. If the test is administered on paper, the test taker could draw a line through it to indicate that it may be ignored; otherwise, the test taker will have to perform this operation mentally or on scratch paper. In either case, once the obviously incorrect answers have been eliminated, the remaining choices may be considered. Sometimes identifying the clearly wrong answers will give the test taker some information about the correct answer. For instance, if one of the remaining answer choices is a direct opposite of one of the eliminated answer choices, it may well be the correct answer. The opposite of obviously wrong is obviously right! Of course, this is not always the case. Some answers are obviously incorrect simply because they are irrelevant to the question being asked. Still, identifying and eliminating some incorrect answer choices is a good way to simplify a multiple-choice question.

4. Don't Overanalyze

Anxious test takers often overanalyze questions. When you are nervous, your brain will often run wild, causing you to make associations and discover clues that don't actually exist. If you feel that this may be a problem for you, do whatever you can to slow down during the test. Try taking a deep breath or counting to ten. As you read and consider the question, restrict yourself to the particular words used by the author. Avoid thought tangents about what the author *really* meant, or what he or she was *trying* to say. The only things that matter on a multiple-choice test are the words that are actually in the question. You must avoid reading too much into a multiple-choice question, or supposing that the writer meant something other than what he or she wrote.

5. No Need for Panic

It is wise to learn as many strategies as possible before taking a multiple-choice test, but it is likely that you will come across a few questions for which you simply don't know the answer. In this situation, avoid panicking. Because most multiple-choice tests include dozens of questions, the relative value of a single wrong answer is small. Moreover, your failure on one question has no effect on your success elsewhere on the test. As much as possible, you should compartmentalize each question on a multiple-choice test. In other words, you should not allow your feelings about one question to affect your success on the others. When you find a question that you either don't understand or don't know how to answer, just take a deep breath and do your best. Read the entire question slowly and carefully. Try rephrasing the question a couple of different ways. Then, read all of the answer choices carefully. After eliminating obviously wrong answers, make a selection and move on to the next question.

6. Confusing Answer Choices

When working on a difficult multiple-choice question, there may be a tendency to focus on the answer choices that are the easiest to understand. Many people, whether consciously or not, gravitate to the answer choices that require the least concentration, knowledge, and memory. This is a mistake. When you come across an answer choice that is confusing, you should give it extra attention. A question might be confusing because you do not know the subject matter to which it refers. If this is the case, don't eliminate the answer before you have affirmatively settled on another. When you come across an answer choice of this type, set it aside as you look at the remaining choices. If you can confidently assert that one of the other choices is correct, you can leave the confusing answer aside. Otherwise, you will need to take a moment to try to better understand the confusing answer choice. Rephrasing is one way to tease out the sense of a confusing answer choice.

7. Your First Instinct

Many people struggle with multiple-choice tests because they overthink the questions. If you have studied sufficiently for the test, you should be prepared to trust your first instinct once you have carefully and completely read the question and all of the answer choices. There is a great deal of research suggesting that the mind can come to the correct conclusion very quickly once it has obtained all of the relevant information. At times, it may seem to you as if your intuition is working faster even than your reasoning mind. This may in fact be true. The knowledge you obtain while studying may be retrieved from your subconscious before you have a chance to work out the associations that support it. Verify your instinct by working out the reasons that it should be trusted.

8. Key Words

Many test takers struggle with multiple-choice questions because they have poor reading comprehension skills. Quickly reading and understanding a multiple-choice question requires a mixture of skill and experience. To help with this, try jotting down a few key words and phrases on a piece of scrap paper. Doing this concentrates the process of reading and forces the mind to weigh the relative importance of the question's parts. In selecting words and phrases to write down, the test taker thinks about the question more deeply and carefully. This is especially true for multiple-choice questions that are preceded by a long prompt.

9. Subtle Negatives

One of the oldest tricks in the multiple-choice test writer's book is to subtly reverse the meaning of a question with a word like *not* or *except.* If you are not paying attention to each word in the question, you can easily be led astray by this trick. For instance, a common question format is, "Which of the following is...?" Obviously, if the question instead is, "Which of the following is not...?," then the answer will be quite different. Even worse, the test makers are aware of the potential for this mistake and will include one answer choice that would be correct if the question were not negated or reversed. A test taker who misses the reversal will find what he or she believes to be a correct answer and will be so confident that he or she will fail to reread the question and discover the original error. The only way to avoid this is to practice a wide variety of multiple-choice questions and to pay close attention to each and every word.

10. Reading Every Answer Choice

It may seem obvious, but you should always read every one of the answer choices! Too many test takers fall into the habit of scanning the question and assuming that they understand the question because they recognize a few key words. From there, they pick the first answer choice that answers the question they believe they have read. Test takers who read all of the answer choices might discover that one of the latter answer choices is actually *more* correct. Moreover, reading all of the answer choices can remind you of facts related to the question that can help you arrive at the correct answer. Sometimes, a misstatement or incorrect detail in one of the latter answer choices will trigger your memory of the subject and will enable you to find the right answer. Failing to read all of the answer choices is like not reading all of the items on a restaurant menu: you might miss out on the perfect choice.

11. Spot the Hedges

One of the keys to success on multiple-choice tests is paying close attention to every word. This is never more true than with words like *almost, most, some,* and *sometimes.* These words are called "hedges" because they indicate that a statement is not totally true or not true in every place and time. An absolute statement will contain no hedges, but in many subjects, like literature and history, the answers are not always straightforward or absolute. There are always exceptions to the rules in these subjects. For this reason, you should favor those multiple-choice questions that contain hedging language. The presence of qualifying words indicates that the author is taking special care with his or her words, which is certainly important when composing the right answer. After all, there are many ways to be wrong, but there is only one way to be right! For this reason, it is wise to avoid answers that are absolute when taking a multiple-choice test. An absolute answer is one that says things are either all one way or all another. They often include words like *every, always, best,* and *never.* If you are taking a multiple-choice test in a subject that doesn't lend itself to absolute answers, be on your guard if you see any of these words.

12. Long Answers

In many subject areas, the answers are not simple. As already mentioned, the right answer often requires hedges. Another common feature of the answers to a complex or subjective question are qualifying clauses, which are groups of words that subtly modify the meaning of the sentence. If the question or answer choice describes a rule to which there are exceptions or the subject matter is complicated, ambiguous, or confusing, the correct answer will require many words in order to be expressed clearly and accurately. In essence, you should not be deterred by answer choices that seem excessively long. Oftentimes, the author of the text will not be able to write the correct answer without offering some qualifications and modifications. Your job is to read the answer choices thoroughly and completely and to select the one that most accurately and precisely answers the question.

13. Restating to Understand

Sometimes, a question on a multiple-choice test is difficult not because of what it asks but because of how it is written. If this is the case, restate the question or answer choice in different words. This process serves a couple of important purposes. First, it forces you to concentrate on the core of the question. In order to rephrase the question accurately, you have to understand it well. Rephrasing the question will concentrate your mind on the key words and ideas. Second, it will present the information to your mind in a fresh way. This process may trigger your memory and render some useful scrap of information picked up while studying.

14. True Statements

Sometimes an answer choice will be true in itself, but it does not answer the question. This is one of the main reasons why it is essential to read the question carefully and completely before proceeding to the answer choices. Too often, test takers skip ahead to the answer choices and look for true statements. Having found one of these, they are content to select it without reference to the question above. Obviously, this provides an easy way for test makers to play tricks. The savvy test taker will always read the entire question before turning to the answer choices. Then, having settled on a correct answer choice, he or she will refer to the original question and ensure that the selected answer is relevant. The mistake of choosing a correct-but-irrelevant answer choice is especially common on questions related to specific pieces of objective knowledge, like historical or scientific facts. A prepared test taker will have a wealth of factual knowledge at his or her disposal, and should not be careless in its application.

15. No Patterns

One of the more dangerous ideas that circulates about multiple-choice tests is that the correct answers tend to fall into patterns. These erroneous ideas range from a belief that B and C are the most common right answers, to the idea that an unprepared test-taker should answer "A-B-A-C-A-D-A-B-A." It cannot be emphasized enough that pattern-seeking of this type is exactly the WRONG way to approach a multiple-choice test. To begin with, it is highly unlikely that the test maker will plot the correct answers according to some predetermined pattern. The questions are scrambled and delivered in a random order. Furthermore, even if the test maker was following a pattern in the assignation of correct answers, there is no reason why the test taker would know which pattern he or she was using. Any attempt to discern a pattern in the answer choices is a waste of time and a distraction from the real work of taking the test. A test taker would be much better served by extra preparation before the test than by reliance on a pattern in the answers.

FREE DVD OFFER

Don't forget that doing well on your exam includes both understanding the test content and understanding how to use what you know to do well on the test. We offer a completely FREE Test Taking Tips DVD that covers world class test taking tips that you can use to be even more successful when you are taking your test.

All that we ask is that you email us your feedback about your study guide. To get your **FREE Test Taking Tips DVD**, email freedvd@studyguideteam.com with "FREE DVD" in the subject line and the following information in the body of the email:

- The title of your study guide.
- Your product rating on a scale of 1-5, with 5 being the highest rating.
- Your feedback about the study guide. What did you think of it?
- Your full name and shipping address to send your free DVD.

Introduction to FTCE General Knowledge Test

Function of the Test

In order to become a certified teacher in the state of Florida, a candidate must pass the Florida Teacher Certification Examinations (FTCE). In 2001, the No Child Left Behind Act began the administration of the FTCE. These exams are part of a teacher's certification process in the state of Florida. The Bureau of Educator Certification (BEC) determines the specific exams that a candidate needs to take to teach and become certified in Florida. The required tests depend on certifications that a candidate holds in other states or countries, his or her change of career status, and whether the candidate graduated from a teaching institute in Florida. In order to determine which tests to take, a candidate must submit an application to the BEC, whom will then determine a candidate's testing requirements.

The FTCE General Knowledge (GK) exam is a computer-based test (CBT) that assesses the general knowledge of prospective teachers in the state of Florida and is designed to verify that teachers of all grades and subjects have the minimum necessary skills and knowledge across the general curricular areas. As such, all teachers seeking licensure in the state of Florida typically need to pass the GK exam. In some cases, sufficient scores on previously taken GRE exams may satisfy the GK requirement. Candidates must contact the BEC for an individual determination of exam requirements. The GK exam consists of four subtests: an Essay, English Language Skills, Reading, and Mathematics. The subtests may be attempted individually or combined in one testing appointment.

Test Administration

After the BEC determines which tests a candidate needs to take, an applicant can then register for a test; this application process is required prior to registering for the GK exam. Admission tickets are sent via email and must be presented at the test appointment along with proper identification. Exam sites are available throughout Florida and the United States.

A candidate must report to the test site 30 minutes before the appointment time on the admission ticket in order to complete pre-administration activities, such as an identity verification procedure, which includes a photo and palm scan. If a candidate wears glasses, a visual inspection is conducted, but the candidate's glasses will not be handled or touched. All personal items are kept in a secure storage area and a candidate receives an erasable notepad and pen. Then, a tutorial is given on how to take a computer-based test, as well as a test agreement and waiver. These processes need to be completed in 5 minutes. If the waiver is not accepted within 5 minutes, the candidate will be required to wait 31 calendar days before a retest, and he or she will not be given a refund. Breaks for the restroom are counted as part of the test time, unless scheduled breaks are given.

Candidates with disabilities need to complete an Alternative Testing Arrangements Request Form. The form must be submitted to FTCE customer service as soon as possible because test appointment cannot be made until approval.

Test Format

The FTCE GK exam is administered via computer and consists of four subtests. As mentioned, the subtests may be taken individually or in combination at a given testing appointment. A reference sheet with formulas and an on-screen calculator are provided for the Mathematics subtest.

The following table shows the breakdown of the subtests

Subtest	Allotted Time	Approximate Format
Essay	50 minutes	1 essay
English Language Skills	40 minutes	40 multiple choice questions
Reading	55 minutes	40 multiple choice questions
Mathematics	100 minutes	45 multiple choice questions

Test takers are permitted to take a 15-munte break if they are attempting all four subtests in one testing appointment.

Scoring

Test takers receive unofficial notification of their passing status for the multiple-choice subtests immediately upon completion. Official score reports are released within a month of the testing date for the multiple-choice subtests and within 6 weeks for the Essay subtest. Candidates must pass all four subtests in order to pass the General Knowledge exam. The Essay subtest is scored on a 12-point scale and test takers must receive at least an 8 to pass the section. The passing scaled score on each of the other three subtests is 200. Scaled scores are converted from raw scores, based on the number of correct responses. Score reports include an analysis of the test taker's performance for sections that he or she does not pass, as well as the numeric score that was achieved. For subtests that are passed, test takers simply receive the passing status notification but no numerical score is reported. Candidates wishing to take a retest must wait 31 calendar days after the most recent attempt before taking a retest.

English Language Skills

Language Structure

Dangling and Misplaced Modifiers

A *modifier* is a phrase that describes, alters, limits, or gives more information about a word in the sentence. The two most common issues are dangling and misplaced modifiers.

A *dangling modifier* is created when the phrase modifies a word that is not clearly stated in the sentence.

> Dangling modifier: Having finished dinner, the dishes were cleared from the table.
>
> Correction: Having finished dinner, Amy cleared the dishes from the table.

In the first sentence, *having finished dinner* appears to modify *the dishes*, which obviously can't finish dinner. The second sentence adds the subject *Amy*, to make it clear who has finished dinner.

> Dangling modifier: Hoping to improve test scores, all new books were ordered for the school.
>
> Correction: Hoping to improve test scores, administrators ordered all new books for the school.
>
> Without the subject *administrators*, it appears the books are hoping to improve test scores, which doesn't make sense.

Misplaced modifiers are placed incorrectly in the sentence, which can cause confusion. Compare these examples:

> Misplaced modifier: Rory purchased a new flat screen television and placed it on the wall above the fireplace, with all the bells and whistles.
>
> Revised: Rory purchased a new flat screen television, with all the bells and whistles, and placed it on the wall above the fireplace.

The bells and whistles should modify the television, not the fireplace.

> Misplaced modifier: The delivery driver arrived late with the pizza, who was usually on time.
>
> Revised: The delivery driver, who usually was on time, arrived late with the pizza.

This suggests that the delivery driver was usually on time, instead of the pizza.

Misplaced modifier: We saw a family of ducks on the way to church.

Revised: On the way to church, we saw a family of ducks.

The misplaced modifier, here, suggests the *ducks* were on their way to church, instead of the pronoun *we*.

Split Infinitives

An infinitive is made up of the word *to* and a verb, such as: to run, to jump, to ask. A *split infinitive* is created when a word comes between *to* and the verb.

Split infinitive: To quickly run

Correction: To run quickly

Split infinitive: To quietly ask

Correction: To ask quietly

Double Negatives

A *double negative* is a negative statement that includes two negative elements. This is incorrect in Standard English.

Incorrect: She hasn't never come to my house to visit.

Correct: She has never come to my house to visit.

The intended meaning is that she has never come to the house, so the double negative is incorrect. However, it is possible to use two negatives to create a positive statement.

Correct: She was not unhappy with her performance on the quiz.

In this case, the double negative, *was not unhappy*, is intended to show a positive, so it is correct. This means that she was somewhat happy with her performance.

Faulty Parallelism

It is necessary to use parallel construction in sentences that have multiple similar ideas. Using parallel structure provides clarity in writing. *Faulty parallelism* is created when multiple ideas are joined using different sentence structures. Compare these examples:

Incorrect: We start each practice with stretches, a run, and fielding grounders.
Correct: We start each practice with stretching, running, and fielding grounders.

Incorrect: I watched some television, reading my book, and fell asleep.
Correct: I watched some television, read my book, and fell asleep.

Incorrect: *Some of the readiness skills for Kindergarten are to cut with scissors, to tie shoes, and dressing independently.*
Correct: *Some of the readiness skills for Kindergarten are being able to cut with scissors, to tie shoes, and to dress independently.*

Subordination

If multiple pieces of information in a sentence are not equal, they can be joined by creating an independent clause and a dependent clause. The less important information becomes the *subordinate clause*:

Draft: The hotel was acceptable. We wouldn't stay at the hotel again.

Revised: Though the hotel was acceptable, we wouldn't stay there again.

The more important information (*we wouldn't stay there again*) becomes the main clause, and the less important information (*the hotel was acceptable*) becomes the subordinate clause.

Homonyms

Homonyms are words that sound the same but are spelled differently, and they have different meanings. There are several common homonyms that give writers trouble.

<u>*There, They're*, and *Their*</u>
The word *there* can be used as an adverb, adjective, or pronoun:

There are ten children on the swim team this summer.

I put my book over *there*, but now I can't find it.

The word *they're* is a contraction of the words *they* and *are*:

They're flying in from Texas on Tuesday.

The word *their* is a possessive pronoun:

I store *their* winter clothes in the attic.

<u>*Its* and *It's*</u>
Its is a possessive pronoun:

The cat licked *its* injured paw.

It's is the contraction for the words *it* and *is*:

It's unbelievable how many people opted not to vote in the last election.

<u>Your and You're</u>
Your is a possessive pronoun:

Can I borrow *your* lawnmower this weekend?

You're is a contraction for the words *you* and *are*:

You're about to embark on a fantastic journey.

To, Too, and *Two*

To is an adverb or a preposition used to show direction, relationship, or purpose:

We are going *to* New York.

They are going *to* see a show.

Too is an adverb that means more than enough, also, and very:

You have had *too* much candy.

We are on vacation that week, *too*.

Two is the written-out form of the numeral 2:

Two of the shirts didn't fit, so I will have to return them.

New and *Knew*

New is an adjective that means recent:

There's a *new* customer on the phone.

Knew is the past tense of the verb *know*:

I *knew* you'd have fun on this ride.

Affect and *Effect*

Affect and *effect* are complicated because they are used as both nouns and verbs, have similar meanings, and are pronounced the same.

	Affect	**Effect**
Noun Definition	emotional state	result
Noun Example	The patient's affect was flat.	The effects of smoking are well documented.
Verb Definition	to influence	to bring about
Verb Example	The pollen count affects my allergies.	The new candidate hopes to effect change.

Independent and Dependent Clauses

Independent and *dependent* clauses are strings of words that contain both a subject and a verb. An independent clause *can* stand alone as complete thought, but a dependent clause *cannot*. A dependent clause relies on other words to be a complete sentence.

Independent clause: The keys are on the counter.
Dependent clause: If the keys are on the counter

Notice that both clauses have a subject (*keys*) and a verb (*are*). The independent clause expresses a complete thought, but the word *if* at the beginning of the dependent clause makes it *dependent* on other words to be a complete thought.

Independent clause: If the keys are on the counter, please give them to me.

This presents a complete sentence since it includes at least one verb and one subject and is a complete thought. In this case, the independent clause has two subjects (*keys* & an implied *you*) and two verbs (*are* & *give*).

Independent clause: I went to the store.
Dependent clause: Because we are out of milk,

Complete Sentence: Because we are out of milk, I went to the store.
Complete Sentence: I went to the store because we are out of milk.

Phrases

A *phrase* is a group of words that do not make a complete thought or a clause. They are parts of sentences or clauses. Phrases can be used as nouns, adjectives, or adverbs. A phrase does not contain both a subject and a verb.

Prepositional Phrases

A *prepositional phrase* shows the relationship between a word in the sentence and the object of the preposition. The object of the preposition is a noun that follows the preposition.

The orange pillows are on the couch.

On is the preposition, and *couch* is the object of the preposition.

She brought her friend with the nice car.

With is the preposition, and *car* is the object of the preposition. Here are some common prepositions:

about	as	at	after
by	for	from	in
of	on	to	with

Verbals and Verbal Phrases

Verbals are forms of verbs that act as other parts of speech. They can be used as nouns, adjectives, or adverbs. Though they are use verb forms, they are not to be used as the verb in the sentence. A word group that is based on a verbal is considered a *verbal phrase*. There are three major types of verbals: *participles, gerunds,* and *infinitives.*

Participles are verbals that act as adjectives. The present participle ends in *–ing*, and the past participle ends in *–d*, *-ed*, *-n*, or *-t*.

Verb	**Present Participle**	**Past Participle**
walk	walking	walked
share	sharing	shared

Participial phrases are made up of the participle and modifiers, complements, or objects.

Crying for most of an hour, the baby didn't seem to want to nap.

Having already taken this course, the student was bored during class.

Crying for most of an hour and *Having already taken this course* are the participial phrases.

Gerunds are verbals that are used as nouns and end in *–ing*. A gerund can be the subject or object of the sentence like a noun. Note that a present participle can also end in *–ing*, so it is important to distinguish between the two. The gerund is used as a noun, while the participle is used as an adjective.

Swimming is my favorite sport.

I wish I were sleeping.

A *gerund phrase* includes the gerund and any modifiers or complements, direct objects, indirect objects, or pronouns.

Cleaning the house is my least favorite weekend activity.

Cleaning the house is the gerund phrase acting as the subject of the sentence.

The most important goal this year is raising money for charity.

Raising money for charity is the gerund phrase acting as the direct object.

The police accused the woman of stealing the car.

The *gerund* phrase *stealing the car* is the object of the preposition in this sentence.

An *infinitive* is a verbal made up of the word to and a verb. Infinitives can be used as nouns, adjectives, or adverbs.

Examples: To eat, to jump, to swim, to lie, to call, to work

An *infinitive phrase* is made up of the infinitive plus any complements or modifiers. The infinitive phrase *to wait* is used as the subject in this sentence:

To wait was not what I had in mind.

The infinitive phrase *to sing* is used as the subject complement in this sentence:

Her dream is to sing.

The infinitive phrase *to grow* is used as an adverb in this sentence:

Children must eat to grow.

Appositive Phrases

An *appositive* is a noun or noun phrase that renames a noun that comes immediately before it in the sentence. An appositive can be a single word or several words. These phrases can be *essential* or *nonessential*. An essential appositive phrase is necessary to the meaning of the sentence and a nonessential appositive phrase is not. It is important to be able to distinguish these for purposes of comma use.

Essential: My sister Christina works at a school.

Naming which sister is essential to the meaning of the sentence, so no commas are needed.

Nonessential: My sister, who is a teacher, is coming over for dinner tonight.

Who is a teacher is not essential to the meaning of the sentence, so commas are required.

Absolute Phrases

An *absolute phrase* modifies a noun without using a conjunction. It is not the subject of the sentence and is not a complete thought on its own. Absolute phrases are set off from the independent clause with a comma.

Arms outstretched, she yelled at the sky.

All things considered, this has been a great day.

The Four Types of Sentence Structures

A *simple sentence* has one independent clause.

I am going to win.

A *compound sentence* has two independent clauses. A conjunction—*for, and, nor, but, or, yet, so*—links them together. Note that each of the independent clauses has a subject and a verb.

I am going to win, but the odds are against me.

A *complex sentence* has one independent clause and one or more dependent clauses.

I am going to win, even though I don't deserve it.

Even though I don't deserve it is a dependent clause. It does not stand on its own. Some conjunctions that link an independent and a dependent clause are *although, because, before, after, that, when, which*, and *while*.

A *compound-complex sentence* has at least three clauses, two of which are independent and at least one that is a dependent clause.

While trying to dance, I tripped over my partner's feet, but I regained my balance quickly.

The dependent clause is *While trying to dance*.

Sentence Fragments

A *sentence fragment* is an incomplete sentence. An independent clause is made up of a subject and a predicate, and both are needed to make a complete sentence.

Sentence fragments often begin with *relative pronouns* (when, which), *subordinating conjunctions* (because, although) or *gerunds* (trying, being, seeing). They might be missing the subject or the predicate.

The most common type of fragment is the isolated dependent clause, which can be corrected by joining it to the independent clause that appears before or after the fragment:

> Fragment: While the cookies baked.
>
> Correction: While the cookies baked, we played cards. (We played cards while the cookies baked.)

Run-on Sentences

A *run-on sentence* is created when two independent clauses (complete thoughts) are joined without correct punctuation or a conjunction. Run-on sentences can be corrected in the following ways:

- Join the independent clauses with a comma and coordinating conjunction.

  > Run-on: We forgot to return the library books we had to pay a fine.
  >
  > Correction: We forgot to return the library books, so we had to pay a fine.

- Join the independent clauses with a semicolon, dash, or colon when the clauses are closely related in meaning.

  > Run-on: I had a salad for lunch every day this week I feel healthier already.
  >
  > Correction: I had a salad for lunch every day this week; I feel healthier already.

- Join the independent clauses with a semicolon and a conjunctive adverb.

  > Run-on: We arrived at the animal shelter on time however the dog had already been adopted.
  >
  > Correction: We arrived at the animal shelter on time; however, the dog had already been adopted.

- Separate the independent clauses into two sentences with a period.

  > Run-on: He tapes his favorite television show he never misses an episode.
  >
  > Correction: He tapes his favorite television show. He never misses an episode.

- Rearrange the wording of the sentence to create an independent clause and a dependent clause.

Run-on: My wedding date is coming up I am getting more excited to walk down the aisle.

Correction: As my wedding date approaches, I am getting more excited to walk down the aisle.

Identifying Modes of Writing

Distinguishing Between Common Modes of Writing

To distinguish between the common modes of writing, it is important to identify the primary purpose of the work. This can be determined by considering what the author is trying to say to the reader. Although there are countless different styles of writing, all written works tend to fall under four primary categories: argumentative/persuasive, informative expository, descriptive, and narrative.

The below table highlights the purpose, distinct characteristics, and examples of each rhetorical mode.

Writing Mode	Purpose	Distinct Characteristics	Examples
Argumentative	To persuade	Opinions, loaded or subjective language, evidence, suggestions of what the reader should do, calls to action	Critical reviews Political journals Letters of recommendation Cover letters Advertising
Informative	To teach or inform	Objective language, definitions, instructions, factual information	Business and scientific reports Textbooks Instruction manuals News articles Personal letters Wills Informative essays Travel guides Study guides
Descriptive	To deliver sensory details to the reader	Heavy use of adjectives and imagery, language that appeals to any of the five senses	Poetry Journal entries Often used in narrative mode
Narrative	To tell a story, share an experience, entertain	Series of events, plot, characters, dialogue, conflict	Novels Short stories Novellas Anecdotes Biographies Epic poems Autobiographies

Identifying Common Types of Writing

The following steps help to identify examples of common types within the modes of writing:

1. 1. Identifying the audience—to whom or for whom the author is writing
2. 2. Determining the author's purpose—why the author is writing the piece
3. 3. Analyzing the word choices and how they are used

To demonstrate, the following passage has been marked to illustrate *the addressee*, the author's purpose, and word choices:

> *To Whom It May Concern*:
>
> I am extraordinarily excited to be applying to the Master of Environmental Science program at Australian National University. I believe the richness in biological and cultural diversity, as well as Australia's close proximity to the Great Barrier Reef, would provide a deeply fulfilling educational experience. *I am writing to express why I believe I would be an excellent addition to the program.*
>
> While in college, I participated in a three-month public health internship in Ecuador, where I spent time both learning about medicine in a third world country and also about the Ecuadorian environment, including the Amazon Jungle and the Galápagos Islands. My favorite experience through the internship, besides swimming with sea lions in San Cristóbal, was helping to neutralize parasitic potable water and collect samples for analysis in Puyo.
>
> Though my undergraduate studies related primarily to the human body, I took several courses in natural science, including a year of chemistry, biology, and physics as well as a course in a calculus. I am confident that my fundamental knowledge in these fields will prepare me for the science courses integral to the Masters of Environmental Science.

Having identified the *addressee*, it is evident that this selection is a letter of some kind. Further inspection into the author's purpose, seen in *bold*, shows that the author is trying to explain why he or she should be accepted into the environmental science program, which automatically places it into the argumentative mode as the writer is trying to persuade the reader to agree and to incite the reader into action by encouraging the program to accept the writer as a candidate. In addition to revealing the purpose, the use of emotional language—extraordinarily, excellent, deeply fulfilling, favorite experience, confident—illustrates that this is a persuasive piece. It also provides evidence for why this person would be an excellent addition to the program—his/her experience in Ecuador and with scientific curriculum.

The following passage presents an opportunity to solidify this method of analysis and practice the steps above to determine the mode of writing:

> The biological effects of laughter have long been an interest of medicine and psychology. Laughing is often speculated to reduce blood pressure because it induces feelings of relaxation and elation. Participating students watched a series of videos that elicited laughter, and their blood pressure was taken before and after the viewings. An average decrease in blood pressure was observed, though resulting p-values attest that the results were not significant.

This selection contains factual and scientific information, is devoid of any adjectives or flowery descriptions, and is not trying to convince the reader of any particular stance. Though the audience is not directly addressed, the purpose of the passage is to present the results of an experiment to those who would be interested in the biological effects of laughter—most likely a scientific community. Thus, this passage is an example of informative writing.

Below is another passage to help identify examples of the common writing modes, taken from *The Endeavor Journal of Sir Joseph Banks*:

10th May 1769 – THE ENGLISH CREW GET TAHITIAN NAMES

> We have now got the Indian name of the Island, Otahite, so therefore for the future I shall call it. As for our own names the Indians find so much difficulty in pronouncing them that we are forced to indulge them in calling us what they please, or rather what they say when they attempt to pronounce them. I give here the List: Captn Cooke *Toote*, Dr Solander *Torano*, Mr. Hicks *Hete*, Mr. Gore *Toárro*, Mr. Molineux *Boba* from his Christian name Robert, Mr. Monkhouse *Mato*, and myself *Tapáne*. In this manner, they have names for almost every man in the ship.

This extract contains no elements of an informative or persuasive intent and does not seem to follow any particular line of narrative. The passage gives a list of the different names that the Indians have given the crew members, as well as the name of an island. Although there is no context for the selection, through the descriptions, it is clear that the author and his comrades are on an island trying to communicate with the native inhabitants. Hence, this passage is a journal that reflects the descriptive mode.

These are only a few of the many examples that can be found in the four primary modes of writing.

<u>Determining the Appropriate Mode of Writing</u>
The author's *primary purpose* is defined as the reason an author chooses to write a selection, and it is often dependent on his or her *audience*. A biologist writing a textbook, for example, does so to communicate scientific knowledge to an audience of people who want to study biology. An audience can be as broad as the entire global population or as specific as women fighting for equal rights in the bicycle repair industry. Whatever the audience, it is important that the author considers its demographics—age, gender, culture, language, education level, etc.

If the author's purpose is to persuade or inform, he or she will consider how much the intended audience knows about the subject. For example, if an author is writing on the importance of recycling to anyone who will listen, he or she will use the informative mode—including background information on recycling—and the argumentative mode—evidence for why it works, while also using simple diction so that it is easy for everyone to understand. If, on the other hand, the writer is proposing new methods for recycling using solar energy, the audience is probably already familiar with standard recycling processes and will require less background information, as well as more technical language inherent to the scientific community.

If the author's purpose is to entertain through a story or a poem, he or she will need to consider whom he/she is trying to entertain. If an author is writing a script for a children's cartoon, the plot, language, conflict, characters, and humor would align with the interests of the age demographic of that audience. On the other hand, if an author is trying to entertain adults, he or she may write content not suitable for children. The author's purpose and audience are generally interdependent.

Vocabulary Application

Basic Components of Vocabulary and Strategies to Help Students Determine the Meaning of Unknown Words

Vocabulary

Vocabulary consists of the bank of words that students can understand and apply fluently in order to communicate effectively. A strong vocabulary and word recognition base enables students to access prior knowledge and experiences in order to make connections in written texts. A strong vocabulary also allows students to express ideas, learn new concepts, and decode the meanings of unfamiliar words by using context clues. Conversely, if a child's vocabulary knowledge is limited and does not steadily increase, reading comprehension will be negatively affected. If students become frustrated with their lack of understanding of written texts, they will likely choose to only read texts at their comfort level or refuse to read altogether. With direct instruction, educators introduce specific words to pre-teach before reading, or examine word roots, prefixes, and suffixes. Through indirect instruction, educators ensure that students are regularly exposed to new words. This engages students in high-quality conversations and social interactions and provides access to a wide variety of challenging and enjoyable reading material.

Morphology

The study of morphology generally deals with the structure and formation of words. A phoneme is the smallest unit of sound that does not necessarily carry meaning. Essentially, phonemes are combined to form words, and words are combined to form sentences. Morphology looks at the smallest meaningful part of a word, known as a morpheme. In contrast to a phoneme, a morpheme must carry a sound and a meaning. Free morphemes are those that can stand alone, carrying both sound and meaning, as in the following words: girl, boy, man, and lady. Just as the name suggests, bound morphemes are bound to other morphemes in order to carry meaning. Examples of bound morphemes include: ish, ness, ly, and dis.

Semantics

Semantics is the branch of linguistics that addresses meanings. Morphemes, words, phrases, and sentences all carry distinct meanings. The way these individual parts are arranged can have a significant effect on meaning. In order to construct language, students must be able to use semantics to arrange and rearrange words to achieve the particular meaning they are striving for. Activities that teach semantics revolve around teaching the arrangement of word parts (morphology) and root words, and then the teaching of vocabulary. Moving from vocabulary words into studying sentences and sentence structure leads students to learn how to use context clues to determine meaning and to understand anomalies such as metaphors, idioms, and allusions. There are five types of semantic relationships that are critical to understand:

Hyponyms refer to a relationship between words where general words have multiple more-specific words (hyponyms) that fall into the same category (e.g., horse: mare, stallion, foal, Appaloosa, Clydesdale).

Meronyms refer to a relationship between words where a whole word has multiple parts (meronyms) that comprise it (e.g., horse: tail, mane, hooves, ears).

Synonyms refer to words that have the same meaning as another word (e.g., instructor/teacher/educator, canine/dog, feline/cat, herbivore/vegetarian).

Antonyms refer to words that have the opposite meaning as another word (e.g., true/false, up/down, in/out, right/wrong).

Homonyms refer to words that are spelled the same (homographs) or sound the same (homophones) but mean different things (e.g., there/their/they're, two/too/to, principal/principle, plain/plane, (kitchen) sink/ sink (down as in water)).

<u>Syntax</u>

With its origins from the Greek word, "syntaxis," which means arrangement, *syntax* is the study of phrase and sentence formation. The study of syntax focuses on the ways in which specific words can be combined to create coherent meaning. For example: the simple rearrangement of the words, "I can run," is different from the question, "Can I run?" which is also different from the meaningless "Run I can."

The following methods can be used to teach syntax:

Proper Syntax Modeling: Students don't need to be corrected for improper syntax. Instead, they should be shown ways to rephrase what they said with proper syntax. If a student says, "Run I can," then the teacher should say, "Oh, you can run how fast?" This puts syntax in place with conversational skills.

Open-Ended Sentences: Students can complete open-ended sentences with proper syntax both orally and in written format, or they can correct sentences that have improper syntax so that they make sense.

Listening for Syntax: Syntax is auditory. Students can often hear a syntax error before they can see it in writing. Teachers should have students use word cards or word magnets to arrange and rearrange simple sentences and read them aloud to check for syntax.

Repetition: Syntax can be practiced by using songs, poems, and rhymes for repetitive automation.

<u>Pragmatics</u>

Pragmatics is the study of what words mean in certain situations. It helps to understand the intentions and interpretations of intentions through words used in human interaction. Different listeners and different situations call for different language and intonations of language. When people engage in a conversation, it is usually to convey a certain message, and the message (even using the same words) can change depending on the setting and the audience. The more fluent the speaker, the more success she or he will have in conveying the intended message.

The following methods can be used to teach pragmatics:

When students state something incorrectly, a response can be given to what they intended to say in the first place. For instance, if a student says, "That's how it didn't happen." Then the teacher might say, "Of course, that's not how it happened." Instead of putting students on defense by being corrected, this method puts them at ease and helps them learn.

Role-playing conversations with different people in different situations can help teach pragmatics. For example, pretend playing can be used where a situation remains the same but the audience changes, or the audience stays the same but the situations change. This can be followed with a discussion about how language and intonations change too.

Different ways to convey a message can be used, such as asking vs. persuading, or giving direct vs. indirect requests and polite vs. impolite messages.

Various non-verbal signals can be used to see how they change pragmatics. For example, students can be encouraged to use mismatched words and facial expressions, such as angry words while smiling or happy words while pretending to cry.

Strategies to Help Read New and/or Difficult Words

Students who are developing reading fluency and comprehension skills can become frustrated when presented with unfamiliar words in a given text. With direct phonics instruction, educators can teach students to decode words and then use context clues to define the words while reading. If students have a strong enough understanding of language structures, including nouns and verbs, educators can ask them to consider what part of speech the unknown word might be based on and where it might fit into the sentence. Other useful strategies involve self-monitoring, in which students are asked to think as they read and ask themselves if what they have just read makes sense. Focusing on visual clues, such as drawings and photographs, may give students valuable insight into deciphering unknown words. Looking for the word in another section of the text to see how it relates to the overall meaning could give a clue to the new vocabulary word. Spelling the word out loud or looking for word chunks, prefixes, and suffixes, as well as demonstrating how to segment the unknown word into its individual syllables, may also be effective strategies to employ.

One of the most valuable strategies, however, for helping students to read and understand new words is pre-teaching. In this strategy, educators select what they evaluate to be the unfamiliar words in the text and then introduce them to the class before reading. Educators using this method should be careful not to simply ask the students to read the text and then spell the new words correctly. They should also provide clear definitions and give the students the opportunity to read these words in various sentences to decipher word meaning. This method can dramatically reduce how often students stop reading in order to reflect on unknown words. Educators are often unsure as to whether to correct every mispronounced word a student makes when reading. If the mispronounced word still makes sense, it is sometimes better to allow the student to continue to read, since the more the student stops, the more the student's reading comprehension and fluency are negatively affected.

Identifying Dialect and Diction

Identifying Variation in Dialect and Diction

Language arts educators often seem to be in the position of teaching the "right" way to use English, particularly in lessons about grammar and vocabulary. However, all it takes is back-to-back viewings of speeches by the queen of England and the president of the United States or side-by-side readings of a contemporary poem and one written in the 1600s to come to the conclusion that there is no single, fixed, correct form of spoken or written English. Instead, language varies and evolves across different regions and time periods. It also varies between cultural groups depending on factors such as race, ethnicity, age, and socioeconomic status. Students should come away from a language arts class with more than a strictly prescriptive view of language; they should have an appreciation for its rich diversity.

It is important to understand some key terms in discussing linguistic variety.

Language is a tool for communication. It may be spoken, unspoken—as with body language—written, or codified in other ways. Language is symbolic in the sense that it can describe objects, ideas, and events that are not actually present, have not actually occurred, or only exist in the mind of the speaker. All languages are governed by systematic rules of grammar and semantics. These rules allow speakers to manipulate a finite number of elements, such as sounds or written symbols, to create an infinite number of meanings.

A *dialect* is a distinct variety of a language in terms of patterns of grammar, vocabulary, and/or *phonology*—the sounds used by its speakers—that distinguish it from other forms of that language. Two dialects are not considered separate languages if they are *mutually intelligible*—if speakers of each dialect are able to understand one another. A dialect is not a subordinate version of a language. Examples of English dialects include Scottish English and American Southern English.

By definition, *Standard English* is a dialect. It is one variety of English with its own usage of grammar, vocabulary, and pronunciation. Given that Standard English is taught in schools and used in places like government, journalism, and other professional workplaces, it is often elevated above other English dialects. Linguistically, though, there is nothing that makes Standard English more correct or advanced than other dialects.

A *pidgin* is formed when speakers of different languages begin utilizing a simplified mixture of elements from both languages to communicate with each other. In North America, pidgins occurred when Africans were brought to European colonies as slaves, leading to a mixture of African and European languages. Historically, pidgins also sprung up in areas of international trade. A pidgin is communication born of necessity and lacks the full complexity or standardized rules that govern a language.

When a pidgin becomes widely used and is taught to children as their native language, it becomes a *Creole*. An example is Haitian Creole, a language based on French and including elements of West African languages.

An *accent* is a unique speech pattern, particularly in terms of tone or intonation. Speakers from different regions tend to have different accents, as do learners of English from different native languages. In some cases, accents are mutually intelligible, but in other cases, speakers with different accents might have some difficulty in understanding one another.

Colloquial language is language that is used conversationally or familiarly—e.g., "What's up?"—in contrast to formal, professional, or academic language— "How are you this evening?"

Vernacular refers to the native, everyday language of a place. Historically, for instance, Bibles and religious services across Europe were primarily offered in Latin, even centuries after the fall of the Roman Empire. After the revolution of the printing press and the widespread availability of vernacular translations of the Bible in the fifteenth and sixteenth centuries, everyday citizens were able to study from Bibles in their own language without needing specialized training in Latin.

A *regionalism* is a word or expression used in a particular region. In the United States, for instance, examples of regionalisms might be *soda*, *pop*, or *Coke*—terms that vary in popularity according to region.

Jargon is vocabulary used within a specialized field, such as computer programming or mechanics. Jargon may consist of specialized words or of everyday words that have a different meaning in this specialized context.

Slang refers to non-standard expressions that are not used in elevated speech and writing. Slang creates linguistic in-groups and out-groups of people, those who can understand the slang terms and those who can't. Slang is often tied to a specific time period. For example, "groovy" and "far out" are connected to the 1970s, and "as if!" and "4-1-1-" are connected to the 1990s.

A language arts classroom should demonstrate the history and evolution of language, rather than presenting fixed, unchangeable linguistic regulations. Particularly for students who feel intimidated or excluded by Standard English, instructors can make lessons more relatable or inclusive by allowing students to share or explore their own patterns of language. Students can be encouraged to act as linguists or anthropologists by getting involved in projects. Some examples include asking them to identify and compare slang in their generation to slang from their parents' generation, to exchange information about their dialect with students who come from different cultural backgrounds, or to conduct a linguistic survey of their friends, family, or neighbors. Language arts class can also be integrated with history topics by having students research unfamiliar slang or words that have shifted in meaning from the past until now—a type of study particularly useful when reading a text from a past era.

Understanding Dialect and its Appropriateness

While students should come away from class feeling supported in their linguistic diversity, the reality is that certain forms of language are viewed differently depending on the context. Lessons learned in the classroom have a real-life application to a student's future, so he or she should know where, when, and how to utilize different forms of language.

For students preparing for college, knowledge of the conventions of Standard English is essential. The same is true for students who plan to enter professional job fields. Without necessarily having a word for it, many students are already familiar with the concept of *code-switching*—altering speech patterns depending upon context. For example, a person might use a different accent or slang with neighborhood friends than with coworkers or pick up new vocabulary and speech patterns after moving to a new region, either unconsciously or consciously. In this way, speakers have an innate understanding of how their language use helps them fit into any given situation.

Instructors can design activities that help students pay attention to their language use in a given context. When discussing a novel in class, students might be encouraged to spend a few minutes freewriting in a journal to generate ideas and express their unedited thoughts. Later, though, students will then be asked to present those thoughts in a formal writing assignment that requires adherence to Standard English grammar, employing academic vocabulary and expressions appropriate to literary discussions. Alternatively, students might design an advertisement that appeals to teenagers and another one that appeals to adults, utilizing different language in each. In this way, students can learn how to reformulate their thoughts using the language appropriate to the task at hand.

Awareness of dialect can also help students as readers, too. Many writers of literary fiction and nonfiction utilize dialect and colloquialisms to add verisimilitude to their writing. This is especially true for authors who focus on a particular region or cultural group in their works, also known as *regionalism* or *local color literature*. Examples include Zora Neale Hurston's *Their Eyes Were Watching God* and the short stories of Kate Chopin. Students can be asked to consider how the speech patterns in a text affect a reader's understanding of the characters—how the pattern reflects a character's background and place in society. They might consider a reader's impression of the region—how similar or different it is from the reader's region or what can be inferred about the region based on how people speak. In some cases, unfamiliar dialect may be very difficult for readers to understand on the page but becomes much more intelligible when read aloud—as in the reading of Shakespeare.

Reading passages together in class and then finding recordings or videos of the dialect presented in the text can help familiarize students with different speech patterns. And of course, students should also consider how use of dialect affects the audience or if it is directed to a specific audience. Who was the intended audience for *Their Eyes Were Watching God*, a novel that recreates the speech patterns of African Americans in early 1900s Florida? How might the novel be understood differently by readers who recognize that dialect than by readers who are encountering it for the first time? What would be lost if the characters didn't converse in their local dialect? Being alert to these questions creates students who are attuned to the nuances of language use in everyday life.

Standard English Conventions

Understanding the Conventions of Standard English

<u>Parts of Speech</u>
The English language has eight parts of speech, each serving a different grammatical function.

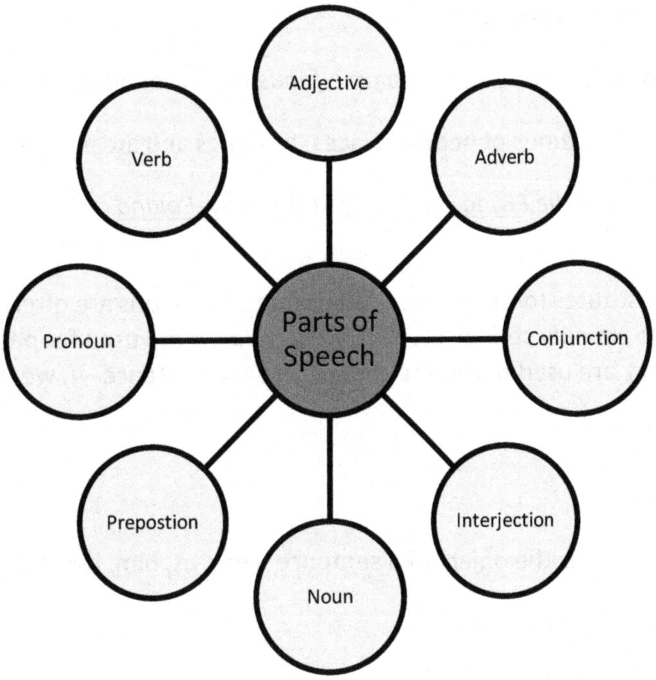

Verb
Verbs describe an action—e.g., *run, play, eat*—or a state of being—e.g., *is, are, was*. It is impossible to make a grammatically-complete sentence without a verb.

He *runs* to the store.

She *is* eight years old.

Noun

Nouns can be a person, place, or thing. They can refer to concrete objects—e.g., chair, apple, house—or abstract things—love, knowledge, friendliness.

Look at the *dog*!

Where are my *keys*?

Some nouns are *countable*, meaning they can be counted as separate entities—one chair, two chairs, three chairs. They can be either singular or plural. Others nouns, usually substances or concepts, are *uncountable*—e.g., air, information, wealth—and some nouns can be both countable and uncountable depending on how they are used.

I bought three *dresses*.

Respect is important to me.

I ate way too much *food* last night.

At the international festival, you can sample *foods* from around the world.

Proper nouns are the specific names of people, places, or things and are almost always capitalized.

Marie Curie studied at the Flying University in Warsaw, Poland.

Pronoun

Pronouns function as substitutes for nouns or noun phrases. Pronouns are often used to avoid constant repetition of a noun or to simplify sentences. *Personal pronouns* are used for people. Some pronouns are *subject pronouns*; they are used to replace the subject in a sentence—I, we, he, she, they.

Is *he* your friend?

We work together.

Object pronouns can function as the object of a sentence—me, us, him, her, them.

Give the documents to *her*.

Did you call *him* back yet?

Some pronouns can function as either the subject or the object—e.g., you, it. The subject of a sentence is the noun of the sentence that is doing or being something.

You should try it.

It tastes great.

Possessive pronouns indicate ownership. They can be used alone—mine, yours, his, hers, theirs, ours—or with a noun—my, your, his, her, their, ours. In the latter case, they function as a determiner, which is described in detail in the below section on adjectives.

This table is *ours*.

I can't find *my* phone!

Reflexive pronouns refer back to the person being spoken or written about. These pronouns end in -*self/-selves*.

I've heard that New York City is gorgeous in the autumn, but I've never seen it for *myself*.

After moving away from home, young people have to take care of *themselves*.

Indefinite pronouns are used for things that are unknown or unspecified. Some examples are *anybody, something,* and *everything*.

I'm looking for *someone* who knows how to fix computers.

I wanted to buy some shoes today, but I couldn't find *any* that I liked.

Adjective
An adjective modifies a noun, making it more precise or giving more information about it. Adjectives answer these questions: What kind? Which one?

I just bought a *red* car.

I don't like *cold* weather.

One special type of word that modifies a noun is a *determiner.* In fact, some grammarians classify determiners as a separate part of speech because whereas adjectives simply describe additional qualities of a noun, a determiner is often a necessary part of a noun phrase, without which the phrase is grammatically incomplete. A determiner indicates whether a noun is definite or indefinite, and can identify which noun is being discussed. It also introduces context to the noun in terms of quantity and possession. The most commonly-used determiners are *articles*— a, an, the.

I ordered *a* pizza.

She lives in *the* city.

Possessive pronouns discussed above, such as *my*, *your*, and *our*, are also determiners, along with *demonstratives*—this, that—and *quantifiers*—much, many, some. These determiners can take the place of an article.

Are you using *this* chair?

I need *some* coffee!

Adverb
Adverbs modify verbs, adjectives, and other adverbs. Words that end in –ly are usually adverbs. Adverbs answer these questions: When? Where? In what manner? To what degree?

> She talks *quickly*.
>
> The mountains are *incredibly* beautiful!
>
> The students arrived *early*.
>
> Please take your phone call *outside*.

Preposition
Prepositions show the relationship between different elements in a phrase or sentence and connect nouns or pronouns to other words in the sentence. Some examples of prepositions are words such as *after, at, behind, by, during, from, in, on, to*, and *with*.

> Let's go *to* class.
>
> Starry Night was painted *by* Vincent van Gogh *in* 1889.

Conjunction
Conjunctions join words, phrases, clauses, or sentences together, indicating the type of connection between these elements.

> I like pizza, *and* I enjoy spaghetti.
>
> I like to play baseball, *but* I'm allergic to mitts.

Some conjunctions are *coordinating*, meaning they give equal emphasis to two main clauses. Coordinating conjunctions are short, simple words that can be remembered using the mnemonic FANBOYS: for, and, nor, but, or, yet, so. Other conjunctions are *subordinating*. Subordinating conjunctions introduce dependent clauses and include words such as *because, since, before, after, if*, and *while*.

Interjection
An *interjection* is a short word that shows greeting or emotion. Examples of interjections include *wow, ouch, hey, oops, alas*, and *hey*.

> *Wow*! Look at that sunset!
>
> Was it your birthday yesterday? *Oops*! I forgot.

<u>Errors in Standard English Grammar, Usage, Syntax, and Mechanics</u>
Sentence Fragments
A *complete sentence* requires a verb and a subject that expresses a complete thought. Sometimes, the subject is omitted in the case of the implied *you*, used in sentences that are the command or imperative form—e.g., "Look!" or "Give me that." It is understood that the subject of the command is *you*, the listener or reader, so it is possible to have a structure without an explicit subject. Without these elements, though, the sentence is incomplete—it is a *sentence fragment.* While sentence fragments often occur in conversational English or creative writing, they are generally not appropriate in academic

writing. Sentence fragments often occur when dependent clauses are not joined to an independent clause:

Sentence fragment: Because the airline overbooked the flight.

The sentence above is a dependent clause that does not express a complete thought. What happened as a result of this cause? With the addition of an independent clause, this now becomes a complete sentence:

Complete sentence: Because the airline overbooked the flight, several passengers were unable to board.

Sentences fragments may also occur through improper use of conjunctions:

I'm going to the Bahamas for spring break. And to New York City for New Year's Eve.

While the first sentence above is a complete sentence, the second one is not because it is a prepositional phrase that lacks a subject [I] and a verb [am going]. Joining the two together with the coordinating conjunction forms one grammatically-correct sentence:

I'm going to the Bahamas for spring break and to New York City for New Year's Eve.

Run-ons

A *run-on* is a sentence with too many independent clauses that are improperly connected to each other:

This winter has been very cold some farmers have suffered damage to their crops.

The sentence above has two subject-verb combinations. The first is "this winter has been"; the second is "some farmers have suffered." However, they are simply stuck next to each other without any punctuation or conjunction. Therefore, the sentence is a run-on.

Another type of run-on occurs when writers use inappropriate punctuation:

This winter has been very cold, some farmers have suffered damage to their crops.

Though a comma has been added, this sentence is still not correct. When a comma alone is used to join two independent clauses, it is known as a *comma splice*. Without an appropriate conjunction, a comma cannot join two independent clauses by itself.

Run-on sentences can be corrected by either dividing the independent clauses into two or more separate sentences or inserting appropriate conjunctions and/or punctuation. The run-on sentence can be amended by separating each subject-verb pair into its own sentence:

This winter has been very cold. Some farmers have suffered damage to their crops.

The run-on can also be fixed by adding a comma and conjunction to join the two independent clauses with each other:

This winter has been very cold, so some farmers have suffered damage to their crops.

Parallelism

Parallel structure occurs when phrases or clauses within a sentence contain the same structure. Parallelism increases readability and comprehensibility because it is easy to tell which sentence elements are paired with each other in meaning.

> Jennifer enjoys cooking, knitting, and to spend time with her cat.

This sentence is not parallel because the items in the list appear in two different forms. Some are *gerunds***,** which is the verb + ing: *cooking, knitting.* The other item uses the *infinitive* form, which is to + verb: *to spend.* To create parallelism, all items in the list may reflect the same form:

> Jennifer enjoys cooking, knitting, and spending time with her cat.

All of the items in the list are now in gerund forms, so this sentence exhibits parallel structure. Here's another example:

> The company is looking for employees who are responsible and with a lot of experience.

Again, the items that are listed in this sentence are not parallel. "Responsible" is an adjective, yet "with a lot of experience" is a prepositional phrase. The sentence elements do not utilize parallel parts of speech.

> The company is looking for employees who are responsible and experienced**.**

"Responsible" and "experienced" are both adjectives, so this sentence now has parallel structure.

Dangling and Misplaced Modifiers

Modifiers enhance meaning by clarifying or giving greater detail about another part of a sentence. However, incorrectly-placed modifiers have the opposite effect and can cause confusion. A *misplaced modifier* is a modifier that is not located appropriately in relation to the word or phrase that it modifies:

> Because he was one of the greatest thinkers of Renaissance Italy, John idolized Leonardo da Vinci.

In this sentence, the modifier is "because he was one of the greatest thinkers of Renaissance Italy," and the noun it is intended to modify is "Leonardo da Vinci." However, due to the placement of the modifier next to the subject, John, it seems as if the sentence is stating that John was a Renaissance genius, not Da Vinci.

> John idolized Leonard da Vinci because he was one of the greatest thinkers of Renaissance Italy.

The modifier is now adjacent to the appropriate noun, clarifying which of the two men in this sentence is the greatest thinker.

Dangling modifiers modify a word or phrase that is not readily apparent in the sentence. That is, they "dangle" because they are not clearly attached to anything:

> After getting accepted to college, Amir's parents were proud.

The modifier here, "after getting accepted to college," should modify who got accepted. The noun immediately following the modifier is "Amir's parents"—but they are probably not the ones who are going to college.

After getting accepted to college, Amir made his parents proud.

The subject of the sentence has been change to Amir himself, and now the subject and its modifier are appropriately matched.

Inconsistent Verb Tense

Verb tense reflects when an action occurred or a state existed. For example, the tense known as *simple present* expresses something that is happening right now or that happens regularly:

She *works* in a hospital.

Present continuous tense expresses something in progress. It is formed by to be + verb + -ing.

Sorry, I can't go out right now. I *am doing* my homework.

Past tense is used to describe events that previously occurred. However, in conversational English, speakers often use present tense or a mix of past and present tense when relating past events because it gives the narrative a sense of immediacy. In formal written English, though, consistency in verb tense is necessary to avoid reader confusion.

I traveled to Europe last summer. As soon as I stepped off the plane, I feel like I'm in a movie! I'm surrounded by quaint cafes and impressive architecture.

The passage above abruptly switches from past tense—*traveled, stepped*—to present tense—*feel, am surrounded*.

I *traveled* to Europe last summer. As soon as I *stepped* off the plane, I *felt* like I was in a movie! I *was surrounded* by quaint cafes and impressive architecture.

All verbs are in past tense, so this passage now has consistent verb tense.

Split Infinitives

The *infinitive form* of a verb consists of "to + base verb"—e.g., to walk, to sleep, to approve. A *split infinitive* occurs when another word, usually an adverb, is placed between *to* and the verb:

I decided *to simply walk* to work to get more exercise every day.

The infinitive *to walk* is split by the adverb *simply*.

It was a mistake *to hastily approve* the project before conducting further preliminary research.

The infinitive *to approve* is split by *hastily*.

Although some grammarians still advise against split infinitives, this syntactic structure is common in both spoken and written English and is widely accepted in standard usage.

Subject-Verb Agreement

In English, verbs must agree with the subject. The form of a verb may change depending on whether the subject is singular or plural, or whether it is first, second, or third person. For example, the verb *to be* has various forms:

I am a student.

You are a student.

She is a student.

We are students.

They are students.

Errors occur when a verb does not agree with its subject. Sometimes, the error is readily apparent:

We is hungry.

Is is not the appropriate form of *to be* when used with the third person plural *we*.

We are hungry.

This sentence now has correct subject-verb agreement.

However, some cases are trickier, particularly when the subject consists of a lengthy noun phrase with many modifiers:

Students who are hoping to accompany the anthropology department on its annual summer trip to Ecuador needs to sign up by March 31st.

The verb in this sentence is *needs*. However, its subject is not the noun adjacent to it—Ecuador. The subject is the noun at the beginning of the sentence—students. Because *students* is plural, *needs* is the incorrect verb form.

Students who are hoping to accompany the anthropology department on its annual summer trip to Ecuador *need* to sign up by March 31st.

This sentence now uses correct agreement between *students* and *need*.

Another case to be aware of is a *collective noun*. A collective noun refers to a group of many things or people but can be singular in itself—e.g., family, committee, army, pair team, council, jury. Whether or not a collective noun uses a singular or plural verb depends on how the noun is being used. If the noun refers to the group performing a collective action as one unit, it should use a singular verb conjugation:

The family is moving to a new neighborhood.

The whole family is moving together in unison, so the singular verb form *is* is appropriate here.

The committee has made its decision.

The verb *has* and the possessive pronoun *its* both reflect the word *committee* as a singular noun in the sentence above; however, when a collective noun refers to the group as individuals, it can take a plural verb:

> The newlywed pair spend every moment together.

This sentence emphasizes the love between two people in a pair, so it can use the plural verb *spend.*

> The council are all newly elected members.

The sentence refers to the council in terms of its individual members and uses the plural verb *are.*

Overall though, American English is more likely to pair a collective noun with a singular verb, while British English is more likely to pair a collective noun with a plural verb.

<u>Grammar, Usage, Syntax, and Mechanics Choices</u>

Colons and Semicolons

In a sentence, *colons* are used before a list, a summary or elaboration, or an explanation related to the preceding information in the sentence:

> There are two ways to reserve tickets for the performance**:** by phone or in person.

> One thing is clear**:** students are spending more on tuition than ever before.

As these examples show, a colon must be preceded by an independent clause. However, the information after the colon may be in the form of an independent clause or in the form of a list.

Semicolons can be used in two different ways—to join ideas or to separate them. In some cases, semicolons can be used to connect what would otherwise be stand-alone sentences. Each part of the sentence joined by a semicolon must be an independent clause. The use of a semicolon indicates that these two independent clauses are closely related to each other:

> The rising cost of childcare is one major stressor for parents**;** healthcare expenses are another source of anxiety.

> Classes have been canceled due to the snowstorm**;** check the school website for updates.

Semicolons can also be used to divide elements of a sentence in a more distinct way than simply using a comma. This usage is particularly useful when the items in a list are especially long and complex and contain other internal punctuation.

> Retirees have many modes of income: some survive solely off their retirement checks**;** others supplement their income through part time jobs, like working in a supermarket or substitute teaching**;** and others are financially dependent on the support of family members, friends, and spouses.

Its and It's

These pronouns are the some of the most confused in the English language as most possessives contain the suffix –'s. However, for *it*, it is the opposite. *Its* is a possessive pronoun:

> The government is reassessing *its* spending plan.

It's is a contraction of the words *it is*:

It's snowing outside.

Saw and Seen
Saw and *seen* are both conjugations of the verb *to see*, but they express different verb tenses. *Saw* is used in the simple past tense. *Seen* is the past participle form of *to see* and can be used in all perfect tenses.

I seen her yesterday.

This sentence is incorrect. Because it expresses a completed event from a specified point in time in the past, it should use simple past tense:

I *saw* her yesterday.

This sentence uses the correct verb tense. Here's how the past participle is used correctly:

I *have seen* her before.

The meaning in this sentence is slightly changed to indicate an event from an unspecific time in the past. In this case, present perfect is the appropriate verb tense to indicate an unspecified past experience. Present perfect conjugation is created by combining *to have* + past participle.

Then and Than
Then is generally used as an adverb indicating something that happened next in a sequence or as the result of a conditional situation:

We parked the car and *then* walked to the restaurant.

If enough people register for the event, *then* we can begin planning.

Than is a conjunction indicating comparison:

This watch is more expensive *than* that one.

The bus departed later *than* I expected.

They're, Their, and There
They're is a contraction of the words *they are*:

They're moving to Ohio next week.

Their is a possessive pronoun:

The baseball players are training for *their* upcoming season.

There can function as multiple parts of speech, but it is most commonly used as an adverb indicating a location:

Let's go to the concert! Some great bands are playing *there*.

Insure and Ensure
These terms are both verbs. *Insure* means to guarantee something against loss, harm, or damage, usually through an insurance policy that offers monetary compensation:

> The robbers made off with her prized diamond necklace, but luckily it was *insured* for one million dollars.

Ensure means to make sure, to confirm, or to be certain:

> *Ensure* that you have your passport before entering the security checkpoint.

Accept and Except
Accept is a verb meaning to take or agree to something:

> I would like to *accept* your offer of employment.

Except is a preposition that indicates exclusion:

> I've been to every state in America *except* Hawaii.

Affect and Effect
Affect is a verb meaning to influence or to have an impact on something:

> The amount of rainfall during the growing season *affects* the flavor of wine produced from these grapes.

Effect can be used as either a noun or a verb. As a noun, *effect* is synonymous with a result:

> If we implement the changes, what will the *effect* be on our profits?

As a verb, *effect* means to bring about or to make happen:

> In just a few short months, the healthy committee has *effected* real change in school nutrition.

<u>Components of Sentences</u>

Clauses
Clauses contain a subject and a verb. An *independent clause* can function as a complete sentence on its own, but it might also be one component of a longer sentence. *Dependent clauses* cannot stand alone as complete sentences. They rely on independent clauses to complete their meaning. Dependent clauses usually begin with a subordinating conjunction. Independent and dependent clauses are sometimes also referred to as *main clauses* and *subordinate clauses*, respectively. The following structure highlights the differences:

> Apiculturists raise honeybees because they love insects.

Apiculturists raise honeybees is an independent or main clause. The subject is *apiculturists*, and the verb is *raise*. It expresses a complete thought and could be a standalone sentence.

Because they love insects is a dependent or subordinate clause. If it were not attached to the independent clause, it would be sentence fragment. While it contains a subject and verb—*they love*—

this clause is dependent because it begins with the subordinate conjunction *because*. Thus, it does not express a complete thought on its own.

Another type of clause is a *relative clause*, and it is sometimes referred to as an *adjective clause* because it gives further description about noun. A relative clause begins with a *relative pronoun*: *that, which, who, whom, whichever, whomever*, or *whoever.* It may also begin with a *relative adverb*: *where, why*, or *when.* Here's an example of relative clause, functioning as an adjective:

> The strawberries that I bought yesterday are already beginning to spoil.

Here, the relative clause is *that I bought yesterday*; the relative pronoun is *that*. The subject is *I*, and the verb is *bought*. The clause modifies the subject *strawberries* by answering the question, "Which strawberries?" Here's an example of a relative clause with an adverb:

> The tutoring center is a place where students can get help with homework.

The relative clause is *where students can get help with homework*, and it gives more information about a place by describing what kind of place it is. It begins with the relative adverb *where* and contains the noun *students* along with its verb phrase *can get.*

Relative clauses may be further divided into two types: essential or nonessential. *Essential clauses* contain identifying information without which the sentence would lose significant meaning or not make sense. These are also sometimes referred to as *restrictive clauses*. The sentence above contains an example of an essential relative clause. Here is what happens when the clause is removed:

> The tutoring center is a place where students can get help with homework.
>
> The tutoring center is a place.

Without the relative clause, the sentence loses the majority of its meaning; thus, the clause is essential or restrictive.

Nonessential clauses—also referred to as *non-restrictive clauses*—offer additional information about a noun in the sentence, but they do not significantly control the overall meaning of the sentence. The following example indicates a nonessential clause:

> New York City, which is located in the northeastern part of the country, is the most populated city in America.
>
> New York City is the most populated city in America.

Even without the relative clause, the sentence is still understandable and continues to communicate its central message about New York City. Thus, it is a nonessential clause.

Punctuation differs between essential and nonessential relative clauses, too. Nonessential clauses are set apart from the sentence using commas whereas essential clauses are not separated with commas. Also, the relative pronoun *that* is generally used for essential clauses, while *which* is used for nonessential clauses. The following examples clarify this distinction:

> *Romeo and Juliet* is my favorite play *that Shakespeare wrote.*

The relative clause *that Shakespeare wrote* contains essential, controlling information about the noun *play*, limiting it to those plays by Shakespeare. Without it, it would seem that *Romeo and Juliet* is the speaker's favorite play out of every play ever written, not simply from Shakespeare's repertoire.

> *Romeo and Juliet, which Shakespeare wrote,* is my favorite play.

Here, the nonessential relative clause—"which Shakespeare wrote"—modifies *Romeo and Juliet*. It doesn't provide controlling information about the play, but simply offers further background details. Thus, commas are needed.

Phrases

Phrases are groups of words that do not contain the subject-verb combination required for clauses. Phrases are classified by the part of speech that begins or controls the phrase.

A *noun phrase* consists of a noun and all its modifiers—adjectives, adverbs, and determiners. Noun phrases can serve many functions in a sentence, acting as subjects, objects, and object complements:

> *The shallow yellow bowl* sits on the top shelf.

> Nina just bought *some incredibly fresh organic produce*.

Prepositional phrases are made up of a preposition and its object. The object of a preposition might be a noun, noun phrase, pronoun, or gerund. Prepositional phrases may function as either an adjective or an adverb:

> Jack picked up the book *in front of him*.

The prepositional phrase *in front of him* acts as an adjective indicating which book Jack picked up.

> The dog ran into the back yard.

The phrase *into the backyard* describes where the dog ran, so it acts as an adverb.

Verb phrases include all of the words in a verb group, even if they are not directly adjacent to each other:

> I *should have woken up* earlier this morning.

> The company **is** now *offering* membership discounts for new enrollers.

This sentence's verb phrase is *is offering*. Even though they are separated by the word *now*, they function together as a single verb phrase.

Structures of Sentences

All sentences contain the same basic elements: a subject and a verb. The *subject* is who or what the sentence is about; the *verb* describes the subject's action or condition. However, these elements, subjects and verbs, can be combined in different ways. The following graphic describes the different types of sentence structures.

Sentence Structure	**Independent Clauses**	**Dependent Clauses**
Simple	1	0
Compound	2 or more	0
Complex	1	1 or more
Compound-Complex	2 or more	1 or more

A *simple sentence* expresses a complete thought and consists of one subject and verb combination:

The children ate pizza.

The subject is *children*. The verb is *ate*.

Either the subject or the verb may be *compound*—that is, it could have more than one element:

The children and their parents ate pizza.

The children *ate pizza and watched a movie*.

All of these are still simple sentences. Despite having either compound subjects or compound verbs, each sentence still has only one subject and verb combination.

Compound sentences combine two or more simple sentences to form one sentence that has multiple subject-verb combinations:

The children ate pizza, and *their parents watched a movie*.

This structure is comprised of two independent clauses: (1) *the children ate pizza* and (2) *their parents watched a movie.* Compound sentences join different subject-verb combinations using a comma and a coordinating conjunction.

I called my mom, *but* she didn't answer the phone.

The weather was stormy, *so* we canceled our trip to the beach.

A *complex sentence* consists of an independent clause and one or more dependent clauses. Dependent clauses join a sentence using *subordinating conjunctions*. Some examples of subordinating conjunctions are *although, unless, as soon as, since, while, when, because, if,* and *before*.

I missed class yesterday *because* my mother was ill.

Before traveling to a new country, you need to exchange your money to the local currency.

The order of clauses determines their punctuation. If the dependent clause comes first, it should be separated from the independent clause with a comma. However, if the complex sentence consists of an independent clause followed by a dependent clause, then a comma is not always necessary.

A *compound-complex sentence* can be created by joining two or more independent clauses with at least one dependent clause:

> After the earthquake struck, thousands of homes were destroyed, and many families were left without a place to live.

The first independent clause in the compound structure includes a subordinating clause—*after the earthquake struck*. Thus, the structure is both complex and compound.

Practice Questions

1. Which of the following sentences has an error in capitalization?
    a. The East Coast has experienced very unpredictable weather this year.
    b. My Uncle owns a home in Florida, where he lives in the winter.
    c. I am taking English Composition II on campus this fall.
    d. There are several nice beaches we can visit on our trip to the Jersey Shore this summer.

2. Julia Robinson, an avid photographer in her spare time, was able to capture stunning shots of the local wildlife on her last business trip to Australia.

Which of the following is an adjective in the preceding sentence?
    a. Time
    b. Capture
    c. Avid
    d. Photographer

3. Which of the following sentences uses correct punctuation?
    a. Carole is not currently working; her focus is on her children at the moment.
    b. Carole is not currently working and her focus is on her children at the moment.
    c. Carole is not currently working, her focus is on her children at the moment.
    d. Carole is not currently working her focus is on her children at the moment.

4. Which of these examples is a compound sentence?
    a. Alex and Shane spent the morning coloring and later took a walk down to the park.
    b. After coloring all morning, Alex and Shane spent the afternoon at the park.
    c. Alex and Shane spent the morning coloring, and then they took a walk down to the park.
    d. After coloring all morning and spending part of the day at the park, Alex and Shane took a nap.

5. Which of these examples shows incorrect use of subject-verb agreement?
    a. Neither of the cars are parked on the street.
    b. Both of my kids are going to camp this summer.
    c. Any of your friends are welcome to join us on the trip in November.
    d. Each of the clothing options is appropriate for the job interview.

6. When it gets warm in the spring, _______ and _______ like to go fishing at Cobbs Creek.

Which of the following word pairs should be used in the blanks above?
    a. me, him
    b. he, I
    c. him, I
    d. he, me

7. Which example shows correct comma usage for dates?
    a. The due date for the final paper in the course is Monday, May 16, 2016.
    b. The due date for the final paper in the course is Monday, May 16 2016.
    c. The due date for the final project in the course is Monday, May, 16, 2016.
    d. The due date for the final project in the course is Monday May 16, 2016.

8. Which of the following uses correct spelling?

a. Leslie knew that training for the Philadelphia Marathon would take dicsipline and perserverance, but she was up to the challenge.

b. Leslie knew that training for the Philadelphia Marathon would take discipline and perseverence, but she was up to the challenge.

c. Leslie knew that training for the Philadelphia Marathon would take disiplin and perservearance, but she was up to the challenge.

d. Leslie knew that training for the Philadelphia Marathon would take discipline and perseverance, but she was up to the challenge.

9. At last night's company function, in honor of Mr. Robertson's retirement, several employees spoke kindly about his career achievements.

In the preceding sentence, what part of speech is the word *function*?

a. Adjective
b. Adverb
c. Verb
d. Noun

10. Which of the examples uses the correct plural form?

a. Tomatos
b. Analysis
c. Cacti
d. Criterion

11. Which of the following examples uses correct punctuation?

a. The moderator asked the candidates, "Is each of you prepared to discuss your position on global warming?".

b. The moderator asked the candidates, "Is each of you prepared to discuss your position on global warming?"

c. The moderator asked the candidates, 'Is each of you prepared to discuss your position on global warming?'

d. The moderator asked the candidates, "Is each of you prepared to discuss your position on global warming"?

12. Based on the words *transfer, transact, translation, transport,* what is the meaning of the prefix *trans*?

a. Separation
b. All, everywhere
c. Forward
d. Across, beyond, over

13. In which of the following sentences does the word *part* function as an adjective?

a. The part Brian was asked to play required many hours of research.
b. She parts ways with the woodsman at the end of the book.
c. The entire team played a part in the success of the project.
d. Ronaldo is part Irish on his mother's side of the family.

14. All of Shannon's family and friends helped her to celebrate her 50th birthday at Café Sorrento. Which of the following is the complete subject of the preceding sentence?

a. Family and friends
b. All
c. All of Shannon's family and friends
d. Shannon's family and friends

15. Which of the following sentences uses second person point of view?

a. I don't want to make plans for the weekend before I see my work schedule.
b. She had to miss the last three yoga classes due to illness.
c. Pluto is no longer considered a planet because it is not gravitationally dominant.
d. Be sure to turn off all of the lights before locking up for the night.

16. As the tour group approached the bottom of Chichen Itza, the prodigious Mayan pyramid, they became nervous about climbing its distant peak.

Based on the context of the sentence, which of the following words shows the correct meaning of the word *prodigious*?

a. Very large
b. Famous
c. Very old
d. Fancy

17. Which of the following sentences correctly uses a hyphen?

a. Last-year, many of the players felt unsure of the coach's methods.
b. Some of the furniture she selected seemed a bit over - the - top for the space.
c. Henry is a beagle-mix and is ready for adoption this weekend.
d. Geena works to maintain a good relationship with her ex-husband to the benefit of their children.

18. Which of the following examples correctly uses quotation marks?

a. "A Wrinkle in Time" was one of my favorite novels as a child.
b. Though he is famous for his roles in films like "The Great Gatsby" and "Titanic," Leonardo DiCaprio has never won an Oscar.
c. Sylvia Plath's poem, "Daddy" will be the subject of this week's group discussion.
d. "The New York Times" reported that many fans are disappointed in some of the trades made by the Yankees this off-season.

19. Which of the following sentences shows correct word usage?

a. It's often been said that work is better then rest.
b. Its often been said that work is better then rest.
c. It's often been said that work is better than rest.
d. Its often been said that work is better than rest.

20. Glorify, fortify, gentrify, acidify

Based on the preceding words, what is the correct meaning of the suffix *–fy*?

a. Marked by, given to
b. Doer, believer
c. Make, cause, cause to have
d. Process, state, rank

21. Which of the following uses correct spelling?

a. Jed was disatisfied with the acommodations at his hotel, so he requested another room.
b. Jed was dissatisfied with the accommodations at his hotel, so he requested another room.
c. Jed was dissatisfied with the accomodations at his hotel, so he requested another room.
d. Jed was disatisfied with the accommodations at his hotel, so he requested another room.

22. Which of the following is an imperative sentence?

a. Pennsylvania's state flag includes two draft horses and an eagle.
b. Go down to the basement and check the hot water heater for signs of a leak.
c. You must be so excited to have a new baby on the way!
d. How many countries speak Spanish?

23. After a long day at work, Tracy had dinner with her family, and then took a walk to the park.

What are the transitional words in the preceding sentence?

a. After, then
b. At, with, to
c. Had, took
d. A, the

24. Which of the following examples is a compound sentence?

a. Shawn and Jerome played soccer in the backyard for two hours.
b. Marissa last saw Elena and talked to her this morning.
c. The baby was sick, so I decided to stay home from work.
d. Denise, Kurt, and Eric went for a run after dinner.

25. Robert needed to find at least four sources for his final project, so he searched several library databases for reliable academic research.

Which words function as nouns in the preceding sentence?

a. Robert, sources, project, databases, research
b. Robert, sources, final, project, databases, academic, research
c. Robert, sources, project, he, library, databases, research
d. Sources, project, databases, research

26. Which of the following sentences uses correct subject-verb agreement?

a. There is two constellations that can be seen from the back of the house.
b. At least four of the sheep needs to be sheared before the end of summer.
c. Lots of people were auditioning for the singing competition on Saturday.
d. Everyone in the group have completed the assignment on time.

27. Philadelphia is home to some excellent walking tours where visitors can learn more about the culture and rich history of the city of brotherly love.

What are the adjectives in the preceding sentence?

a. Philadelphia, tours, visitors, culture, history, city, love
b. Excellent, walking, rich, brotherly
c. Is, can, learn
d. To, about, of

28. The realtor showed __________ and __________ a house on Wednesday afternoon.

Which of the following pronoun pairs should be used in the blanks above?

a. She, I
b. She, me
c. Me, her
d. Her, me

29. Which of the following examples uses correct punctuation?
a. Recommended supplies for the hunting trip include the following: rain gear, large backpack, hiking boots, flashlight, and non-perishable foods.
b. I left the store, because I forgot my wallet.
c. As soon as the team checked into the hotel; they met in the lobby for a group photo.
d. None of the furniture came in on time: so they weren't able to move in to the new apartment.

30. Which of the following sentences shows correct word usage?
a. Your going to have to put you're jacket over their.
b. You're going to have to put your jacket over there.
c. Your going to have to put you're jacket over they're.
d. You're going to have to put you're jacket over their.

Read the selection and answer questions 31-35.

[1]I have to admit that when my father bought an RV, I thought he was making a huge mistake. [2]In fact, I even thought he might have gone a little bit crazy. [3]I did not really know anything about recreational vehicles, but I knew that my dad was as big a "city slicker" as there was. [4]On trips to the beach, he preferred to swim at the pool, and whenever he went hiking, he avoided touching any plants for fear that they might be poison ivy. [5]Why would this man, with an almost irrational fear of the outdoors, want a 40-foot camping behemoth?

[6]The RV was a great purchase for our family and brought us all closer together. [7]Every morning we would wake up, eat breakfast, and broke camp. [8]We laughed at our own comical attempts to back The Beast into spaces that seemed impossibly small. [9]We rejoiced when we figured out how to "hack" a solution to a nagging technological problem. [10]When things inevitably went wrong and we couldn't solve the problems on our own, we discovered the incredible helpfulness and friendliness of the RV community. We even made some new friends in the process.

[11] Above all, it allows us to share adventures travelling across America that we could not have experienced in cars and hotels. [12]Enjoying a campfire on a chilly summer evening with the mountains of Glacier National Park in the background, or waking up early in the morning to see the sun rising over the distant spires of Arches National Park are memories that will always stay with me and our entire family. [13]Those are also memories that my siblings and I have now shared with our own children.

31. How should the author change sentence 11?
    a. Above all, it will allow us to share adventures travelling across America that we could not have experienced in cars and hotels.
    b. Above all, it allows you to share adventures travelling across America that you could not have experienced in cars and hotels.
    c. Above all, it allowed us to share adventures travelling across America that we could not have experienced in cars and hotels.
    d. Above all, it allows them to share adventures travelling across America that they could not have experienced in cars and hotels.

32. Which of the following examples would make a good addition to the selection after sentence 4?
    a. My father is also afraid of seeing insects.
    b. My father is surprisingly good at starting a campfire.
    c. My father negotiated contracts for a living.
    d. My father isn't even bothered by pigeons.

33. Which of the following would correct the error in sentence 7?
    a. Every morning we would wake up, ate breakfast, and broke camp.
    b. Every morning we would wake up, eat breakfast, and broke camp.
    c. Every morning we would wake up, eat breakfast, and break camp.
    d. Every morning we would wake up, ate breakfast, and break camp.

34. What transition word could be added to the beginning of sentence 6?
    a. Not surprisingly,
    b. Furthermore,
    c. As it turns out,
    d. Of course,

35. Which of the following topics would fit well between paragraph 1 and paragraph 2?
    a. A guide to RV holding tanks
    b. Describing how RV travel is actually not as outdoors-oriented as many think
    c. A description of different types of RVs
    d. Some examples of how other RV enthusiasts helped the narrator and his father during their travels

36. Which of the following is a clearer way to describe the following phrase?
    "employee-manager relations improvement guide"
    a. A guide to employing better managers
    b. A guide to improving relations between managers and employees
    c. A relationship between employees, managers, and improvement
    d. An improvement in employees' and managers' use of guides

Read the sentences, and then answer the following question.

Polls show that more and more people in the US distrust the government and view it as dysfunctional and corrupt. Every election, the same people are voted back into office.

37. Which word or words would best link these sentences?
    a. Not surprisingly,
    b. Understandably,
    c. And yet,
    d. Therefore,

38. Which of the following statements would make the best conclusion to an essay about civil rights activist Rosa Parks?
    a. On December 1, 1955, Rosa Parks refused to give up her bus seat to a white passenger, setting in motion the Montgomery bus boycott.
    b. Rosa Parks was a hero to many, and came to symbolize the way that ordinary people could bring about real change in the Civil Rights Movement.
    c. Rosa Parks died in 2005 in Detroit, having moved from Montgomery shortly after the bus boycott.
    d. Rosa Parks' arrest was an early part of the Civil Rights Movement, and helped lead to the passage of the Civil Rights Act of 1964.

Select the best version of the underlined part of the sentence. If you think the original sentence is best, choose the first answer.

39. Since <u>none of the furniture were delivered</u> on time, we have to move in at a later date.
    a. none of the furniture were delivered
    b. none of the furniture was delivered
    c. all of the furniture were delivered
    d. all of the furniture was delivered

40. <u>An important issues stemming from this meeting</u> is that we won't have enough time to meet all of the objectives.
    a. An important issues stemming from this meeting
    b. Important issue stemming from this meeting
    c. An important issue stemming from this meeting
    d. Important issues stemming from this meeting

Answer Explanations

1. B: In choice *B*, the word *Uncle* should not be capitalized, because it is not functioning as a proper noun. If the word named a specific uncle, such as *Uncle Jerry*, then it would be considered a proper noun and should be capitalized. Choice *A* correctly capitalizes the proper noun *East Coast*, and does not capitalize *winter*, which functions as a common noun in the sentence. Choice *C* correctly capitalizes the name of a specific college course, which is considered a proper noun. Choice *D* correctly capitalizes the proper noun *Jersey Shore*.

2. C: In choice C, *avid* is functioning as an adjective that modifies the word photographer. *Avid* describes the photographer Julia Robinson's style. The words *time* and *photographer* are functioning as nouns, and the word *capture* is functioning as a verb in the sentence. Other words functioning as adjectives in the sentence include, *local*, *business*, and *spare*, as they all describe the nouns they precede.

3. A: Choice *A* is correctly punctuated because it uses a semicolon to join two independent clauses that are related in meaning. Each of these clauses could function as an independent sentence. Choice *B* is incorrect because the conjunction is not preceded by a comma. A comma and conjunction should be used together to join independent clauses. Choice *C* is incorrect because a comma should only be used to join independent sentences when it also includes a coordinating conjunction such as *and* or *so*. Choice *D* does not use punctuation to join the independent clauses, so it is considered a fused (same as a run-on) sentence.

4. C: Choice *C* is a compound sentence because it joins two independent clauses with a comma and the coordinating conjunction *and*. The sentences in Choices *B* and D include one independent clause and one dependent clause, so they are complex sentences, not compound sentences. The sentence in Choice *A* has both a compound subject, *Alex and Shane*, and a compound verb, *spent and took*, but the entire sentence itself is one independent clause.

5. A: Choice *A* uses incorrect subject-verb agreement because the indefinite pronoun *neither* is singular and must use the singular verb form *is*. The pronoun *both* is plural and uses the plural verb form of *are*. The pronoun *any* can be either singular or plural. In this example, it is used as a plural, so the plural verb form *are* is used. The pronoun *each* is singular and uses the singular verb form *is*.

6. B: Choice *B* is correct because the pronouns *he* and *I* are in the subjective case. *He* and *I* are the subjects of the verb *like* in the independent clause of the sentence. Choice *A*, *C*, and *D* are incorrect because they all contain at least one objective pronoun (*me* and *him*). Objective pronouns should not be used as the subject of the sentence, but rather, they should come as an object of a verb. To test for correct pronoun usage, try reading the pronouns as if it were the only pronoun in the sentence. For example, *he* and *me* may appear to be the correct answer choices, but try reading them as the only pronoun.

> He like[s] to go fishing...
> Me like to go fishing...
> When looked at that way, *me* is an obviously incorrect choice.

7. A: It is necessary to put a comma between the date and the year. It is also required to put a comma between the day of the week and the month. Choice *B* is incorrect because it is missing the comma between the day and year. Choice *C* is incorrect because it adds an unnecessary comma between the month and date. Choice *D* is missing the necessary comma between day of the week and the month.

8. D: *Discipline* and *perseverance* are both spelled correctly in choice *d*. These are both considered commonly misspelled words. One or both words are spelled incorrectly in choices *A, B,* and *C.*

9. D: In choice *D*, the word *function* is a noun. While the word *function* can also act as a verb, in this particular sentence it is acting as a noun as the object of the preposition *at*. Choices *A* and *B* are incorrect because the word *function* cannot be used as an adjective or adverb.

10. C: Cacti is the correct plural form of the word *cactus*. Choice *A* (*tomatos*) includes an incorrect spelling of the plural of *tomato*. Both *B* (*analysis*) and *D* (*criterion*) are incorrect because they are in singular form. The correct plural form for these choices would be *criteria* and analyses.

11. B: Quotation marks are used to indicate something someone said. The example sentences feature a direct quotation that requires the use of double quotation marks. Also, the end punctuation, in this case a question mark, should always be contained within the quotation marks. Choice *A* is incorrect because there is an unnecessary period after the quotation mark. Choice *C* is incorrect because it uses single quotation marks, which are used for a quote within a quote. Choice *D* is incorrect because it places the punctuation outside of the quotation marks.

12. D: The prefix *trans* means across, beyond, over. Choices *A, B,* and *C* are incorrect because they are the meanings of other prefixes. Choice *A* is a meaning of the prefix *de*. Choice *B* is the meaning of the prefix *omni*. Choice *C* is one of the meanings of the prefix *pro*. The example words are helpful in determining the meaning of *trans*. All of the example words—*transfer, transact, translation, transport*—indicate something being *across, beyond*, or *over* something else. For example, *translation* refers to text going across languages. If no example words were given, you could think of words starting with *trans* and then compare their meanings to try to determine a common definition.

13. D: In choice *D*, the word *part* functions as an adjective that modifies the word *Irish*. Choices *A* and *C* are incorrect because the word *part* functions as a noun in these sentences. Choice *B* is incorrect because the word *part* functions as a verb.

14. C: *All of Shannon's family and friends* is the complete subject because it includes who or what is doing the action in the sentence as well as the modifiers that go with it. Choice *A* is incorrect because it only includes the simple subject of the sentence. Choices *B* and *D* are incorrect because they only include part of the complete subject.

15. D: Choice *D* directly addresses the reader, so it is in second person point of view. This is an imperative sentence since it issues a command; imperative sentences have an *understood you* as the subject. Choice *A* uses first person pronouns *I* and *my*. Choices *B* and *C* are incorrect because they use third person point of view.

16. A: The word *prodigious* is defined as very impressive, amazing, or large. In this sentence, the meaning can be drawn from the words *they became nervous about climbing its distant peak*, as this would be an appropriate reaction upon seeing a very large peak that's far in the distance. Choices *B, C,* and *D* do not accurately define the word *prodigious*, so they are incorrect.

17. D: Choice *D* correctly places a hyphen after the prefix *ex* to join it to the word *husband*. Words that begin with the prefixes *great, trans, ex, all,* and *self*, require a hyphen. Choices *A* and *C* place hyphens in words where they are not needed. *Beagle mix* would only require a hyphen if coming before the word *Henry*, since it would be serving as a compound adjective in that instance. Choice *B* contains hyphens that are in the correct place but are formatted incorrectly since they include spaces between the hyphens and the surrounding words.

18. C: Choice *C* is correct because quotation marks should be used for the title of a short work such as a poem. Choices *A, B,* and *D* are incorrect because the titles of novels, films, and newspapers should be placed in italics, not quotation marks.

19. A: This question focuses on the correct usage of the commonly confused word pairs of *it's/its* and *then/than. It's* is a contraction for *it is* or *it has. Its* is a possessive pronoun. The word *than* shows comparison between two things. *Then* is an adverb that conveys time. Choice *C* correctly uses *it's* and *than. It's* is a contraction for *it has* in this sentence, and *than* shows comparison between *work* and *rest*. None of the other answers choices use both of the correct words.

20. C: The suffix *-fy* means to make, cause, or cause to have. Choices *A, B,* and *D* are incorrect because they show meanings of other suffixes. Choice *A* shows the meaning of the suffix *-ous*. Choice *B* shows the meaning of the suffix *–ist*, and *D* shows the meaning of the suffix *-age*.

21. B: *Dissatisfied* and *accommodations* are both spelled correctly in Choice *B*. These are both considered commonly misspelled words. One or both words are spelled incorrectly in choices *A, C,* and *D*.

22. B: Choice *B* is an imperative sentence because it issues a command. In addition, it ends with a period, and an imperative sentence must end in a period or exclamation mark. Choice *A* is a declarative sentence that states a fact and ends with a period. Choice *C* is an exclamatory sentence that shows strong emotion and ends with an exclamation point. Choice *D* is an interrogative sentence that asks a question and ends with a question mark.

23. A: *After* and *then* are transitional words that indicate time or position. Choice *B* is incorrect because the words *at, with,* and *to* are used as prepositions in this sentence, not transitions. Choice *C* is incorrect because the words *had* and *took* are used as verbs in this sentence. In Choice *D, a* and *the* are used as articles in the sentence.

24. C: Choice *C* is a compound sentence because it joins two independent clauses—*The baby was sick* and *I decided to stay home from work*—with a comma and the coordinating conjunction *so*. Choices *A, B,* and *D*, are all simple sentences, each containing one independent clause with a complete subject and predicate. Choices *A* and *D* each contain a compound subject, or more than one subject, but they are still simple sentences that only contain one independent clause. Choice *B* contains a compound verb (more than one verb), but it's still a simple sentence.

25. A: Choice *A* includes all of the words functioning as nouns in the sentence. Choice *B* is incorrect because it includes the words *final* and *academic,* which are functioning as adjectives in this sentence. The word *he* makes Choice *C* incorrect because it is a pronoun. This example also includes the word *library*, which can function as a noun, but is functioning as an adjective modifying the word *databases* in this sentence. Choice *D* is incorrect because it leaves out the proper noun *Robert*.

26. C: The simple subject of this sentence, the word *lots*, is plural. It agrees with the plural verb form *were*. Choice *A* is incorrect, because the simple subject *there*, referring to the two constellations, is considered plural. It does not agree with the singular verb form *is*. In Choice *B*, the singular subject *four*, does not agree with the plural verb form *needs*. In Choice *D* the plural subject *everyone* does not agree with the singular verb form *have*.

27. B: *Excellent* and *walking* are adjectives modifying the noun *tours. Rich* is an adjective modifying the noun *history*, and *brotherly* is an adjective modifying the noun *love*. Choice *A* is incorrect because all of these words are functioning as nouns in the sentence. Choice *C* is incorrect because all of these words are functioning as verbs in the sentence. Choice *D* is incorrect because all of these words are considered prepositions, not adjectives.

28. D: The object pronouns *her* and *me* act as the indirect objects of the sentence. If *me* is in a series of object pronouns, it should always come last in the series. Choice *A* is incorrect because it uses subject pronouns *she* and *I*. Choice *B* is incorrect because it uses the subject pronoun *she*. Choice *C* uses the correct object pronouns, but they are in the wrong order.

29. A: In this example, a colon is correctly used to introduce a series of items. Choice *B* places an unnecessary comma before the word *because*. A comma is not needed before the word *because* when it introduces a dependent clause at the end of a sentence and provides necessary information to understand the sentence. Choice *C* is incorrect because it uses a semi-colon instead of a comma to join a dependent clause and an independent clause. Choice *D* is incorrect because it uses a colon in place of a comma and coordinating conjunction to join two independent clauses.

30. B: Choice *B* correctly uses the contraction for *you are* as the subject of the sentence, and it correctly uses the possessive pronoun *your* to indicate ownership of the jacket. It also correctly uses the adverb *there*, indicating place. Choice *A* is incorrect because it reverses the possessive pronoun *your* and the contraction for *you are*. It also uses the possessive pronoun *their* instead of the adverb *there*. Choice *C* is incorrect because it reverses *your* and *you're* and uses the contraction for *they are* in place of the adverb *there*. Choice *D* incorrectly uses the possessive pronoun *their* instead of the adverb *there*.

31. C: The sentence should be in the same tense and person as the rest of the selection. The rest of the selection is in past tense and first person. Choice *A* is in future tense. Choice *B* is in second person. Choice *D* is in third person. While none of these sentences are incorrect by themselves, they are written in a tense that is different from the rest of the selection. Only *Choice C* maintains tense and voice consistent with the rest of the selection.

32. A: Choices *B* and *D* go against the point the author is trying to make—that the father is not comfortable in nature. Choice *C* is irrelevant to the topic. Choice *A* is the only choice that emphasizes the father's discomfort with spending time in nature.

33. C: This sentence uses verbs in a parallel series, so each verb must follow the same pattern. In order to fit with the helping verb "would," each verb must be in the present tense. In Choices *A*, *B*, and *D*, one or more of the verbs switches to past tense. Only Choice *C* remains in the same tense, maintaining the pattern.

34. C: In paragraph 2, the author surprises the reader by asserting that the opposite of what was expected was in fact true—the city slicker father actually enjoyed the RV experience. Only Choice *C* indicates this shift in expected outcome, while the other choices indicate a continuation of the previous expectation.

35. B: Choices *A* and *C* are irrelevant to the topic. They deal more with details about RVs while the author is more concerned with the family's experiences with them. Choice *D* is relevant to the topic, but it would fit better between paragraphs 2 and 3, since the author does not mention this point until the end of the second paragraph. Choice *B* would help explain to the reader why the father, who does not enjoy the outdoors, could end up enjoying RVs so much.

36. B: Stacked modifying nouns such as this example are untangled by starting from the end and adding words as necessary to provide meaning. In this case, a *guide* to *improving relations* between *managers* and *employees*. Choices *C* and *D* do not define the item first as a guide. Choice *A* does identify as a guide, but confuses the order of the remaining descriptors. Choice *B* is correct, as it unstacks the nouns in the correct order and also makes logical sense.

37. C: The second sentence tells of an unexpected outcome of the first sentence. Choice *A*, Choice *B*, and Choice *D* indicate a logical progression, which does not match this surprise. Only Choice *C* indicates this unexpected twist.

38. B: Choice *A*, Choice *C*, and Choice *D* all relate facts but do not present the kind of general statement that would serve as an effective summary or conclusion. Choice *B* is correct.

39. B: Answer Choice *A* uses the plural form of the verb, when the subject is the pronoun *none*, which needs a singular verb. *C* also uses the wrong verb form and uses the word *all* in place of *none*, which doesn't make sense in the context of the sentence. *D* uses *all* again, and is missing the comma, which is necessary to set the dependent clause off from the independent clause.

40. C: In this answer, the article and subject agree, and the subject and predicate agree. Answer Choice *A* is incorrect because the article *an* and *issues* do not agree in number. *B* is incorrect because an article is needed before *important issue*. *D* is incorrect because the plural subject *issues* does not agree with the singular verb *is*.

Math

Number Sense, Concepts, and Operations

Place Value

Numbers count in groups of 10. That number is the same throughout the set of natural numbers and whole numbers. It is referred to as working within a base 10 numeration system. Only the numbers from zero to 9 are used to represent any number. The foundation for doing this involves *place value*. Numbers are written side by side. This is to show the amount in each place value.

For place value, let's look at how the number 10 is different from zero to 9. It has two digits instead of just one. The one is in the tens' place, and the zero is in the ones' place. Therefore, there is one group of tens and zero ones. 11 has one 10 and one 1. The introduction of numbers from 11 to 19 should be the next step. Each value within this range of numbers consists of one group of 10 and a specific number of leftover ones. Counting by tens can be practiced once the tens column is understood. This process consists of increasing the number in the tens place by one. For example, counting by 10 starting at 17 would result in the next four values being 27, 37, 47, and 57.

A place value chart can be used for understanding and learning about numbers that have more digits. Here is an example of a place value chart:

	MILLIONS			THOUSANDS			ONES			.	DECIMALS		
billions	hundred millions	ten millions	millions	hundred thousands	ten thousands	thousands	hundreds	tens	ones		tenths	hundredths	thousandths

In the number 1,234, there are 4 ones and 3 tens. The 2 is in the hundreds' place, and the one is in the thousands' place. Note that each group of three digits is separated by a comma. The 2 has a value that is 10 times greater than the 3. Every place to the left has a value 10 times greater than the place to its right. Also, each group of three digits is also known as a *period*. 234 is in the ones' period.

The number 1,234 can be written out as *one-thousand, two hundred thirty-four*. The process of writing out numbers is known as the *decimal system*. It is also based on groups of 10. The place value chart is a helpful tool in using this system. In order to write out a number, it always starts with the digit(s) in the highest period. For example, in the number 23,815,467, the 23 is in highest place and is in the millions' period. The number is read *twenty-three million, eight hundred fifteen thousand, four hundred sixty-seven*. Each period is written separately through the use of commas. Also, no "ands" are used within the number. Another way to think about the number 23,815,467 is through the use of an addition problem. For example, $23{,}815{,}467 = 20{,}000{,}000 + 3{,}000{,}000 + 800{,}000 + 10{,}000 + 5{,}000 + 400 + 60 + 7$.

This expression is known as *expanded form*. The actual number 23,815,467 is known as being in *standard form*.

In order to compare whole numbers with many digits, place value can be used. In each number to be compared, it is necessary to find the highest place value in which the numbers differ and to compare the value within that place value. For example, $4{,}523{,}345 < 4{,}532{,}456$ because of the values in the ten thousands place. A similar process can be used for decimals. However, number lines can also be used. Tick marks can be placed within two whole numbers on the number line that represent tenths, hundredths, etc. Each number being compared can then be plotted. The leftmost value on the number line is the largest.

Mental Math

Mental math should always be considered as problems are worked through. It can save time to work a problem out in your head. If a problem is simple enough, such as $15 + 3 = 18$, it should be completed in your head. It will get easier to do this once you know addition and subtraction in higher place values. Mental math is also important in multiplication and division. The times tables, for multiplying all numbers from one to 12, should be memorized. This will allow for division within those numbers to be memorized as well. For example, $121 \div 11 = 11$ because it should be memorized that $11 \times 11 = 121$. Here is the multiplication table to be memorized:

x	1	2	3	4	5	6	7	8	9	10	11	12	13	14	15
1	1	2	3	4	5	6	7	8	9	10	11	12	13	14	15
2	2	4	6	8	10	12	14	16	18	20	22	24	26	28	30
3	3	6	9	12	15	18	21	24	27	30	33	36	39	42	45
4	4	8	12	16	20	24	28	32	36	40	44	48	52	56	60
5	5	10	15	20	25	30	35	40	45	50	55	60	65	70	75
6	6	12	18	24	30	36	42	48	54	60	66	72	78	84	90
7	7	14	21	28	35	42	49	56	63	70	77	84	91	98	105
8	8	16	24	32	40	48	56	64	72	80	88	96	104	112	120
9	9	18	27	36	45	54	63	72	81	90	99	108	117	126	135
10	10	20	30	40	50	60	70	80	90	100	110	120	130	140	150
11	11	22	33	44	55	66	77	88	99	110	121	132	143	154	165
12	12	24	36	48	60	72	84	96	108	120	132	144	156	168	180
13	13	26	39	52	65	78	91	104	117	130	143	156	169	182	195
14	14	28	42	56	70	84	98	112	126	140	154	168	182	196	210
15	15	30	45	60	75	90	105	120	135	150	165	180	195	210	225

The values in yellow along the diagonal of the table consist of *perfect squares*. A perfect square is a number that represents a product of two equal integers.

Number Line

A *number line* is a visual representation of all real numbers. It is a straight line on which any number can be plotted. The origin is zero, and the values to the right of the origin represent positive numbers. Values to the left of the origin represent negative numbers. Both sides extend forever. Here is an example of a number line:

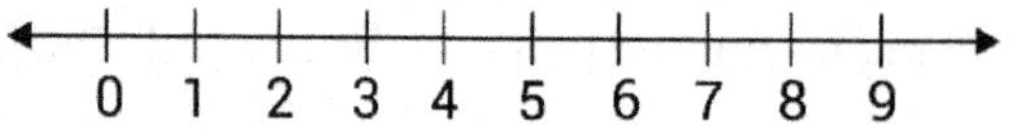

Number lines can be utilized for addition and subtraction. For example, it could be used to add $1 + 3$. Starting at one on the line, adding 3 to one means moving three units to the right to end up at 4. Therefore, $3 + 1$ is equal to 4. $5 - 2$ can also be determined. Start at 5 on the number line. Subtract 2 from 5. This means moving to the left two units from 5 to end up at 3. Therefore, $5 - 2$ is equal to 3.

The number line can also be used to show the identity property of addition and subtraction. What happens on the number line when you add or subtract zero? There is no movement along the line. For example, $5 + 0$ is equal to 5 and $4 - 0$ is equal to 4. Zero is known as both the *additive* and *subtractive identity*. This is because when you add or subtract zero from a number, that number does not change.

Addition adheres to the commutative property. This is because the order of the numbers being added does not matter. For example, both $4 + 5$ and $5 + 4$ equal 9. The *commutative property of addition* states that for any whole numbers *a* and *b*, it is true that $a + b = b + a$. Also, addition follows the associative property because the sum of three or more numbers results in the same answer, no matter what order the numbers are in. Let's look at the following example. Remember that numbers inside parentheses are always calculated first: $1 + (2 + 3)$ and $(1 + 2) + 3$ both equal 6. *The associative property of addition* states that for any whole numbers *a*, *b*, and *c*, $(a + b) + c = a + (b + c)$.

Order of Rational Numbers

A common question type asks to order rational numbers from least to greatest or greatest to least. The numbers will come in a variety of formats, including decimals, percentages, roots, fractions, and whole numbers. These questions test for knowledge of different types of numbers and the ability to determine their respective values.

Whether the question asks to order the numbers from greatest to least or least to greatest, the crux of the question is the same—convert the numbers into a common format. Generally, it's easiest to write the numbers as whole numbers and decimals so they can be placed on a number line. Follow these examples to understand this strategy.

1) Order the following rational numbers from greatest to least:

$$\sqrt{36}, 0.65, 78\%, \frac{3}{4}, 7, 90\%, \frac{5}{2}$$

Of the seven numbers, the whole number (7) and decimal (0.65) are already in an accessible form, so concentrate on the other five.

First, the square root of 36 equals 6. (If the test asks for the root of a non-perfect root, determine which two whole numbers the root lies between.) Next, convert the percentages to decimals. A percentage means "per hundred," so this conversion requires moving the decimal point two places to the left, leaving 0.78 and 0.9. Lastly, evaluate the fractions: $\frac{3}{4} = \frac{75}{100} = 0.75$; $\frac{5}{2} = 2\frac{1}{2} = 2.5$

Now, the only step left is to list the numbers in the request order:

$$7, \sqrt{36}, \frac{5}{2}, 90\%, 78\%, \frac{3}{4}, 0.65$$

2) Order the following rational numbers from least to greatest:

$$2.5, \sqrt{9}, -10.5, 0.853, 175\%, \sqrt{4}, \frac{4}{5}$$

$$\sqrt{9} = 3$$

$$175\% = 1.75$$

$$\sqrt{4} = 2$$

$$\frac{4}{5} = 0.8$$

From least to greatest, the answer is: $-10.5, \frac{4}{5}, 0.853, 175\%, \sqrt{4}, 2.5, \sqrt{9}$.

Patterns

Patterns are an important part of mathematics. When mathematical calculations are completed repeatedly, patterns can be recognized. Recognizing patterns is an integral part of mathematics because it helps you understand relationships between different ideas. For example, a sequence of numbers can be given, and being able to recognize the relationship between the given numbers can help in completing the sequence.

For instance, given the sequence of numbers 7, 14, 21, 28, 35, ..., the next number in the sequence would be 42. This is because the sequence lists all multiples of 7, starting at 7. Sequences can also be built from addition, subtraction, and division. Being able to recognize the relationship between the values that are given is the key to finding out the next number in the sequence.

Patterns within a sequence can come in 2 distinct forms. The items either repeat in a constant order, or the items change from one step to another in some consistent way. The core is the smallest unit, or number of items, that repeats in a repeating pattern. For example, the patternoo ▲oo▲o... has a core that is oo▲. Knowing only the core, the pattern can be extended. Knowing the number of steps in the core allows the identification of an item in each step without drawing/writing the entire pattern out. For example, suppose you must find the tenth item in the previous pattern. Because the core consists of three items (oo▲), the core repeats in multiples of 3. In other words, steps 3, 6, 9, 12, etc. will be ▲ completing the core with the core starting over on the next step. For the above example, the 9th step will be ▲ and the 10th will be o.

The most common patterns where each item changes from one step to the next are arithmetic and geometric sequences. In an arithmetic sequence, the items increase or decrease by a constant difference. In other words, the same thing is added or subtracted to each item or step to produce the next. To determine if a sequence is arithmetic, see what must be added or subtracted to step one to produce step two. Then, check if the same thing is added/subtracted to step two to produce step three. The same thing must be added/subtracted to step three to produce step four, and so on. Consider the pattern 13, 10, 7, 4, … . To get from step one (13) to step two (10) by adding or subtracting requires subtracting by 3. The next step is checking if subtracting 3 from step two (10) will produce step three (7), and subtracting 3 from step three (7) will produce step four (4). In this case, the pattern holds true. Therefore, this is an arithmetic sequence in which each step is produced by subtracting 3 from the previous step. To extend the sequence, 3 is subtracted from the last step to produce the next. The next three numbers in the sequence are 1, -2, -5.

A geometric sequence is one in which each step is produced by multiplying or dividing the previous step by the same number. To see if a sequence is geometric, decide what step one must be multiplied or divided by to produce step two. Then check if multiplying or dividing step two by the same number produces step three, and so on. Consider the pattern 2, 8, 32, 128, … . To get from step one (2) to step two (8) requires multiplication by 4. The next step determines if multiplying step two (8) by 4 produces step three (32), and multiplying step three (32) by 4 produces step four (128). In this case, the pattern holds true. Therefore, this is a geometric sequence in which each step is found by multiplying the previous step by 4. To extend the sequence, the last step is multiplied by 4 and repeated. The next three numbers in the sequence are 512; 2,048; 8,192.

Arithmetic and geometric sequences can also be represented by shapes. For example, an arithmetic sequence could consist of shapes with three sides, four sides, and five sides. A geometric sequence could consist of eight blocks, four blocks, and two blocks (each step is produced by dividing the number of blocks in the previous step by 2).

Relationships Between the Corresponding Terms of Two Numerical Patterns

When given two number patterns, the corresponding terms should be examined to determine if a relationship exists between them. Corresponding terms between patterns are the pairs of numbers which appear in the same step of the two sequences. Consider the following patterns 1, 2, 3, 4,… and 3, 6, 9, 12, … . The corresponding terms are: 1 and 3; 2 and 6; 3 and 9; and 4 and 12. To identify the relationship, each pair of corresponding terms is examined. You can also examine the possibilities of performing an operation (+, −, ×, ÷) to each sequence. In this case:

$$1 + 2 = 3 \text{ or } 1 \times 3 = 3$$

$$2 + 4 = 6 \text{ or } 2 \times 3 = 6$$

$$3 + 6 = 9 \text{ or } 3 \times 3 = 9$$

$$4 + 8 = 12 \text{ or } 4 \times 3 = 12$$

The pattern is that the number from the first sequence multiplied by 3 equals the number in the second sequence. By assigning each sequence a label (input and output) or variable (*x* and *y*), the relationship can be written as an equation. The first sequence represents the inputs, or *x*, and the second sequence represents the outputs, or *y*. So, the relationship can be expressed as: $y = 3x$.

Consider the following sets of numbers:

a	2	4	6	8
b	6	8	10	12

To write a rule for the relationship between the values for *a* and the values for *b*, the corresponding terms (2 and 6; 4 and 8; 6 and 10; 8 and 12) are examined. The possibilities for producing *b* from *a* are:

$2 + 4 = 6$ or $2 \times 3 = 6$

$4 + 4 = 8$ or $4 \times 2 = 8$

$6 + 4 = 10$

$8 + 4 = 12$ or $8 \times 1.5 = 12$

The pattern is that adding 4 to the value of *a* produces the value of *b*. The relationship can be written as the equation $a + 4 = b$.

Rounding

Rounding is an important concept dealing with place value. *Rounding* is the process of either bumping a number up or down, based on a certain place value. First, the place value is specified. Then, the digit to its right is looked at. For example, if rounding to the nearest hundreds place, the digit in the tens place is used. If it is a zero, one, 2, 3, or 4, the digit being rounded to is left alone. If it is a 5, 6, 7, 8 or 9, the digit being rounded to is increased by one. All other digits before the decimal point are then changed to zeros, and the digits in decimal places are dropped. If a decimal place is being rounded to, all digits that come after are just dropped. For example, if 845,231.45 was to be rounded to the nearest thousands place, the answer would be 845,000. The 5 would remain the same due to the 2 in the hundreds place. Also, if 4.567 were to be rounded to the nearest tenths place, the answer would be 4.6. The 5 increased to 6 due to the 6 in the hundredths place, and the rest of the decimal is dropped.

Structure of the Number System

The mathematical number system is made up of two general types of numbers: real and complex. *Real numbers* are those that are used in normal settings, while *complex numbers* are those composed of both a real number and an imaginary one. Imaginary numbers are the result of taking the square root of -1, and $\sqrt{-1} = i$.

The real number system is often explained using a Venn diagram similar to the one below. After a number has been labeled as a real number, further classification occurs when considering the other groups in this diagram. If a number is a never-ending, non-repeating decimal, it falls in the irrational category. Otherwise, it is rational. More information on these types of numbers is provided in the previous section. Furthermore, if a number does not have a fractional part, it is classified as an integer, such as -2, 75, or 0. Whole numbers are an even smaller group that only includes positive integers and 0. The last group of natural numbers is made up of only positive integers, such as 2, 56, or 12.

Real numbers can be compared and ordered using the number line. If a number falls to the left on the real number line, it is less than a number on the right. For example, $-2 < 5$ because -2 falls to the left of 0, and 5 falls to the right. Numbers to the left of zero are negative while those to the right are positive.

Complex numbers are made up of the sum of a real number and an imaginary number. Some examples of complex numbers include $6 + 2i$, $5 - 7i$, and $-3 + 12i$. Adding and subtracting complex numbers is similar to collecting like terms. The real numbers are added together, and the imaginary numbers are added together. For example, if the problem asks to simplify the expression $6 + 2i - 3 + 7i$, the 6 and -3 are combined to make 3, and the $2i$ and $7i$ combine to make $9i$. Multiplying and dividing complex numbers is similar to working with exponents. One rule to remember when multiplying is that $i * i = -1$. For example, if a problem asks to simplify the expression $4i(3 + 7i)$, the $4i$ should be distributed throughout the 3 and the $7i$. This leaves the final expression $12i - 28$. The 28 is negative because $i * i$ results in a negative number. The last type of operation to consider with complex numbers is the conjugate. The *conjugate* of a complex number is a technique used to change the complex number into a real number. For example, the conjugate of $4 - 3i$ is $4 + 3i$. Multiplying $(4 - 3i)(4 + 3i)$ results in $16 + 12i - 12i + 9$, which has a final answer of $16 + 9 = 25$.

The order of operations—PEMDAS—simplifies longer expressions with real or imaginary numbers. Each operation is listed in the order of how they should be completed in a problem containing more than one operation. Parenthesis can also mean grouping symbols, such as brackets and absolute value. Then, exponents are calculated. Multiplication and division should be completed from left to right, and addition and subtraction should be completed from left to right.

Simplification of another type of expression occurs when radicals are involved. As explained previously, root is another word for radical. For example, the following expression is a radical that can be simplified: $\sqrt{24x^2}$. First, the number must be factored out to the highest perfect square. Any perfect square can be taken out of a radical. Twenty-four can be factored into 4 and 6, and 4 can be taken out of the radical. $\sqrt{4} = 2$ can be taken out, and 6 stays underneath. If $x > 0$, x can be taken out of the radical because it is a perfect square. The simplified radical is $2x\sqrt{6}$. An approximation can be found using a calculator.

There are also properties of numbers that are true for certain operations. The *commutative* property allows the order of the terms in an expression to change while keeping the same final answer. Both addition and multiplication can be completed in any order and still obtain the same result. However, order does matter in subtraction and division. The *associative* property allows any terms to be "associated" by parenthesis and retain the same final answer. For example, $(4 + 3) + 5 = 4 + (3 + 5)$. Both addition and multiplication are associative; however, subtraction and division do not hold this property. The *distributive* property states that $a(b + c) = ab + ac$. It is a property that involves both addition and multiplication, and the *a* is distributed onto each term inside the parentheses.

Integers can be factored into prime numbers. To *factor* is to express as a product. For example, $6 = 3 \cdot 2$, and $6 = 6 \cdot 1$. Both are factorizations, but the expression involving the factors of 3 and 2 is known as a *prime factorization* because it is factored into a product of two *prime numbers*—integers which do not have any factors other than themselves and 1. A *composite number* is a positive integer that can be divided into at least one other integer other than itself and 1, such as 6. Integers that have a factor of 2 are even, and if they are not divisible by 2, they are odd. Finally, a *multiple* of a number is the product of that number and a counting number—also known as a *natural number*. For example, some multiples of 4 are 4, 8, 12, 16, etc.

Basic Addition, Subtraction, Multiplication, and Division

Gaining more of something relates to addition. While taking something away relates to subtraction. Vocabulary words such as *total, more, less, left,* and *remain* are common when working with these problems. The $+$ sign means plus. This shows that addition is happening. The $-$ sign means minus. This shows that subtraction is happening. The symbols will be important when you write out equations.

Addition can also be defined in equation form. For example, $4 + 5 = 9$ shows that $4 + 5$ is the same as 9. Therefore, $9 = 9$, and "four plus five equals nine." When two quantities are being added together, the result is called the *sum*. Therefore, the sum of 4 and 5 is 9. The numbers being added, such as 4 and 5, are known as the *addends*.

Subtraction can also be in equation form. For example, $9 - 5 = 4$ shows that $9 - 5$ is the same as 4 and that "9 minus 5 is 4." The result of subtraction is known as a *difference*. The difference of $9 - 5$ is 4. 4 represents the amount that is left once the subtraction is done. The order in which subtraction is completed does matter. For example, $9 - 5$ and $5 - 9$ do not result in the same answer. $5 - 9$ results in a negative number. So, subtraction does not adhere to the commutative or associative property. The order in which subtraction is completed is important.

Multiplication is when we add equal amounts. The answer to a multiplication problem is called a *product*. Products stand for the total number of items within different groups. The symbol for multiplication is $\times$ or $\cdot$. We say 2×3 or $2 \cdot 3$ means "2 times 3."

As an example, there are three sets of four apples. The goal is to know how many apples there are in total. Three sets of four apples gives $4 + 4 + 4 = 12$. Also, three times four apples gives $3 \times 4 = 12$. Therefore, for any whole numbers *a* and *b*, where *a* is not equal to zero, $a \times b = b + b + \cdots b$, where *b* is added *a* times. Also, $a \times b$ can be thought of as the number of units in a rectangular block consisting of *a* rows and *b* columns. For example, 3×7 is equal to the number of squares in the following rectangle:

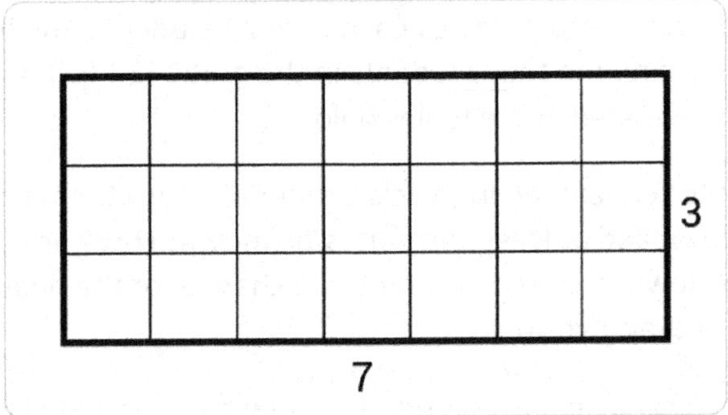

The answer is 21, and there are 21 squares in the rectangle.

With any number times one (for example,$8 \times 1 = 8$) the original amount does not change. Therefore, one is the *multiplicative identity*. For any whole number *a*, $1 \times a = a$. Also, any number multiplied times zero results in zero. Therefore, for any whole number *a*, $0 \times a = 0$.

Division is based on dividing a given number into parts. The simplest problem involves dividing a number into equal parts. For example, a pack of 20 pencils is to be divided among 10 children. You would have to divide 20 by 10. In this example, each child would receive 2 pencils.

The symbol for division is $\div$ or /. The equation above is written as $20 \div 10 = 2$, or 20 / 10 = 2. This means "20 divided by 10 is equal to 2". Division can be explained as the following: for any whole numbers *a* and *b*, where *b* is not equal to zero, $a \div b = c$ if and only if $a = b \times c$. This means, division can be thought of as a multiplication problem with a missing part. For instance, calculating $20 \div 10$ is the same as asking the following: "If there are 20 items in total with 10 in each group, how many are in each group?" Therefore, 20 is equal to ten times what value? This question is the same as asking, "If there are 20 items in total with 2 in each group, how many groups are there?" The answer to each question is 2.

In a division problem, *a* is known as the *dividend*, *b* is the *divisor*, and *c* is the *quotient*. Zero cannot be divided into parts. Therefore, for any nonzero whole number $a, 0 \div a = 0$. Also, division by zero is undefined. Dividing an amount into zero parts is not possible.

Harder division involves dividing a number into equal parts, but having some left over. An example is dividing a pack of 20 pencils among 8 friends so that each friend receives the same number of pencils. In this setting, each friend receives 2 pencils. There are 4 pencils leftover. 20 is the dividend, 8 is the divisor, 2 is the quotient, and 4 is known as the *remainder*. Within this type of division problem, for whole numbers *a*, *b*, *c*, and *d*, $a \div b = c$ with a remainder of *d*. This is true if and only if $a = (b \times c) + d$. When calculating $a \div b$, if there is no remainder, *a* is said to be *divisible* by *b*. *Even numbers* are all divisible by the number 2. *Odd numbers* are not divisible by 2. An odd number of items cannot be paired up into groups of 2 without having one item leftover.

Addition and subtraction are "inverse operations." Adding a number and then subtracting the same number will cancel each other out. This results in the original number, and vice versa. For example,$8 + 7 - 7 = 8$and $137 - 100 + 100 = 137$.

Multiplication and division are also inverse operations. So, multiplying by a number and then dividing by the same number results in the original number. For example,$8 \times 2 \div 2 = 8$ and$12 \div 4 \times 4 = 12$. Inverse operations are used to work backwards to solve problems. In the case that 7 and a number add to 18, the inverse operation of subtraction is used to find the unknown value ($18 - 7 = 11$). If a school's entire 4th grade was divided evenly into 3 classes each with 22 students, the inverse operation of multiplication is used to determine the total students in the grade ($22 \times 3 = 66$). More scenarios involving inverse operations are listed in the tables below.

Word problems take concepts you learned in the classroom and turn them into real-life situations. Some parts of the problem are known and at least one part is unknown. There are three types of instances in which something can be unknown: the starting point, the change, or the final result. These can all be missing from the information they give you.

For an addition problem, the change is the quantity of a new amount added to the starting point.

For a subtraction problem, the change is the quantity taken away from the starting point.

Regarding addition, the given equation is $3 + 7 = 10$.

The number 3 is the starting point. 7 is the change, and 10 is the result from adding a new amount to the starting point. Different word problems can arise from this same equation, depending on which value is the unknown. For example, here are three problems:

- If a boy had 3 pencils and was given 7 more, how many would he have in total?
- If a boy had 3 pencils and a girl gave him more so that he had 10 in total, how many were given to him?
- A boy was given 7 pencils so that he had 10 in total. How many did he start with?

All three problems involve the same equation. Finding out which part of the equation is missing is the key to solving each word problem. The missing answers would be 10, 7, and 3.

In terms of subtraction, the same three scenarios can occur. The given equation is $6 - 4 = 2$.

The number 6 is the starting point. 4 is the change, and 2 is the new amount that is the result from taking away an amount from the starting point. Again, different types of word problems can arise from this equation. For example, here are three possible problems:

- If a girl had 6 quarters and 2 were taken away, how many would be left over?
- If a girl had 6 quarters, purchased a pencil, and had 2 quarters left over, how many did she pay with?
- If a girl paid for a pencil with 4 quarters and had 2 quarters left over, how many did she have to start with?

The three question types follow the structure of the addition word problems. Finding out whether the starting point, the change, or the final result is missing is the goal in solving the problem. The missing answers would be 2, 4, and 6.

The three addition problems and the three subtraction word problems can be solved by using a picture, a number line, or an algebraic equation. If an equation is used, a question mark can be used to show the number we don't know. For example, $6 - 4 = ?$ can be written to show that the missing value is the result. Using equation form shows us what part of the addition or subtraction problem is missing.

Key words within a multiplication problem involve *times, product, doubled*, and *tripled.* Key words within a division problem involve *split, quotient, divided, shared, groups*, and *half*. Like addition and subtraction, multiplication and division problems also have three different types of missing values.

<u>Multiplication</u>
Multiplication consists of a certain number of groups, with the same amount of items within each group, and the total amount within all groups. Therefore, each one of these amounts can be the missing value.

For example, the given equation is $5 \times 3 = 15$.

5 and 3 are interchangeable, so either amount can be the number of groups or the number of items within each group. 15 is the total number of items. Again, different types of word problems can arise from this equation. For example, here are three problems:

- If a classroom is serving 5 different types of apples for lunch and has 3 apples of each type, how many total apples are there to give to the students?
- If a classroom has 15 apples with 5 different types, how many of each type are there?
- If a classroom has 15 apples with 3 of each type, how many types are there to choose from?

Each question involves using the same equation to solve. It is important to decide which part of the equation is the missing value. The answers to the problems are 15, 3, and 5.

<u>Division</u>
Similar to multiplication, division problems involve a total amount, a number of groups having the same amount, and a number of items within each group. The difference between multiplication and division is that the starting point is the total amount. It then gets divided into equal amounts.

For example, the equation is $15 \div 5 = 3$.

15 is the total number of items, which is being divided into 5 different groups. In order to do so, 3 items go into each group. Also, 5 and 3 are interchangeable. So, the 15 items could be divided into 3 groups of

5 items each. Therefore, different types of word problems can arise from this equation. For example, here are three types of problems:

- A boy needs 48 pieces of chalk. If there are 8 pieces in each box, how many boxes should he buy?
- A boy has 48 pieces of chalk. If each box has 6 pieces in it, how many boxes did he buy?
- A boy has partitioned all of his chalk into 8 piles, with 6 pieces in each pile. How many pieces does he have in total?

Each one of these questions involves the same equation. The third question can easily utilize the multiplication equation $8 \times 6 = ?$ instead of division. The answers are 6, 8, and 48.

Another method of multiplication can be done with the use of an *area model*. An area model is a rectangle that is divided into rows and columns that match up to the number of place values within each number. For example, $29 \times 65 = 25 + 4$ and $66 = 60 + 5$. The products of those 4 numbers are found within the rectangle and then summed up to get the answer. The entire process is: $(60 \times 25) + (5 \times 25) + (60 \times 4) + (5 \times 4) = 1{,}500 + 240 + 125 + 20 = 1{,}885$. Here is the actual area model:

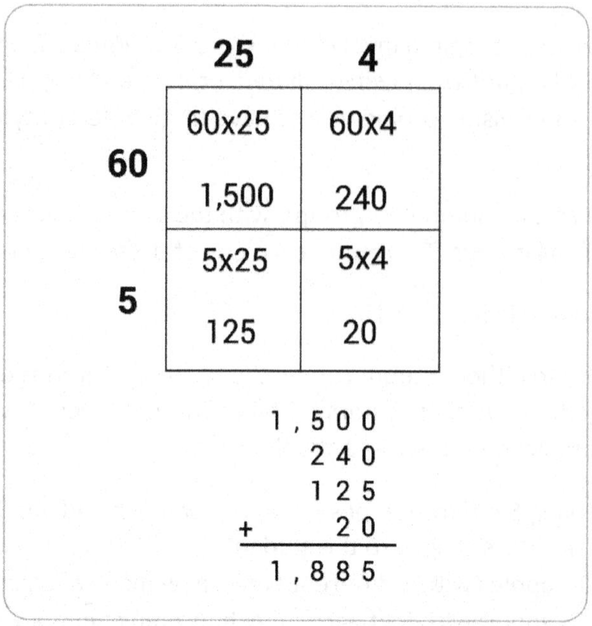

Decimals and fractions are two ways to represent positive numbers less than one. Counting money in coins is a good way to visualize values less than one. This is because problems dealing with change are stories that are used in real life. For example, if a student had 3 quarters and a dime and wanted to purchase a cookie at lunch for 50 cents, how much change would she receive? The answer would be found by first calculating the sum of the change as 85 cents and then subtracting 50 cents to get 35 cents. Money can also be used as a way to understand the transition between decimals and fractions. For example, a dime represents \$0.10 or $\frac{1}{10}$ of a dollar. Problems involving both dollars and cents should also be considered. For example, if someone has 3 dollar bills and 2 quarters, the amount can be represented as a decimal as \$3.50.

Formally, a *decimal* is a number that has a dot in the number. For example, 3.45 is a decimal. The dot is called a *decimal point*. The number to the left of the decimal point is in the ones place. The number to the right of the decimal point represents the part of the number less than one. The first number to the right of the decimal point is the tenths place, and one tenth represents $\frac{1}{10}$, just like a dime. The next place is the hundredths place, and it represents $\frac{1}{100}$, just like a penny. This idea is continued to the right in the hundredths, thousandths, and ten thousandths places. Each place value to the right is ten times smaller than the one to its left.

A number less than one has only digits in some decimal places. For example, 0.53 is less than one. A *mixed number* is a number greater than one that also contains digits in some decimal places. For example, 3.43 is a mixed number. Adding a zero to the right of a decimal does not change the value of the number. For example, 2.75 is the same as 2.750. However, 2.75 is the more accepted representation of the number. Also, zeros are usually placed in the ones column in any value less than one. For example, 0.65 is the same as .65, but 0.65 is more widely used.

In order to read or write a decimal, the decimal point is ignored. The number is read as a whole number. Then the place value unit is stated where the last digit falls. For example, 0.089 is read as *eighty-nine thousandths,* and 0.1345 is read as *one thousand, three hundred forty-five ten thousandths.* In mixed numbers, the word *and* is used to represent the decimal point. For example, 2.56 is read as *two and fifty-six hundredths.*

We multiply decimals the same way we multiply whole numbers. The only difference is that decimal places are included in the end result. For example, given the problem 87.5×0.45, the answer would be found by multiplying 875×45 to get 39,375. Then you would input a decimal point three places to the left because there are three total decimal places in the original problem. Therefore, the answer is 39.375.

Dividing a number by a single digit or two digits can be turned into repeated subtraction problems. An area model can be used throughout the problem that represents multiples of the divisor. For example, the answer to $8580 \div 55$ can be found by subtracting 55 from 8580 one at a time and counting the total number of subtractions necessary.

However, a simpler process involves using larger multiples of 55. First, $100 \times 55 = 5{,}500$ is subtracted from 8,580, and 3,080 is leftover. Next, $50 \times 55 = 2{,}750$ is subtracted from 3,080 to obtain380. $5 \times 55 = 275$ is subtracted from 330 to obtain 55, and finally, $1 \times 55 = 55$ is subtracted from 55 to obtain zero. Therefore, there is no remainder, and the answer is $100 + 50 + 5 + 1 = 156$.

Here is a picture of the area model and the repeated subtraction process:

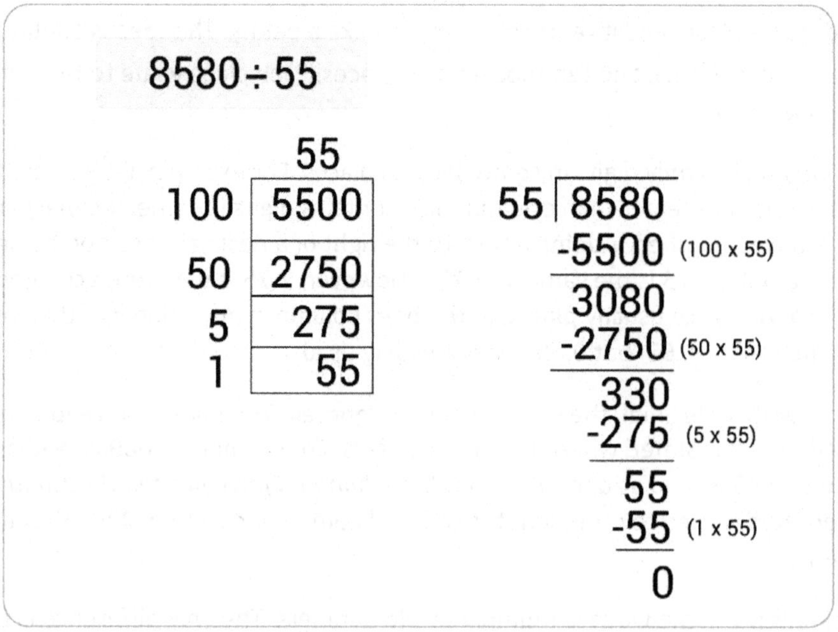

If you want to check the answer of a division problem, multiply the answer times the divisor. This will help you check to see if the dividend is obtained. If there is a remainder, the same process is done, but the remainder is added on at the end to try to match the dividend. In the previous example, $156 \times 64 = 9984$ would be the checking procedure. Dividing decimals involves the same repeated subtraction process. The only difference would be that the subtractions would involve numbers that include values in the decimal places. Lining up decimal places is crucial in this type of problem.

Recognition of Decimals

The *decimal system* is a way of writing out numbers that uses ten different numerals: 0, 1, 2, 3, 4, 5, 6, 7, 8, and 9. This is also called a "base ten" or "base 10" system. Other bases are also used. For example, computers work with a base of 2. This means they only use the numerals 0 and 1.

The *decimal place* denotes how far to the right of the decimal point a numeral is. The first digit to the right of the decimal point is in the *tenths* place. The next is the *hundredths*. The third is the *thousandths*.

So, 3.142 has a 1 in the tenths place, a 4 in the hundredths place, and a 2 in the thousandths place.

The *decimal point* is a period used to separate the *ones* place from the *tenths* place when writing out a number as a decimal.

A *decimal number* is a number written out with a decimal point instead of as a fraction, for example, 1.25 instead of $\frac{5}{4}$. Depending on the situation, it can sometimes be easier to work with fractions and sometimes easier to work with decimal numbers.

A decimal number is *terminating* if it stops at some point. It is called *repeating* if it never stops, but repeats a pattern over and over. It is important to note that every rational number can be written as a terminating decimal or as a repeating decimal.

Addition with Decimals

To add decimal numbers, each number in columns needs to be lined up by the decimal point. For each number being added, the zeros to the right of the last number need to be filled in so that each of the numbers has the same number of places to the right of the decimal. Then, the columns can be added together. Here is an example of 2.45 + 1.3 + 8.891 written in column form:

$$\begin{array}{r} 2.450 \\ 1.300 \\ \underline{+\,8.891} \end{array}$$

Zeros have been added in the columns so that each number has the same number of places to the right of the decimal.

Added together, the correct answer is 12.641:

$$\begin{array}{r} 2.450 \\ 1.300 \\ \underline{+\,8.891} \\ 12.641 \end{array}$$

Subtraction with Decimals

Subtracting decimal numbers is the same process as adding decimals. Here is 7.89 – 4.235 written in column form:

$$\begin{array}{r} 7.890 \\ \underline{-\,4.235} \\ 3.655 \end{array}$$

A zero has been added in the column so that each number has the same number of places to the right of the decimal.

Multiplication with Decimals

Decimals can be multiplied as if there were no decimals points in the problem. For example, 0.5 x 1.25 can be rewritten and multiplied as 5 x 125, which equals 625.

The final answer will have the same number of decimal *points* as the total number of decimal *places* in the problem. The first number has one decimal place, and the second number has two decimal places. Therefore, the final answer will contain three decimal places:

$$0.5 \times 1.25 = 0.625$$

Division with Decimals

Dividing a decimal by a whole number entails using long division first by ignoring the decimal point. Then, the decimal point is moved the number of places given in the problem.

For example, $6.8 \div 4$ can be rewritten as $68 \div 4$, which is 17. There is one non-zero integer to the right of the decimal point, so the final solution would have one decimal place to the right of the solution. In this case, the solution is 1.7.

Dividing a decimal by another decimal requires changing the divisor to a whole number by moving its decimal point. The decimal place of the dividend should be moved by the same number of places as the divisor. Then, the problem is the same as dividing a decimal by a whole number.

For example, $5.72 \div 1.1$ has a divisor with one decimal point in the denominator. The expression can be rewritten as $57.2 \div 11$ by moving each number one decimal place to the right to eliminate the decimal. The long division can be completed as $572 \div 11$ with a result of 52. Since there is one non-zero integer to the right of the decimal point in the problem, the final solution is 5.2.

In another example, $8 \div 0.16$ has a divisor with two decimal points in the denominator. The expression can be rewritten as $800 \div 16$ by moving each number two decimal places to the right to eliminate the decimal in the divisor. The long division can be completed with a result of 50.

Percentages

Percentages can be thought of as fractions that are based on a whole of 100; that is, one whole is equal to 100%. The word percent means "per hundred." Fractions can be expressed as percents by finding equivalent fractions with a denomination of 100. Example: $\frac{7}{10} = \frac{70}{100} = 70\%$; $\frac{1}{4} = \frac{25}{100} = 25\%$.

To express a percentage as a fraction, divide the percentage number by 100 and reduce the fraction to its simplest possible terms. Example: $60\% = \frac{60}{100} = \frac{3}{5}$; $96\% = \frac{96}{100} = \frac{24}{25}$.

Converting decimals to percentages and percentages to decimals is as simple as moving the decimal point. To convert from a decimal to a percent, move the decimal point two places to the right. To convert from a percent to a decimal, move it two places to the left. Example: 0.23 = 23%; 5.34 = 534%; 0.007 = 0.7%; 700% = 7.00; 86% = 0.86; 0.15% = 0.0015.

It may be helpful to remember that the percentage number will always be larger than the equivalent decimal number.

A percentage problem can be presented three main ways: (1) Find what percentage of some number another number is. Example: What percentage of 40 is 8? (2) Find what number is some percentage of a given number. Example: What number is 20% of 40? (3) Find what number another number is a given percentage of.

Example: What number is 8 20% of? The three components in all of these cases are the same: a whole (*W*), a part (*P*), and a percentage (%). These are related by the equation: $P = W \times \%$. This is the form of the equation you would use to solve problems of type (2). To solve types (1) and (3), you would use these two forms:

$$\% = \frac{P}{W} \text{ and } W = \frac{P}{\%}$$

The thing that frequently makes percentage problems difficult is that they are most often also word problems, so a large part of solving them is figuring out which quantities are what. Example: In a school cafeteria, 7 students choose pizza, 9 choose hamburgers, and 4 choose tacos. Find the percentage that chooses tacos. To find the whole, you must first add all of the parts: 7 + 9 + 4 = 20. The percentage can then be found by dividing the part by the whole ($\% = \frac{P}{W}$): $\frac{4}{20} = \frac{20}{100} = 20\%$.

<u>Converting Decimals, Fractions, and Percentages</u>

Percentages are a type of fraction. In a percentage, the denominator, represented by a % sign, is always 100. The sign % stands for per hundred. So, 25% can be read as 25 per hundred. In order to convert a decimal to a percent, move the decimal point two spaces to the right. The decimal 0.45 becomes 45%. In order to convert a percentage into a decimal, move the decimal point two places to the left. The percentage 16% becomes 0.16.

Fractions can also be converted into percentages. The first step is to convert the fraction into a decimal. Next, convert the decimal into a percentage. For example, consider the fraction 3/4. Dividing 3 by 4 yields 0.75, which can be converted into a percentage by shifting the decimal two places to the right (75%).

Numbers and Fractions

Fractions are a vital part of mathematics, and their understanding tends to be extremely challenging for students. Too often, steps are learned without understanding why they are being performed. It is important for teachers to make the concept of fractions less abstract and more tangible by providing concrete examples in the classroom. With this solid foundation and a lot of practice, learning will be easier, and success with fractions in later math classes will occur.

A *fraction* is a part of something that is whole. Items such as apples can be cut into parts to help visualize fractions. If an apple is cut into 2 equal parts, each part represents ½ of the apple. If each half is cut into two parts, the apple now is cut into quarters. Each piece now represents ¼ of the apple. In this example, each part is equal because they all have the same size. Geometric shapes, such as circles and squares, can also be utilized in the classroom to help visualize the idea of fractions.

For example, a circle can be drawn on the board and divided it into 6 equal parts:

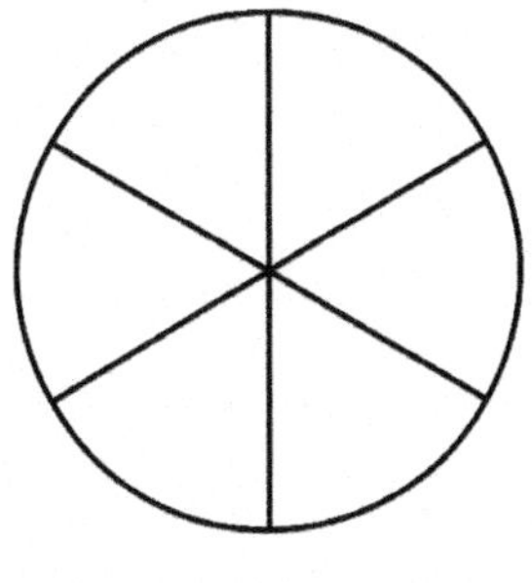

Shading can be used to represent parts of the circle that can be translated into fractions. The top of the fraction, the *numerator*, can represent how many segments are shaded. The bottom of the fraction, the *denominator*, can represent the number of segments that the circle is broken into. A pie is a good analogy to use in this example. If one piece of the circle is shaded, or one piece of pie is cut out, $^1/_6$ of the object is being referred to. An apple, a pie, or a circle can be utilized in order to compare simple fractions. For example, showing that $^1/_2$ is larger than $^1/_4$ and that $^1/_4$ is smaller than $^1/_3$ can be accomplished through shading. A *unit fraction* is a fraction in which the numerator is 1, and the denominator is a positive whole number. It represents one part of a whole—one piece of pie.

A *proper fraction* is a fraction in which the numerator is less than the denominator. An *improper fraction* is a fraction in which the numerator is greater than the denominator. An example of a proper fraction is $^5/_6$, and an improper fraction is $^6/_5$. A proper fraction represents less than a whole pie or circle, and an improper fraction represents more than one whole pie or circle. Improper fractions can be written using whole numbers as *mixed numbers.* The bar in a fraction represents division. Therefore $^6/_5$ is the same as $6 \div 5$. In order to rewrite it as a mixed number, division is performed to obtain $6 \div 5 = 1\, R1$. The remainder is then converted into fraction form. The actual remainder becomes the numerator of a fraction, and the divisor becomes the denominator. Therefore 1 *R*1 is written as $1\frac{1}{5}$, a mixed number. A mixed number can also decomposed into the addition of a whole number and a fraction. For example,

$$1\frac{1}{5} = 1 + \frac{1}{5} \text{ and } 4\frac{5}{6} = 4 + \frac{1}{6} + \frac{1}{6} + \frac{1}{6} + \frac{1}{6} + \frac{1}{6}$$

Every fraction can be built from a combination of unit fractions.

Like fractions, or *equivalent fractions*, represent two fractions that are made up of different numbers, but represent the same quantity. For example, the given fractions are $^4/_8$ and $^3/_6$. If a pie was cut into 8 pieces and 4 pieces were removed, half of the pie would remain. Also, if a pie was split into 6 pieces and 3 pieces were eaten, half of the pie would also remain. Therefore, both of the fractions represent half of a pie. These two fractions are referred to as like fractions. *Unlike fractions* are fractions that are different and cannot be thought of as representing equal quantities. When working with fractions in mathematical expressions, like fractions should be simplified. Both $^4/_8$ and $^3/_6$ can be simplified into $^1/_2$.

Comparing fractions can be completed through the use of a number line. For example, if $\frac{3}{5}$ and $\frac{6}{10}$ need to be compared, each fraction should be plotted on a number line. To plot $\frac{3}{5}$, the area from 0 to 1 should be broken into 5 equal segments, and the fraction represents 3 of them. To plot $\frac{4}{10}$, the area from 0 to 1 should be broken into 10 equal segments and the fraction represents 6 of them.

It can be seen that $\frac{3}{5} = \frac{6}{10}$

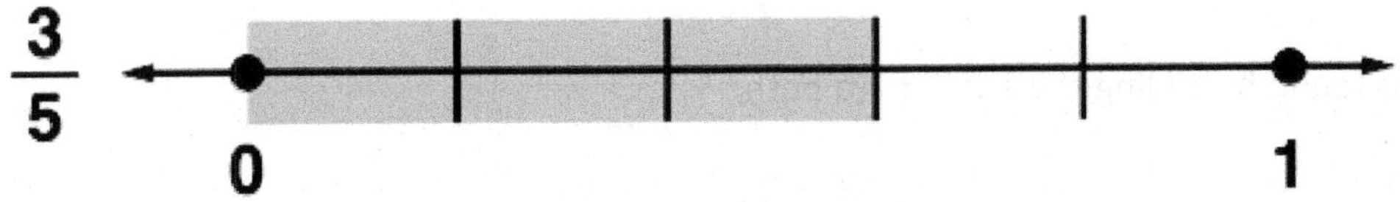

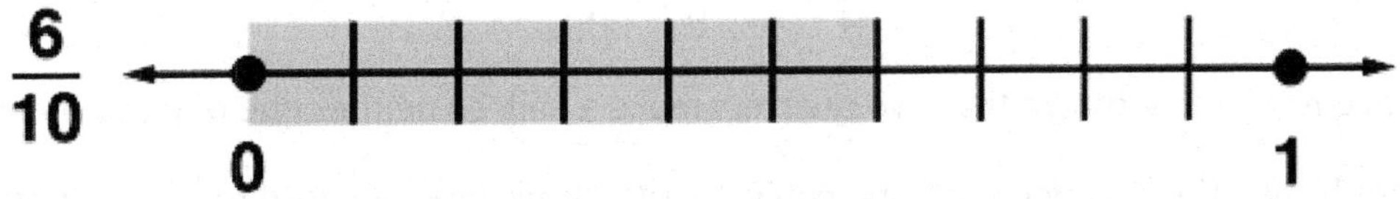

Like fractions are plotted at the same point on a number line. Baseline fractions can also be used to compare fractions. For example, if it is known that

$$\frac{4}{5} > \frac{1}{2}$$

and

$$\frac{1}{2} > \frac{4}{10}$$

Also, converting improper fractions to mixed numbers can be helpful in comparing fractions because the whole number portion of the number is more visible.

Adding and subtracting mixed numbers and fractions can be completed by decomposing fractions into a sum of whole numbers and unit fractions. For example, the given problem is

$$5\frac{3}{7} + 2\frac{1}{7}$$

Decomposing into

$$5 + \frac{1}{7} + \frac{1}{7} + \frac{1}{7} + 2 + \frac{1}{7}$$

This shows that the whole numbers can be added separately from the unit fractions. The answer is

$$5 + 2 + \frac{1}{7} + \frac{1}{7} + \frac{1}{7} + \frac{1}{7} = 7 + \frac{4}{7} = 7\frac{4}{7}$$

Adding and subtracting fractions that have the same denominators involve adding or subtracting the numerators. The denominator will stay the same. Therefore, the decomposition process can be made simpler, and the fractions do not have to be broken into unit fractions.

For example, the given problem is:

$$4\frac{7}{8} - 2\frac{6}{8}$$

The answer is found by adding the answers to both

$$4 - 2 \text{ and } \frac{7}{8} - \frac{6}{8}$$

$$2 + \frac{1}{8} = 2\frac{1}{8}$$

A common mistake would be to add the denominators so that

$$\frac{1}{4} + \frac{1}{4} = \frac{1}{8} \text{ or } \frac{2}{8}$$

However, conceptually, it is known that two quarters make a half, so neither one of these are correct.

If two fractions have different denominators, equivalent fractions must be used to add or subtract them. The fractions must be converted into fractions that have common denominators. A *least common denominator* or the product of the two denominators can be used as the common denominator. For example, in the problem $\frac{5}{6} + \frac{2}{3}$, both 6, which is the least common denominator, and 18, which is the product of the denominators, can be used. In order to use 6, $\frac{2}{3}$ must be converted to sixths. A number line can be used to show the equivalent fraction is $\frac{4}{6}$. What happens is that $\frac{2}{3}$ is multiplied times a fractional form of 1 to obtain a denominator of 6. Hence, $\frac{2}{3} \times \frac{2}{2} = \frac{4}{6}$. Therefore, the problem is now $\frac{5}{6} + \frac{4}{6} = \frac{9}{6}$, which can be simplified into $\frac{3}{2}$. In order to use 18, both fractions must be converted into having 18 as their denominator. $\frac{5}{6}$ would have to be multiplied times $\frac{3}{3}$, and $\frac{2}{3}$ would need to be multiplied times $\frac{6}{6}$.The addition problem would be $\frac{15}{18} + \frac{12}{18} = \frac{27}{18}$, which reduces into $\frac{3}{2}$.

When referring to coins, a dime is equal to $\frac{1}{10}$ of a dollar, and a penny is $\frac{1}{100}$ of a dollar. In decimal form, $\frac{1}{10} = 0.1$, *one-tenth*, and $\frac{1}{100} = 0.01$, *one-hundredth*. Other decimals can be expressed over a denominator of 10 and 100. For example, $\frac{3}{10} = 0.3$, *three-tenths*, and $\frac{56}{100} = 0.56$, *fifty-six hundredths*. Decimals can also be compared using a number line. The region from 0 to 1 can be broken up into either 10 or 100 segments, and the numbers can be plotted accordingly for comparison.

Multiplying and Dividing Fractions

Because multiplication is commutative, multiplying a fraction times a whole number is the same as multiplying a whole number times a fraction. The problem involves adding a fraction a specific number of times. The problem $3 \times \frac{1}{4}$ can be translated into adding the unit fraction 3 times: $\frac{1}{4} + \frac{1}{4} + \frac{1}{4} = \frac{3}{4}$. In the problem $4 \times \frac{2}{5}$, the fraction can be decomposed into $\frac{1}{5} + \frac{1}{5}$ and then added 4 times to obtain $\frac{8}{5}$. Also, both of these answers can be found by just multiplying the whole number times the numerator of the fraction being multiplied.

The whole numbers can be written in fraction form as:

$$\frac{3}{1} \times \frac{1}{4} = \frac{3}{4}$$

$$\frac{4}{1} \times \frac{2}{5} = \frac{8}{5}$$

Multiplying a fraction times a fraction involves multiplying the numerators together separately and the denominators together separately. For example,

$$\frac{3}{8} \times \frac{2}{3} = \frac{3 \times 2}{8 \times 3} = \frac{6}{24}$$

This can then be reduced to $^1/_4$. Dividing a fraction by a fraction is actually a multiplication problem. It involves flipping the divisor and then multiplying normally. For example,

$$\frac{22}{5} \div \frac{1}{2} = \frac{22}{5} \times \frac{2}{1} = \frac{44}{5}$$

The same procedure can be implemented for division problems involving fractions and whole numbers. The whole number can be rewritten as a fraction over a denominator of 1, and then division can be completed.

A common denominator approach can also be used in dividing fractions. Considering the same problem, $\frac{22}{5} \div \frac{1}{2}$, a common denominator between the two fractions is 10. $\frac{22}{5}$ would be rewritten as $\frac{22}{5} \times \frac{2}{2} = \frac{44}{10}$, and $\frac{1}{2}$ would be rewritten as $\frac{1}{2} \times \frac{5}{5} = \frac{5}{10}$. Dividing both numbers straight across results in $\frac{44}{10} \div \frac{5}{10} = \frac{^{44}/_5}{^{10}/_{10}} = \frac{^{44}/_5}{1} = {^{44}/_5}$.

Many real-world problems will involve the use of fractions. Key words include actual fraction values, such as half, quarter, third, fourth, etc. The best approach to solving word problems involving fractions is to draw a picture or diagram that represents the scenario being discussed, while deciding which type of operation is necessary in order to solve the problem. A phrase such as "one fourth of 60 pounds of coal" creates a scenario in which multiplication should be used, and the mathematical form of the phrase is $\frac{1}{4} \times 60$.

Algebraic Expressions and Equations

Algebraic expressions look similar to equations, but they do not include the equal sign. Algebraic expressions are comprised of numbers, variables, and mathematical operations. Some examples of algebraic expressions are $8x + 7y - 12z$, $3a^2$, and $5x^3 - 4y^4$.

Algebraic expressions and equations can be used to represent real-life situations and model the behavior of different variables. For example, $2x + 5$ could represent the cost to play games at an arcade. In this case, 5 represents the price of admission to the arcade and 2 represents the cost of each game played. To calculate the total cost, use the number of games played for x, multiply it by 2, and add 5.

Solving for a Variable

Similar to order of operation rules, algebraic rules must be obeyed to ensure a correct answer. Begin by locating all parentheses and brackets, and then solving the equations within them. Then, perform the operations necessary to remove all parentheses and brackets. Next, convert all fractions into whole numbers and combine common terms on each side of the equation.

Beginning on the left side of the expression, solve operations involving multiplication and division. Then, work left to right solving operations involving addition and subtraction. Finally, cross-multiply if necessary to reach the final solution.

Example 1

$4a$-10=10

Constants are the numbers in equations that do not change. The variable in this equation is a. Variables are most commonly presented as either x or y, but they can be any letter. Every variable is equal to a number; one must solve the equation to determine what that number is. In an algebraic expression, the answer will usually be the number represented by the variable. In order to solve this equation, keep in mind that what is done to one side must be done to the other side as well. The first step will be to remove 10 from the left side by adding 10 to both sides. This will be expressed as $4a$-10+10=10+10, which simplifies to $4a$=20. Next, remove the 4 by dividing both sides by 4. This step will be expressed as $4a$÷4=20÷4. The expression now becomes a=5.

Since variables are the letters that represent an unknown number, you must solve for that unknown number in single variable problems. The main thing to remember is that you can do anything to one side of an equation as long as you do it to the other.

Example 2

Solve for x in the equation 2x + 3 = 5.

Answer: First you want to get the "2x" isolated by itself on one side. To do that, first get rid of the 3. Subtract 3 from both sides of the equation 2x + 3 – 3 = 5 – 3 or 2x = 2. Now since the x is being multiplied by the 2 in "2x", you must divide by 2 to get rid of it. So, divide both sides by 2, which gives 2x / 2 = 2 / 2 or x = 1.

Word Problems and Applications

In word problems, multiple quantities are often provided with a request to find some kind of relation between them. This often will mean that one variable (the dependent variable whose value needs to be found) can be written as a function of another variable (the independent variable whose value can be figured from the given information). The usual procedure for solving these problems is to start by giving each quantity in the problem a variable, and then figuring the relationship between these variables.

For example, suppose a car gets 25 miles per gallon. How far will the car travel if it uses 2.4 gallons of fuel? In this case, y would be the distance the car has traveled in miles, and x would be the amount of fuel burned in gallons (2.4). Then the relationship between these variables can be written as an algebraic equation, $y = 25x$. In this case, the equation is $y = 25 \cdot 2.4 = 60$, so the car has traveled 60 miles.

Some word problems require more than just one simple equation to be written and solved. Consider the following situations and the linear equations used to model them.

Suppose Margaret is 2 miles to the east of John at noon. Margaret walks to the east at 3 miles per hour. How far apart will they be at 3 p.m.? To solve this, *x* would represent the time in hours past noon, and *y* would represent the distance between Margaret and John. Now, noon corresponds to the equation where *x* is 0, so the *y* intercept is going to be 2. It's also known that the slope will be the rate at which the distance is changing, which is 3 miles per hour. This means that the slope will be 3 (be careful at this point: if units were used, other than miles and hours, for *x* and *y* variables, a conversion of the given information to the appropriate units would be required first). The simplest way to write an equation given the *y*-intercept, and the slope is the Slope-Intercept form, is $y = mx + b$. Recall that *m* here is the slope and *b* is the *y* intercept. So, $m = 3$ and $b = 2$. Therefore, the equation will be $y = 3x + 2$. The word problem asks how far to the east Margaret will be from John at 3 p.m., which means when *x* is 3. So, substitute $x = 3$ into this equation to obtain $y = 3 \cdot 3 + 2 = 9 + 2 = 11$. Therefore, she will be 11 miles to the east of him at 3 p.m.

For another example, suppose that a box with 4 cans in it weighs 6 lbs., while a box with 8 cans in it weighs 12 lbs. Find out how much a single can weighs. To do this, let *x* denote the number of cans in the box, and *y* denote the weight of the box with the cans in lbs. This line touches two pairs: $(4, 6)$ and (8, 12). A formula for this relation could be written using the two-point form, with $x_1 = 4, y_1 = 6, x_2 = 8, y_2 = 12$. This would yield $\frac{y-6}{x-4} = \frac{12-6}{8-4}$, or $\frac{y-6}{x-4} = \frac{6}{4} = \frac{3}{2}$. However, only the slope is needed to solve this problem, since the slope will be the weight of a single can. From the computation, the slope is $\frac{3}{2}$. Therefore, each can weighs $\frac{3}{2}$ lb.

Translating Words into Math

When asked rewrite a mathematical expression as a situation or translate a word problem into an expression, look for a series of key words indicating addition, subtraction, multiplication, or division:

Addition: add, altogether, together, plus, increased by, more than, in all, sum, and total

Subtraction: minus, less than, difference, decreased by, fewer than, remain, and take away

Multiplication: *times*, *twice*, *of*, *double*, and *triple*

Division: divided by, cut up, half, quotient of, split, and shared equally

If a question asks to give words to a mathematical expression and says "equals," then an = sign must be included in the answer. Similarly, "less than or equal to" is expressed by the inequality symbol≤, and "greater than or equal" to is expressed as ≥. Furthermore, "less than" is represented by <, and "greater than" is expressed by >.

Word Problems

Word problems can appear daunting, but don't let the verbiage psyche you out. No matter the scenario or specifics, the key to answering them is to translate the words into a math problem. Always keep in mind what the question is asking and what operations could lead to that answer. The following word problems highlight the most commonly tested question types.

Working with Money

Walter's Coffee Shop sells a variety of drinks and breakfast treats.

Price List	
Hot Coffee	$2.00
Slow-Drip Iced Coffee	$3.00
Latte	$4.00
Muffin	$2.00
Crepe	$4.00
Egg Sandwich	$5.00

Costs	
Hot Coffee	$0.25
Slow-Drip Iced Coffee	$0.75
Latte	$1.00
Muffin	$1.00
Crepe	$2.00
Egg Sandwich	$3.00

Walter's utilities, rent, and labor costs him $500 per day. Today, Walter sold 200 hot coffees, 100 slow-drip iced coffees, 50 lattes, 75 muffins, 45 crepes, and 60 egg sandwiches. What was Walter's total profit today?

To accurately answer this type of question, determine the total cost of making his drinks and treats, then determine how much revenue he earned from selling those products. After arriving at these two totals, the profit is measured by deducted the total cost from the total revenue.

Walter's costs for today:

Item	Quantity	Cost Per Unit	Total Cost
Hot Coffee	200	$0.25	$50
Slow-Drip Iced Coffee	100	$0.75	$75
Latte	50	$1.00	$50
Muffin	75	$1.00	$75
Crepe	45	$2.00	$90
Egg Sandwich	60	$3.00	$180
Utilities, rent, and labor			$500
Total Costs			$1,020

Walter's revenue for today:

Item	Quantity	Revenue Per Unit	Total Revenue
Hot Coffee	200	$2.00	$400
Slow-Drip Iced Coffee	100	$3.00	$300
Latte	50	$4.00	$200
Muffin	75	$2.00	$150
Crepe	45	$4.00	$180
Egg Sandwich	60	$5.00	$300
Total Revenue			$1,530

Walter's Profit = *Revenue* – *Costs* = $1,530 – $1,020 = $510

This strategy is applicable to other question types. For example, calculating salary after deductions, balancing a checkbook, and calculating a dinner bill are common word problems similar to business planning. Just remember to use the correct operations. When a balance is increased, use addition.

When a balance is decreased, use subtraction. Common sense and organization are your greatest assets when answering word problems.

Unit Rate

Unit rate word problems will ask to calculate the rate or quantity of something in a different value. For example, a problem might say that a car drove a certain number of miles in a certain number of minutes and then ask how many miles per hour the car was traveling. These questions involve solving proportions. Consider the following examples:

1) Alexandra made $96 during the first 3 hours of her shift as a temporary worker at a law office. She will continue to earn money at this rate until she finishes in 5 more hours. How much does Alexandra make per hour? How much will Alexandra have made at the end of the day?

This problem can be solved in two ways. The first is to set up a proportion, as the rate of pay is constant. The second is to determine her hourly rate, multiply the 5 hours by that rate, and then add the $96.

To set up a proportion, put the money already earned over the hours already worked on one side of an equation. The other side has x over 8 hours (the total hours worked in the day). It looks like this: $\frac{96}{3} = \frac{x}{8}$. Now, cross-multiply to get $768 = 3x$. To get x, divide by 3, which leaves $x = 256$. Alternatively, as x is the numerator of one of the proportions, multiplying by its denominator will reduce the solution by one step. Thus, Alexandra will make $256 at the end of the day. To calculate her hourly rate, divide the total by 8, giving $32 per hour.

Alternatively, it is possible to figure out the hourly rate by dividing $96 by 3 hours to get $32 per hour. Now her total pay can be figured by multiplying $32 per hour by 8 hours, which comes out to $256.

2) Jonathan is reading a novel. So far, he has read 215 of the 335 total pages. It takes Jonathan 25 minutes to read 10 pages, and the rate is constant. How long does it take Jonathan to read one page? How much longer will it take him to finish the novel? Express the answer in time.

To calculate how long it takes Jonathan to read one page, divide the 25 minutes by 10 pages to determine the page per minute rate. Thus, it takes 2.5 minutes to read one page.

Jonathan must read 120 more pages to complete the novel. (This is calculated by subtracting the pages already read from the total.) Now, multiply his rate per page by the number of pages. Thus, $120 \div 2.5 = 300$. Expressed in time, 300 minutes is equal to 5 hours.

3) At a hotel, $\frac{4}{5}$ of the 120 rooms are booked for Saturday. On Sunday, $\frac{3}{4}$ of the rooms are booked. On which day are more of the rooms booked, and by how many more?

The first step is to calculate the number of rooms booked for each day. Do this by multiplying the fraction of the rooms booked by the total number of rooms.

Saturday: $\frac{4}{5} \times 120 = \frac{4}{5} \times \frac{120}{1} = \frac{480}{5} = 96$ rooms

Sunday: $\frac{3}{4} \times 120 = \frac{3}{4} \times \frac{120}{1} = \frac{360}{4} = 90$ rooms

Thus, more rooms were booked on Saturday by 6 rooms.

4) In a veterinary hospital, the veterinarian-to-pet ratio is 1:9. The ratio is always constant. If there are 45 pets in the hospital, how many veterinarians are currently in the veterinary hospital?

Set up a proportion to solve for the number of veterinarians: $\frac{1}{9} = \frac{x}{45}$

Cross-multiplying results in $9x = 45$, which works out to 5 veterinarians.

Alternatively, as there are always 9 times as many pets as veterinarians, is it possible to divide the number of pets (45) by 9. This also arrives at the correct answer of 5 veterinarians.

5) At a general practice law firm, 30% of the lawyers work solely on tort cases. If 9 lawyers work solely on tort cases, how many lawyers work at the firm?

First, solve for the total number of lawyers working at the firm, which will be represented here with x. The problem states that 9 lawyers work solely on torts cases, and they make up 30% of the total lawyers at the firm. Thus, 30% multiplied by the total, x, will equal 9. Written as equation, this is: $30\% \times x = 9$.

It's easier to deal with the equation after converting the percentage to a decimal, leaving $0.3x = 9$. Thus, $x = \frac{9}{0.3} = 30$ lawyers working at the firm.

6) Xavier was hospitalized with pneumonia. He was originally given 35mg of antibiotics. Later, after his condition continued to worsen, Xavier's dosage was increased to 60mg. What was the percent increase of the antibiotics? Round the percentage to the nearest tenth.

An increase or decrease in percentage can be calculated by dividing the difference in amounts by the original amount and multiplying by 100. Written as an equation, the formula is:

$$\frac{new\ quantity - old\ quantity}{old\ quantity} \times 100$$

Here, the question states that the dosage was increased from 35mg to 60mg, so these are plugged into the formula to find the percentage increase.

$$\frac{60 - 35}{35} \times 100 = \frac{25}{35} \times 100 = .7142 \times 100 = 71.4\%$$

Parentheses

Parentheses separate different parts of an equation, and operations within them should be thought of as taking place before the outside operations take place. Practically, this means that the distinction between what is inside and outside of the parentheses decides the order of operations that the equation follows. Failing to solve operations inside the parentheses before addressing the part of the equation outside of the parentheses will lead to incorrect results.

For example, let's analyze $5 - (3 + 25)$. The addition operation within the parentheses must be solved first. So $3 + 25 = 28$, leaving $5 - (28) = -23$. If this was solved in the incorrect order of operations, the solution might be found to be $5 - 3 + 25 = 2 + 25 = 27$, which would be wrong.

Equations often feature multiple layers of parentheses. To differentiate them, square brackets [ ] and braces { } are used in addition to parentheses. The innermost parentheses must be solved before working outward to larger brackets. For example, in $\{2 \div [5 - (3 + 1)]\}$, solving the innermost parentheses (3 + 1) leaves $\{2 \div [5 - (4)]\}$. $[5 - (4)]$ is now the next smallest, which leaves $\{2 \div [1]\}$ in the final step, and 2 as the answer.

Order of Operations

Exponents are shorthand for longer multiplications or divisions. The exponent is written to the upper right of a number. In the expression 2^3, the exponent is 3. The number with the exponent is called the *base*.

When the exponent is a whole number, it means to multiply the base by itself as many times as the number in the exponent. So, $2^3 = 2 \times 2 \times 2 = 8$.

If the exponent is a negative number, it means to take the reciprocal of the positive exponent:

$$2^{-3} = \frac{1}{2^3} = \frac{1}{8}$$

When the exponent is 0, the result is always 1: $2^0 = 1, 5^0 = 1$, and so on.

When the exponent is 2, the number is *squared*, and when the exponent is 3, it is *cubed*.

When working with longer expressions, parentheses are used to show the order in which the operations should be performed. Operations inside the parentheses should be completed first. Thus, $(3 - 1) \div 2$ means one should first subtract 1 from 3, and then divide that result by 2.

The *order of operations* gives an order for how a mathematical expression is to be simplified:

- Parentheses
- Exponents
- Multiplication
- Division
- Addition
- Subtraction

To help remember this, many students like to use the mnemonic PEMDAS. Some students associate this word with a phrase to help them, such as "Pirates Eat Many Donuts at Sea." Here is a quick example:

Evaluate $2^2 \times (3 - 1) \div 2 + 3$.

Parenthesis: $2^2 \times 2 \div 2 + 3$.

Exponents: $4 \times 2 \div 2 + 3$

Multiply: $8 \div 2 + 3$.

Divide: $4 + 3$.

Addition: 7

Positive and Negative Numbers

Signs

Aside from 0, numbers can be either positive or negative. The sign for a positive number is the plus sign or the + symbol, while the sign for a negative number is minus sign or the – symbol. If a number has no designation, then it's assumed to be positive.

Absolute Values

Both positive and negative numbers are valued according to their distance from 0. Look at this number line for +3 and -3:

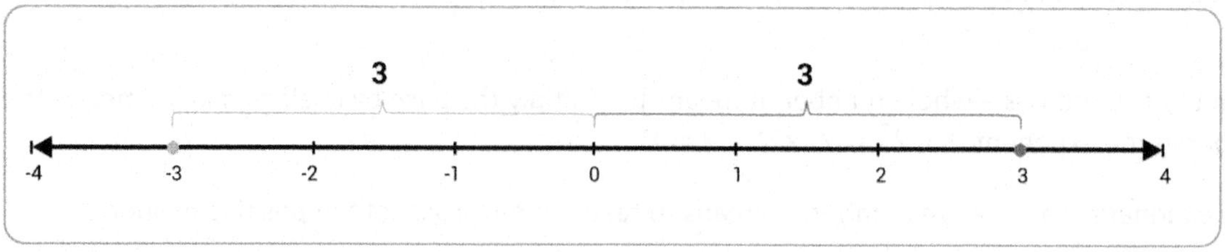

Both 3 and -3 are three spaces from 0. The distance from 0 is called its absolute value. Thus, both -3 and 3 have an absolute value of 3 since they're both three spaces away from 0.

An absolute number is written by placing | | around the number. So, $|3|$ and $|-3|$ both equal 3, as that's their common absolute value.

Implications for Addition and Subtraction

For addition, if all numbers are either positive or negative, simply add them together. For example, 4 + 4 = 8 and -4 + -4 = -8. However, things get tricky when some of the numbers are negative and some are positive.

Take 6 + (-4) as an example. First, take the absolute values of the numbers, which are 6 and 4. Second, subtract the smaller value from the larger. The equation becomes $6-4=2$. Third, place the sign of the original larger number on the sum. Here, 6 is the larger number, and it's positive, so the sum is 2.

Here's an example where the negative number has a larger absolute value: (-6) + 4. The first two steps are the same as the example above. However, on the third step, the negative sign must be placed on the sum, as the absolute value of (-6) is greater than 4. Thus, -6 + 4 = -2.

The absolute value of numbers implies that subtraction can be thought of as flip the sign of the number following the subtraction sign and simply adding the two numbers. This means that subtracting a negative number will in fact be adding the positive absolute value of the negative number. Here are some examples:

$$-6-4=-6+-4=-10$$

$$3--6=3+9=12$$

$$-3-2=-3+-2=-5$$

Implications for Multiplication and Division

For multiplication and division, if both numbers are positive, then the product or quotient is always positive. If both numbers are negative, then the product or quotient is also positive. However, if the numbers have opposite signs, the product or quotient is always negative.

Simply put, the product in multiplication and quotient in division is always positive, unless the numbers have opposing signs, in which case it's negative. Here are some examples:

$$(-6) \times (-5) = 30$$

$$(-50) \div 10 = -5$$

$$8 \times |-7| = 56$$

$$(-48) \div (-6) = 8$$

If there are more than two numbers in a multiplication or division problem, then whether the product or quotient is positive or negative depends on the number of negative numbers in the problem. If there is an odd number of negatives, then the product or quotient is negative. If there is an even number of negative numbers, then the result is positive.

Here are some examples:

$$(-6) \times 5 \times (-2) \times (-4) = -240$$

$$(-6) \times 5 \times 2 \times (-4) = 240$$

Geometry and Measurement

Plane Geometry

Locations on the plane that have no width or breadth are called *points*. These points usually will be denoted with capital letters such as *P*.

Any pair of points *A*, *B* on the plane will determine a unique straight line between them. This line is denoted *AB*. Sometimes to emphasize a line is being considered, this will be written as $\overleftrightarrow{AB}$.

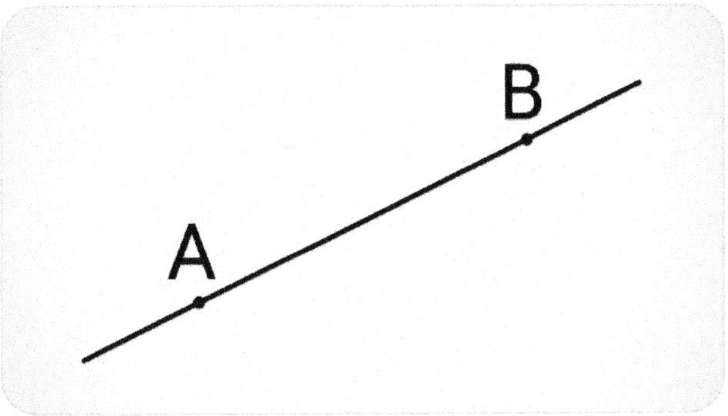

If the Cartesian coordinates for A and B are known, then the distance $d(A, B)$ along the line between them can be measured using the *Pythagorean formula*, which states that if $A = (x_1, y_1)$ and $B = (x_2, y_2)$, then the distance between them is $d(A, B) = \sqrt{(x_2 - x_1)^2 + (y_2 - y_1)^2}$.

The part of a line that lies between A and B is called a *line segment*. It has two endpoints, one at A and one at B. *Rays* also can be formed. Given points A and B, a *ray* is the portion of a line that starts at one of these points, passes through the other, and keeps on going. Therefore, a ray has a single endpoint, but the other end goes off to infinity.

Given a pair of points A and B, a circle centered at A and passing through B can be formed. This is the set of points whose distance from A is exactly $d(A, B)$. The radius of this circle will be $d(A, B)$.

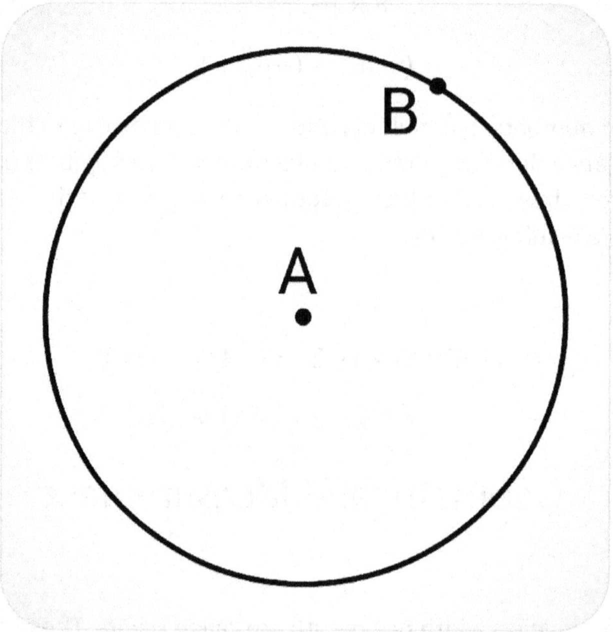

The *circumference* of a circle is the distance traveled by following the edge of the circle for one complete revolution, and the length of the circumference is given by $2\pi r$, where r is the radius of the circle. The formula for circumference is $C = 2\pi r$.

When two lines cross, they form an *angle*. The point where the lines cross is called the *vertex* of the angle. The angle can be named by either just using the vertex, $\angle A$, or else by listing three points $\angle BAC$, as shown in the diagram below.

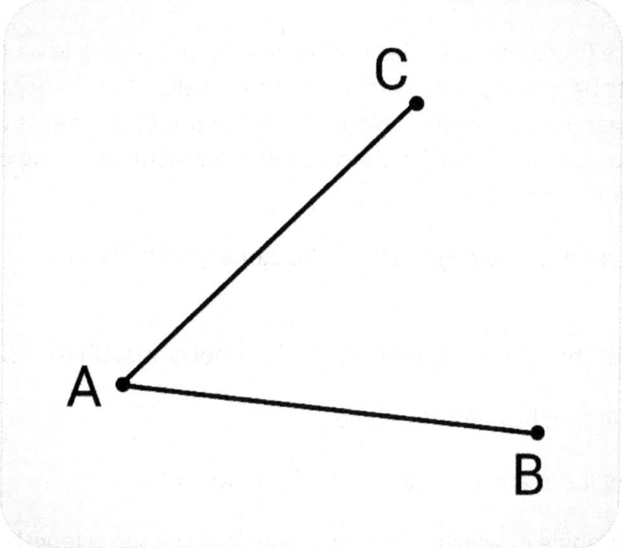

The measurement of an angle can be given in degrees or in radians. In degrees, a full circle is 360 degrees, written 360°. In radians, a full circle is 2π radians.

Given two points on the circumference of a circle, the path along the circle between those points is called an *arc* of the circle. For example, the arc between B and C is denoted by a thinner line:

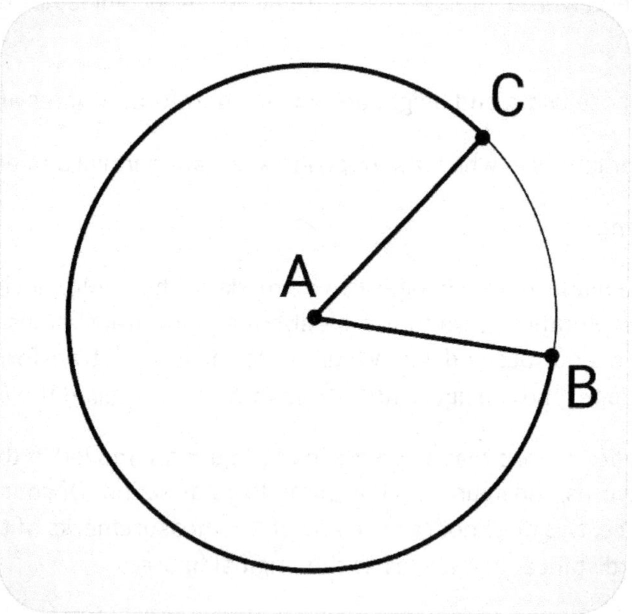

The length of the path along an arc is called the *arc length*. If the circle has radius r, then the arc length is given by multiplying the measure of the angle in radians by the radius of the circle.

Two lines are said to be *parallel* if they never intersect. If the lines are *AB* and *CD*, then this is written as $AB \parallel CD$.

If two lines cross to form four quarter-circles, that is, 90° angles, the two lines are *perpendicular*. If the point at which they cross is *B*, and the two lines are *AB* and *BC*, then this is written as $AB \perp BC$.

A *polygon* is a closed figure (meaning it divides the plane into an inside and an outside) consisting of a collection of line segments between points. These points are called the *vertices* of the polygon. These line segments must not overlap one another. Note that the number of sides is equal to the number of angles, or vertices of the polygon. The angles between line segments meeting one another in the polygon are called *interior angles*.

A *regular polygon* is a polygon whose edges are all the same length and whose interior angles are all of equal measure.

A *triangle* is a polygon with three sides. A *quadrilateral* is a polygon with four sides.

A *right triangle* is a triangle that has one 90° angle.

The sum of the interior angles of any triangle must add up to 180°.

An *isosceles triangle* is a triangle in which two of the sides are the same length. In this case, it will always have two congruent interior angles. If a triangle has two congruent interior angles, it will always be isosceles.

An *equilateral triangle* is a triangle whose sides are all the same length and whose angles are all equivalent to one another, equal to 60°. Equilateral triangles are examples of regular polygons. Note that equilateral triangles are also isosceles.

A *rectangle* is a quadrilateral whose interior angles are all 90°. A rectangle has two sets of sides that are equal to one another.

A *square* is a rectangle whose width and height are equal. Therefore, squares are regular polygons.

A *parallelogram* is a quadrilateral in which the opposite sides are parallel and equivalent to each other.

Transformations of a Plane

Given a figure drawn on a plane, many changes can be made to that figure, including *rotation*, *translation*, and *reflection*. Rotations turn the figure about a point, translations slide the figure, and reflections flip the figure over a specified line. When performing these transformations, the original figure is called the *pre-image*, and the figure after transformation is called the *image*.

More specifically, *translation* means that all points in the figure are moved in the same direction by the same distance. In other words, the figure is slid in some fixed direction. Of course, while the entire figure is slid by the same distance, this does not change any of the measurements of the figures involved. The result will have the same distances and angles as the original figure.

In terms of Cartesian coordinates, a translation means a shift of each of the original points (x, y) by a fixed amount in the *x* and *y* directions, to become $(x + a, y + b)$.

Another procedure that can be performed is called *reflection*. To do this, a line in the plane is specified, called the *line of reflection*. Then, take each point and flip it over the line so that it is the same distance from the line but on the opposite side of it. This does not change any of the distances or angles involved, but it does reverse the order in which everything appears.

To reflect something over the *x*-axis, the points (x, y) are sent to $(x, -y)$. To reflect something over the *y*-axis, the points (x, y) are sent to the points $(-x, y)$. Flipping over other lines is not something easy to express in Cartesian coordinates. However, by drawing the figure and the line of reflection, the distance to the line and the original points can be used to find the reflected figure.

Example: Reflect this triangle with vertices (-1, 0), (2, 1), and (2, 0) over the *y*-axis. The pre-image is shown below.

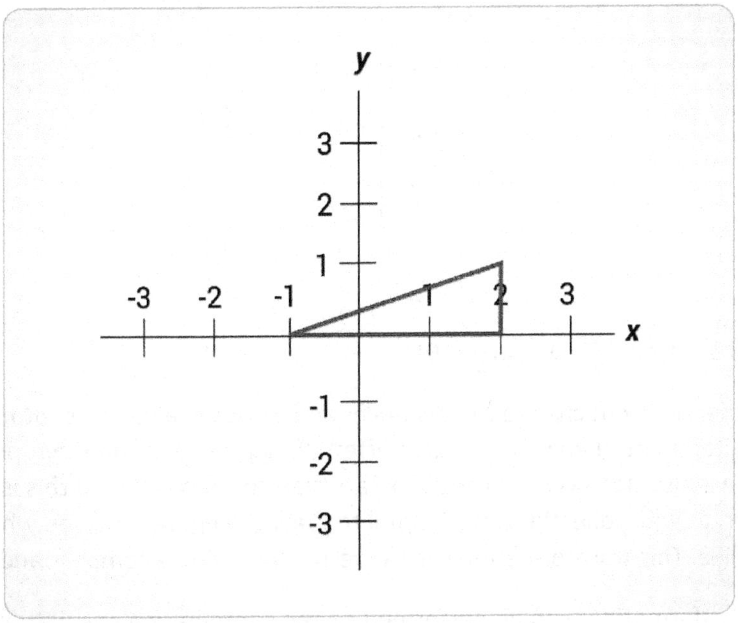

To do this, flip the *x* values of the points involved to the negatives of themselves, while keeping the *y* values the same. The image is shown here.

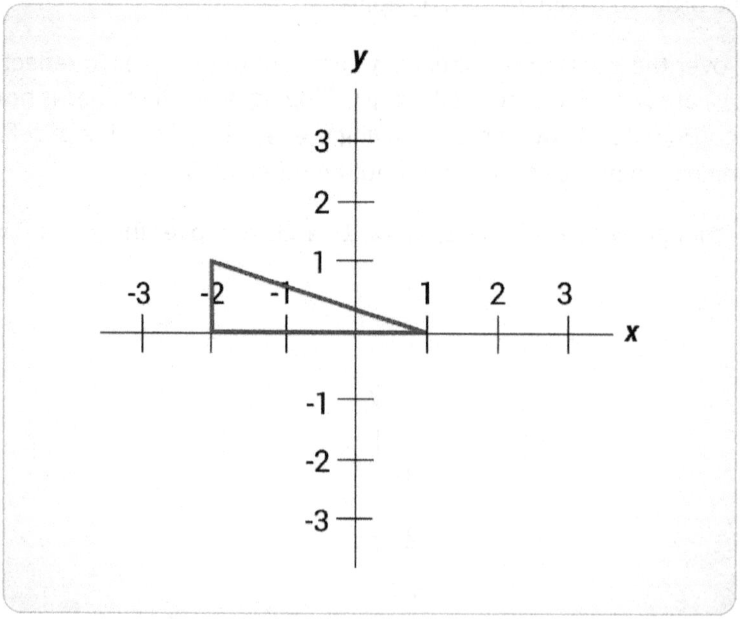

The new vertices will be (1, 0), (-2, 1), and (-2, 0).

Another procedure that does not change the distances and angles in a figure is *rotation*. In this procedure, pick a center point, then rotate every vertex along a circle around that point by the same angle. This procedure is also not easy to express in Cartesian coordinates, and this is not a requirement on this test. However, as with reflections, it's helpful to draw the figures and see what the result of the rotation would look like. This transformation can be performed using a compass and protractor.

Each one of these transformations can be performed on the coordinate plane without changes to the original dimensions or angles.

If two figures in the plane involve the same distances and angles, they are called *congruent figures*. In other words, two figures are congruent when they go from one form to another through reflection, rotation, and translation, or a combination of these.

Remember that rotation and translation will give back a new figure that is identical to the original figure, but reflection will give back a mirror image of it.

To recognize that a figure has undergone a rotation, check to see that the figure has not been changed into a mirror image, but that its orientation has changed (that is, whether the parts of the figure now form different angles with the *x* and *y* axes).

To recognize that a figure has undergone a translation, check to see that the figure has not been changed into a mirror image, and that the orientation remains the same.

To recognize that a figure has undergone a reflection, check to see that the new figure is a mirror image of the old figure.

Keep in mind that sometimes a combination of translations, reflections, and rotations may be performed on a figure.

Dilation

A *dilation* is a transformation that preserves angles, but not distances. This can be thought of as stretching or shrinking a figure. If a dilation makes figures larger, it is called an *enlargement*. If a dilation makes figures smaller, it is called a *reduction*. The easiest example is to dilate around the origin. In this case, multiply the *x* and *y* coordinates by a *scale factor*, k, sending points (x, y) to (kx, ky).

As an example, draw a dilation of the following triangle, whose vertices will be the points (-1, 0), (1, 0), and (1, 1).

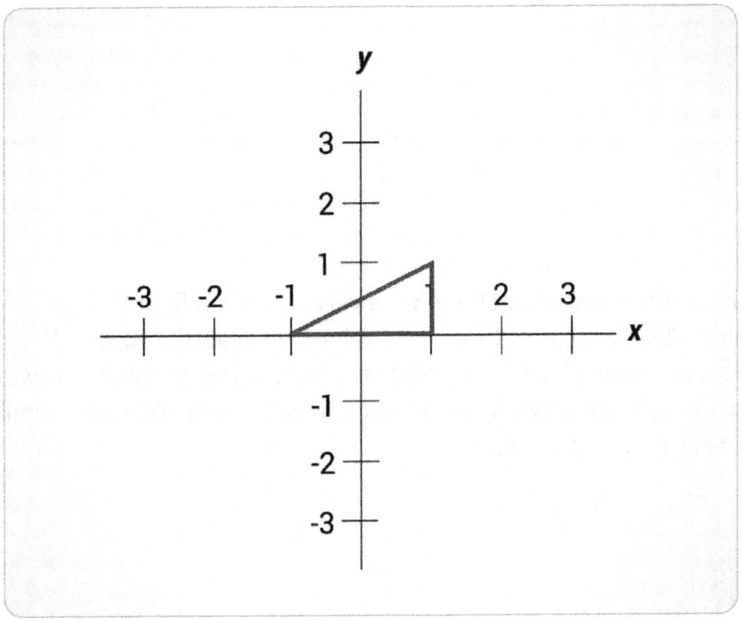

For this problem, dilate by a scale factor of 2, so the new vertices will be (-2, 0), (2, 0), and (2, 2).

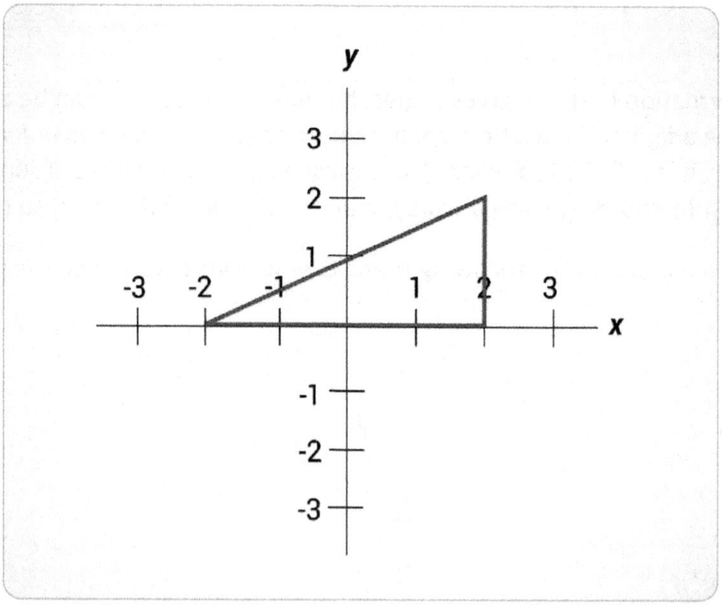

Note that after a dilation, the distances between the vertices of the figure will have changed, but the angles remain the same. The two figures that are obtained by dilation, along with possibly translation, rotation, and reflection, are all *similar* to one another. Another way to think of this is that similar figures have the same number of vertices and edges, and their angles are all the same. Similar figures have the same basic shape, but are different in size.

Symmetry

Using the types of transformations above, if an object can undergo these changes and not appear to have changed, then the figure is symmetrical. If an object can be split in half by a line and flipped over that line to lie directly on top of itself, it is said to have *line symmetry*. An example of both types of figures is seen below.

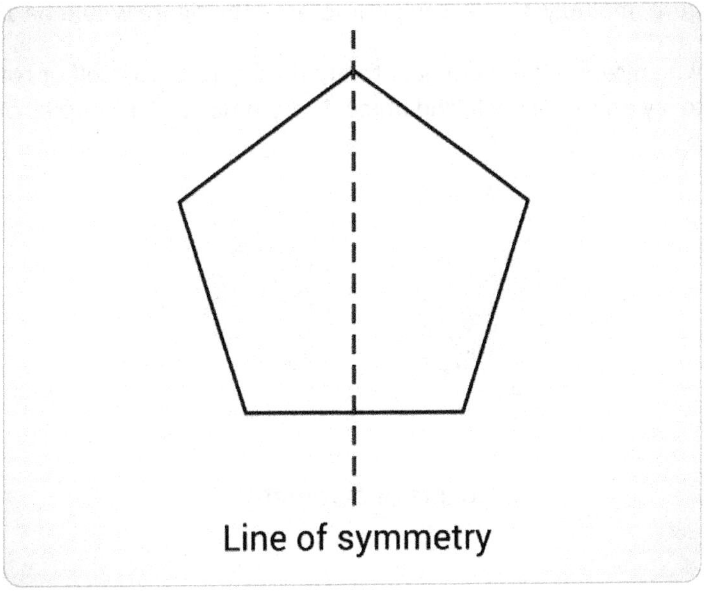

If an object can be rotated about its center to any degree smaller than 360, and it lies directly on top of itself, the object is said to have *rotational symmetry*. An example of this type of symmetry is shown below. The pentagon has an order of 5.

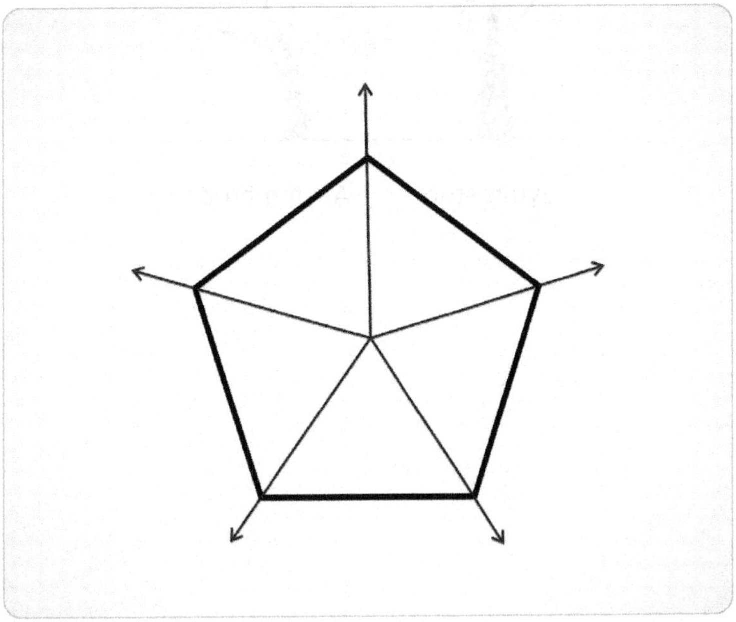

The rotational symmetry lines in the figure above can be used to find the angles formed at the center of the pentagon. Knowing that all of the angles together form a full circle, at 360 degrees, the figure can be split into 5 angles equally. By dividing the 360° by 5, each angle is 72°.

Given the length of one side of the figure, the perimeter of the pentagon can also be found using rotational symmetry. If one side length was 3 cm, that side length can be rotated onto each other side length four times. This would give a total of 5 side lengths equal to 3 cm. To find the perimeter, or distance around the figure, multiply 3 by 5. The perimeter of the figure would be 15 cm.

If a line cannot be drawn anywhere on the object to flip the figure onto itself or rotated less than or equal to 180 degrees to lay on top of itself, the object is asymmetrical. Examples of these types of figures are shown below.

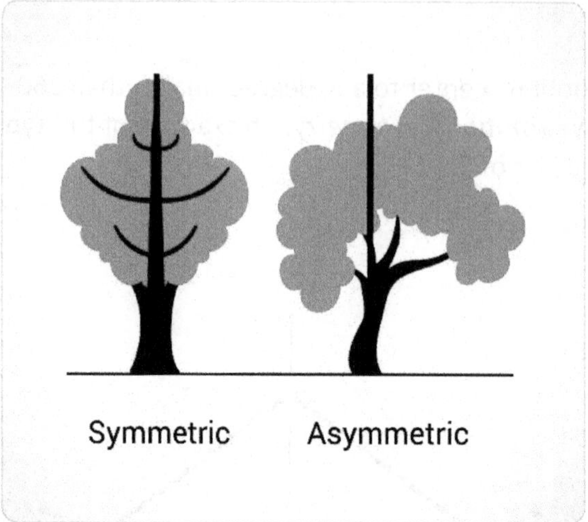

Perimeters and Areas

The *perimeter* of a polygon is the total length of a trip around the whole polygon, starting and ending at the same point. It is found by adding up the lengths of each line segment in the polygon. For a rectangle with sides of length *x* and *y*, the perimeter will be $2x + 2y$.

The area of a polygon is the area of the region that it encloses. Regarding the area of a rectangle with sides of length *x* and *y*, the area is given by xy. For a triangle with a base of length *b* and a height of length *h*, the area is $\frac{1}{2}bh$.

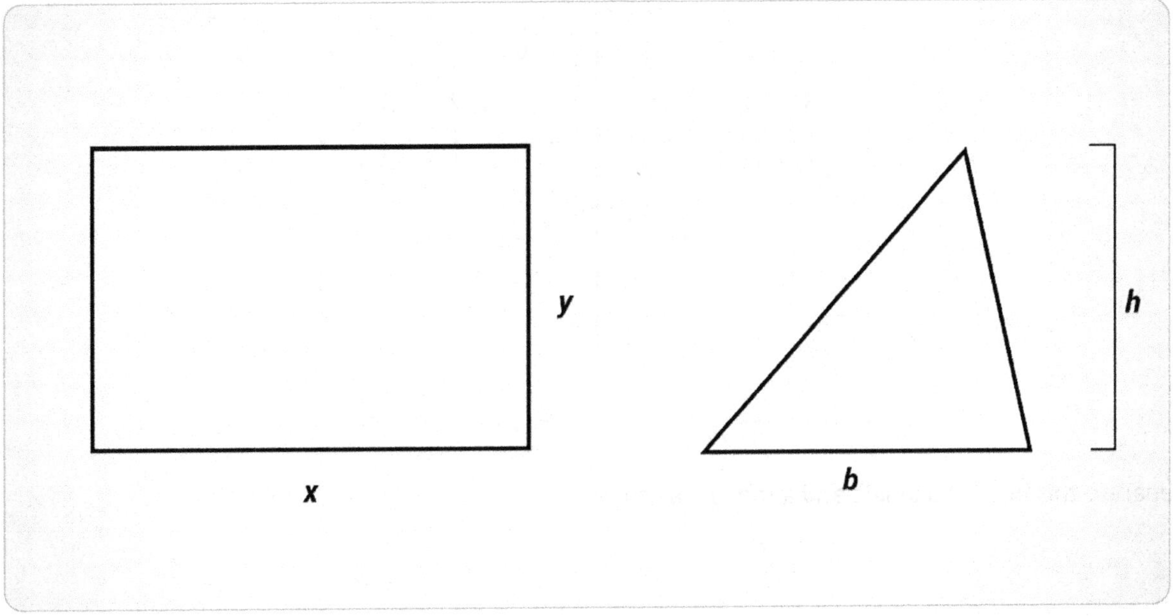

To find the areas of more general polygons, it is usually easiest to break up the polygon into rectangles and triangles. For example, find the area of the following figure whose vertices are (-1, 0), (-1, 2), (1, 3), and (1, 0).

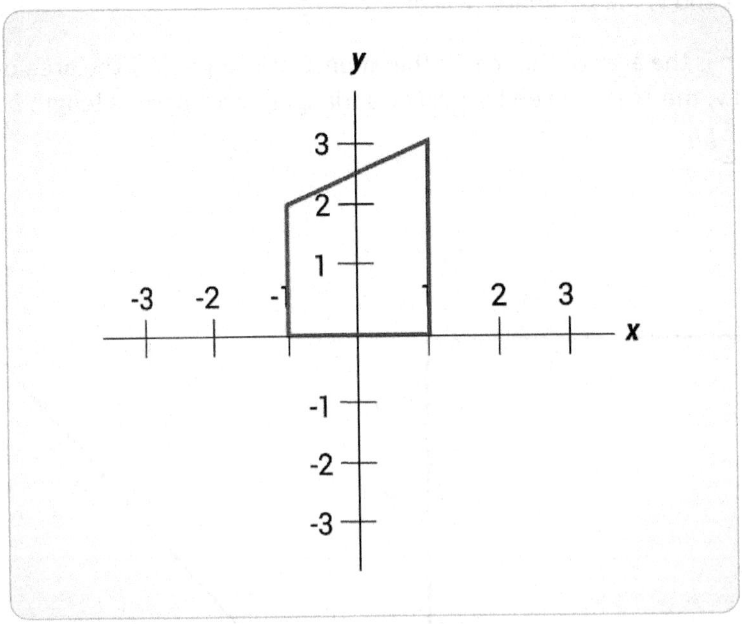

Separate this into a rectangle and a triangle as shown:

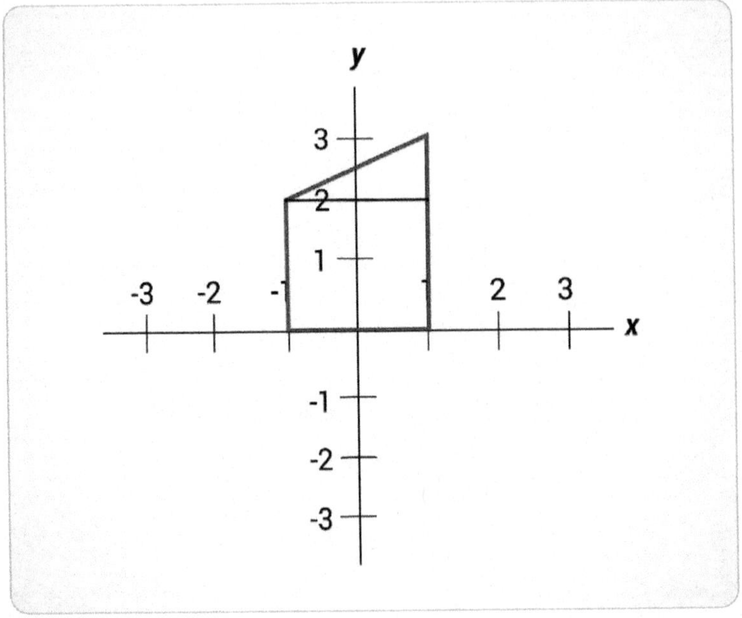

The rectangle has a height of 2 and a width of 2, so it has a total area of $2 \cdot 2 = 4$. The triangle has a width of 2 and a height of 1, so it has an area of $\frac{1}{2} 2 \cdot 1 = 1$. Therefore, the entire quadrilateral has an area of 4 + 1 = 5.

As another example, suppose someone wants to tile a rectangular room that is 10 feet by 6 feet using triangular tiles that are 12 inches by 6 inches. How many tiles would be needed? To figure this, first find the area of the room, which will be $10 \cdot 6 = 60$ square feet. The dimensions of the triangle are 1 foot by ½ foot, so the area of each triangle is $\frac{1}{2} \cdot 1 \cdot \frac{1}{2} = \frac{1}{4}$ square feet. Notice that the dimensions of the triangle had to be converted to the same units as the rectangle. Now, take the total area divided by the area of one tile to find the answer: $\frac{60}{\frac{1}{4}} = 60 \cdot 4 = 240$ tiles required.

Volumes and Surface Areas

Geometry in three dimensions is similar to geometry in two dimensions. The main new feature is that three points now define a unique *plane* that passes through each of them. Three dimensional objects can be made by putting together two dimensional figures in different surfaces. Below, some of the possible three dimensional figures will be provided, along with formulas for their volumes and surface areas.

A rectangular prism is a box whose sides are all rectangles meeting at 90° angles. Such a box has three dimensions: length, width, and height. If the length is *x*, the width is *y*, and the height is *z*, then the volume is given by $V = xyz$.

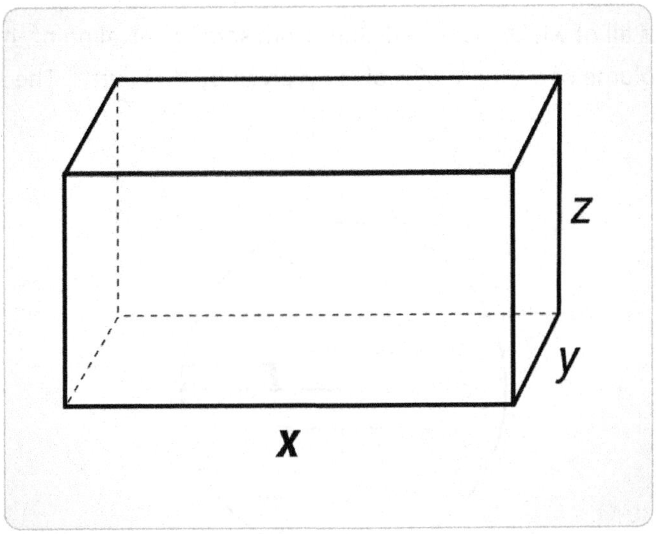

The surface area will be given by computing the surface area of each rectangle and adding them together. There are a total of six rectangles. Two of them have sides of length *x* and *y*, two have sides of length *y* and *z*, and two have sides of length *x* and *z*. Therefore, the total surface area will be given by $SA = 2xy + 2yz + 2xz$.

A *rectangular pyramid* is a figure with a rectangular base and four triangular sides that meet at a single vertex. If the rectangle has sides of length *x* and *y*, then the volume will be given by $V = \frac{1}{3}xyh$.

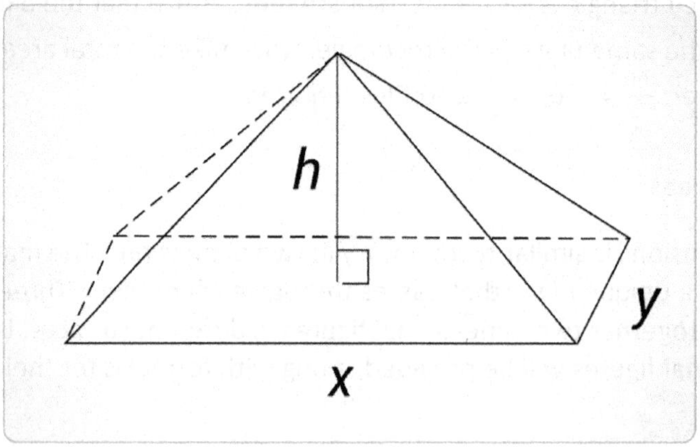

To find the surface area, the dimensions of each triangle need to be known. However, these dimensions can differ depending on the problem in question. Therefore, there is no general formula for calculating total surface area.

A *sphere* is a set of points all of which are equidistant from some central point. It is like a circle, but in three dimensions. The volume of a sphere of radius *r* is given by $V = \frac{4}{3}\pi r^3$. The surface area is given by $A = 4\pi r^2$.

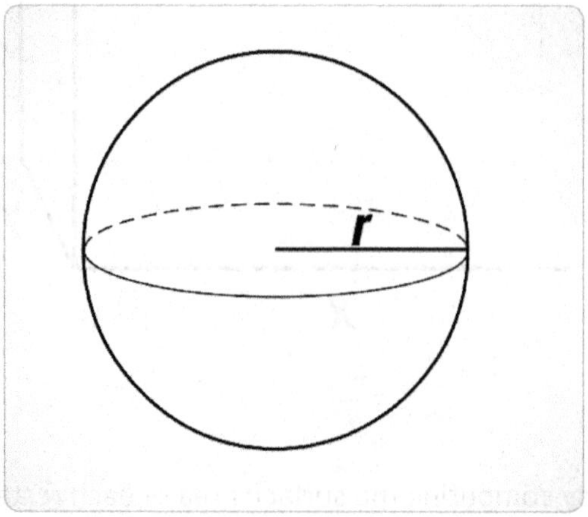

The Pythagorean Theorem

The Pythagorean theorem is an important result in geometry. It states that for right triangles, the sum of the squares of the two shorter sides will be equal to the square of the longest side (also called the *hypotenuse*). The longest side will always be the side opposite to the 90° angle. If this side is called c, and the other two sides are a and b, then the Pythagorean theorem states that $c^2 = a^2 + b^2$. Since lengths are always positive, this also can be written as $c = \sqrt{a^2 + b^2}$. A diagram to show the parts of a triangle using the Pythagorean theorem is below.

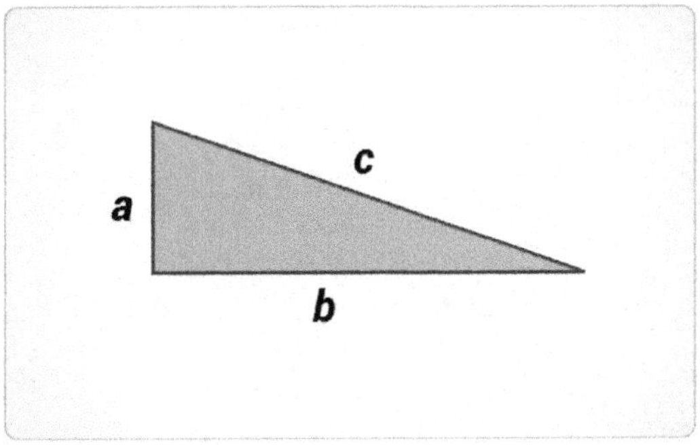

As an example of the theorem, suppose that Shirley has a rectangular field that is 5 feet wide and 12 feet long, and she wants to split it in half using a fence that goes from one corner to the opposite corner. How long will this fence need to be? To figure this out, note that this makes the field into two right triangles, whose hypotenuse will be the fence dividing it in half. Therefore, the fence length will be given by $\sqrt{5^2 + 12^2} = \sqrt{169} = 13$ feet long.

Similar Figures and Proportions

Sometimes, two figures are similar, meaning they have the same basic shape and the same interior angles, but they have different dimensions. If the ratio of two corresponding sides is known, then that ratio, or scale factor, holds true for all of the dimensions of the new figure.

Here is an example of applying this principle. Suppose that Lara is 5 feet tall and is standing 30 feet from the base of a light pole, and her shadow is 6 feet long. How high is the light on the pole? To figure this, it helps to make a sketch of the situation:

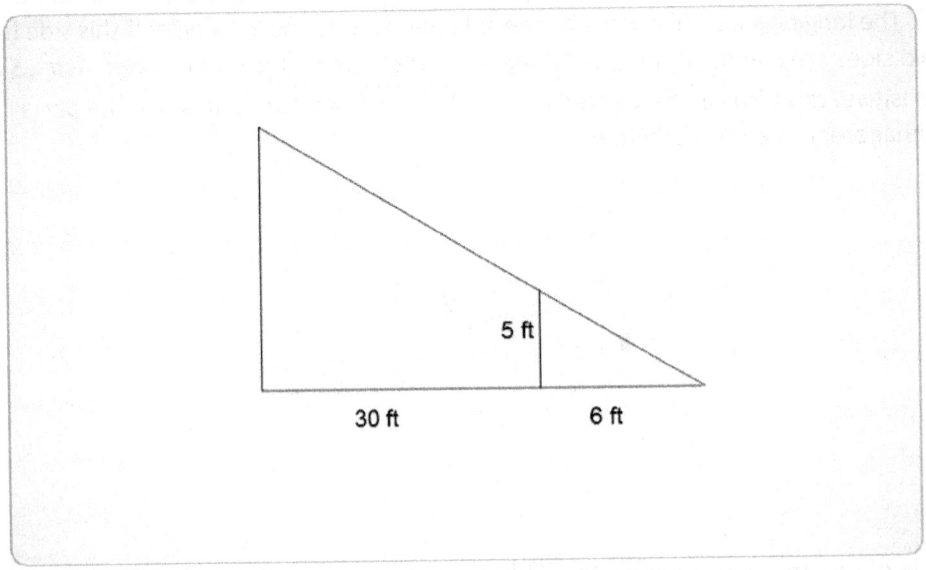

The light pole is the left side of the triangle. Lara is the 5-foot vertical line. Notice that there are two right triangles here, and that they have all the same angles as one another. Therefore, they form similar triangles. So, figure the ratio of proportionality between them.

The bases of these triangles are known. The small triangle, formed by Lara and her shadow, has a base of 6 feet. The large triangle, formed by the light pole along with the line from the base of the pole out to the end of Lara's shadow is $30 + 6 = 36$ feet long. So, the ratio of the big triangle to the little triangle will be $\frac{36}{6} = 6$. The height of the little triangle is 5 feet. Therefore, the height of the big triangle will be $6 \cdot 5 = 30$ feet, meaning that the light is 30 feet up the pole.

Notice that the perimeter of a figure changes by the ratio of proportionality between two similar figures, but the area changes by the *square* of the ratio. This is because if the length of one side is doubled, the area is quadrupled.

As an example, suppose two rectangles are similar, but the edges of the second rectangle are three times longer than the edges of the first rectangle. The area of the first rectangle is 10 square inches. How much more area does the second rectangle have than the first?

To answer this, note that the area of the second rectangle is $3^2 = 9$ times the area of the first rectangle, which is 10 square inches. Therefore, the area of the second rectangle is going to be $9 \cdot 10 = 90$ square inches. This means it has $90 - 10 = 80$ square inches more area than the first rectangle.

As a second example, suppose X and Y are similar right triangles. The hypotenuse of X is 4 inches. The area of Y is $\frac{1}{4}$ the area of X. What is the hypotenuse of Y?

First, realize the area has changed by a factor of $\frac{1}{4}$. The area changes by a factor that is the *square* of the ratio of changes in lengths, so the ratio of the lengths is the square root of the ratio of areas. That means that the ratio of lengths must be is $\sqrt{\frac{1}{4}} = \frac{1}{2}$, and the hypotenuse of *Y* must be $\frac{1}{2} \cdot 4 = 2$ inches.

Volumes between similar solids change like the cube of the change in the lengths of their edges. Likewise, if the ratio of the volumes between similar solids is known, the ratio between their lengths is known by finding the cube root of the ratio of their volumes.

For example, suppose there are two similar rectangular pyramids *X* and *Y*. The base of *X* is 1 inch by 2 inches, and the volume of *X* is 8 inches. The volume of *Y* is 64 inches. What are the dimensions of the base of *Y*?

To answer this, first find the ratio of the volume of *Y* to the volume of *X*. This will be given by $\frac{64}{8} = 8$. Now the ratio of lengths is the cube root of the ratio of volumes, or $\sqrt[3]{8} = 2$. So, the dimensions of the base of *Y* must be 2 inches by 4 inches.

Ratios and Proportions

A ratio is a comparison of two quantities in a particular order. Example: If there are 14 computers in a lab, and the class has 20 students, there is a student to computer ratio of 20 to 14, commonly written as 20:14. Ratios are normally reduced to their smallest whole number representation, so 20:14 would be reduced to 10:7 by dividing both sides by 2.

A proportion is a relationship between two quantities that dictates how one changes when the other changes. A direct proportion describes a relationship in which a quantity increases by a set amount for every increase in the other quantity, or decreases by that same amount for every decrease in the other quantity. Example: Assuming a constant driving speed, the time required for a car trip increases as the distance of the trip increases. The distance to be traveled and the time required to travel are directly proportional.

Inverse proportion is a relationship in which an increase in one quantity is accompanied by a decrease in the other, or vice versa. Example: the time required for a car trip decreases as the speed increases, and increases as the speed decreases, so the time required is inversely proportional to the speed of the car.

Solving for x in a Proportion

Solve for *x* in this proportion: $\frac{10}{15} = \frac{x}{30}$.

There are two ways to solve for *x*.

Method 1: Cross multiply; then, solve for x.

$$\frac{10}{15} = \frac{x}{30}$$

$10(30) = 15(x)$

$300 = 15x$

$300 \div 15 = 15x \div 15$

$x = 20$

Method 2: Notice that 30 is twice as much as 15, so *x* should be twice as much as 10. Therefore, $x = 10 \times 2 = 20$.

American Measuring System

The measuring system used today in the United States developed from of the British units of measurement during colonial times. The most typically used units in this customary system are those used to measure weight, liquid volume, and length, whose common units are found below. In the customary system, the basic unit for measuring weight is the ounce (oz.); there are 16 ounces (oz.) in 1 pound (lb.) and 2000 pounds in 1 ton. The basic unit for measuring liquid volume is the ounce (oz.); 1 ounce is equal to 2 tablespoons (tbsp.) or 6 teaspoons (tsp), and there are 8 ounces in 1 cup, 2 cups in 1 pint (pt.), 2 pints in 1 quart (qt.), and 4 quarts in 1 gallon (gal). For measurements of length, the inch (in) is the base unit; 12 inches make up 1 foot (ft.), 3 feet make up 1 yard (yd.), and 5280 feet make up 1 mile (mi). However, as there are only a set number of units in the customary system, with extremely large or extremely small amounts of material, the numbers can become awkward and difficult to compare.

Common Customary Measurements		
Length	**Weight**	**Capacity**
1 foot = 12 inches	1 pound = 16 ounces	1 cup = 8 fluid ounces
1 yard = 3 feet	1 ton = 2,000 pounds	1 pint = 2 cups
1 yard = 36 inches		1 quart = 2 pints
1 mile = 1,760 yards		1 quart = 4 cups
1 mile = 5,280 feet		1 gallon = 4 quarts
		1 gallon = 16 cups

Metric System

Aside from the United States, most countries in the world have adopted the metric system embodied in the International System of Units (SI). The three main SI base units used in the metric system are the meter (m), the kilogram (kg), and the liter (L); meters measure length, kilograms measure mass, and liters measure volume.

These three units can use different prefixes, which indicate larger or smaller versions of the unit by powers of ten. This can be thought of as making a new unit which is sized by multiplying the original unit in size by a factor.

These prefixes and associated factors are:

Metric Prefixes			
Prefix	**Symbol**	**Multiplier**	**Exponential**
giga	G	1,000,000,000	10^9
mega	M	1,000,000	10^6
kilo	k	1,000	10^3
hecto	h	100	10^2
deca	da	10	10^1
no prefix		1	10^0
deci	d	0.1	10^{-1}
centi	c	0.01	10^{-2}
milli	m	0.001	10^{-3}
micro	µ	0.000001	10^{-6}
nano	n	0.000000001	10^{-9}

The correct prefix is then attached to the base. Some examples:

1 milliliter equals .001 liters.
1,000,000,000 nanometers equals 1 meter.
1 kilogram equals 1,000 grams.

Choosing the Appropriate Measuring Unit

Some units of measure are represented as square or cubic units depending on the solution. For example, perimeter is measured in units, area is measured in square units, and volume is measured in cubic units.

It is important to use the most appropriate unit for the thing being measured. A building's height might be measured in feet or meters while the length of a nail might be measured in inches or centimeters. Additionally, for SI units, the prefix should be chosen to provide the most succinct available value. For example, the mass of a bag of fruit would likely be measured in kilograms rather than grams or milligrams, and the length of a bacteria cell would likely be measured in micrometers rather than centimeters or kilometers.

Algebraic Thinking and the Coordinate Plane

Algebraic Expressions and Equations

Algebraic expressions look similar to equations, but they do not include the equal sign. Algebraic expressions are comprised of numbers, variables, and mathematical operations. Some examples of algebraic expressions are $8x + 7y - 12z$, $3a^2$, and $5x^3 - 4y^4$.

Algebraic expressions and equations can be used to represent real-life situations and model the behavior of different variables. For example, $2x + 5$ could represent the cost to play games at an arcade. In this case, 5 represents the price of admission to the arcade and 2 represents the cost of each game played. To calculate the total cost, use the number of games played for x, multiply it by 2, and add 5.

Properties Involving Algebraic Expressions

Properties such as associativity and commutativity that hold among operations between real numbers also hold between algebraic expressions. Addition and multiplication are associative and commutative; therefore, addition and multiplication can be completed in any order inside an algebraic expression. This is helpful when it comes to solving equations. The addition and multiplication principles state that anything can be added to or multiplied by both sides of an equation to maintain equality. This process is helpful when it comes to isolating the variable. The only time there might be an issue is multiplying times a rational expression with a variable in the denominator. One must make sure that the denominator cannot equal zero. Therefore, it would not be appropriate to multiply both sides of the equation $x^2 = 1$ by $\frac{1}{x}$ to solve for x. The solution $x = 0$ would be lost.

Rewriting Expressions

Algebraic expressions are made up of numbers, variables, and combinations of the two, using mathematical operations. Expressions can be rewritten based on their factors. For example, the expression $6x + 4$ can be rewritten as $2(3x + 2)$ because 2 is a factor of both $6x$ and 4. More complex expressions can also be rewritten based on their factors. The expression $x^4 - 16$ can be rewritten as $(x^2 - 4)(x^2 + 4)$. This is a different type of factoring, where a difference of squares is factored into a sum and difference of the same two terms. With some expressions, the factoring process is simple and only leads to a different way to represent the expression. With others, factoring and rewriting the expression leads to more information about the given problem.

In the following quadratic equation, factoring the binomial leads to finding the zeros of the function: $x^2 - 5x + 6 = y$. This equations factors into $(x - 3)(x - 2) = y$, where 2 and 3 are found to be the zeros of the function when y is set equal to zero. The zeros of any function are the x-values where the graph of the function on the coordinate plane crosses the x-axis.

Factoring an equation is a simple way to rewrite the equation and find the zeros, but factoring is not possible for every quadratic. Completing the square is one way to find zeros when factoring is not an option. The following equation cannot be factored: $x^2 + 10x - 9 = 0$. The first step in this method is to move the constant to the right side of the equation, making it $x^2 + 10x = 9$. Then, the coefficient of x is divided it by 2 and squared. This number is then added to both sides of the equation, to make the equation still true. For this example, $\left(\frac{10}{2}\right)^2 = 25$ is added to both sides of the equation to obtain:

$x^2 + 10x + 25 = 9 + 25$. This expression simplifies to $x^2 + 10x + 25 = 34$, which can then be factored into $(x + 5)^2 = 34$. Solving for x then involves taking the square root of both sides and subtracting 5. This leads to two zeros of the function: $x = \pm\sqrt{34} - 5$. Depending on the type of answer the question seeks, a calculator may be used to find exact numbers.

Given a quadratic equation in standard form— $ax^2 + bx + c = 0$—the sign of a tells whether the function has a minimum value or a maximum value. If $a > 0$, the graph opens up and has a minimum value. If $a < 0$, the graph opens down and has a maximum value. Depending on the way the quadratic equation is written, multiplication may need to occur before a max/min value is determined.

Exponential expressions can also be rewritten, just as quadratic equations. Properties of exponents must be understood. Multiplying two exponential expressions with the same base involves adding the exponents: $a^m a^n = a^{m+n}$. Dividing two exponential expressions with the same base involves subtracting the exponents: $\frac{a^m}{a^n} = a^{m-n}$. Raising an exponential expression to another exponent includes multiplying the exponents: $(a^m)^n = a^{mn}$. The zero power always gives a value of 1: $a^0 = 1$. Raising either a product or a fraction to a power involves distributing that power: $(ab)^m = a^m b^m$ and $\left(\frac{a}{b}\right)^m = \frac{a^m}{b^m}$. Finally, raising a number to a negative exponent is equivalent to the reciprocal including the positive exponent: $a^{-m} = \frac{1}{a^m}$.

Defining Linear Equations

A function is called *linear* if it can take the form of the equation $f(x) = ax + b$, or $y = ax + b$, for any two numbers *a* and *b*. A linear equation forms a straight line when graphed on the coordinate plane. An example of a linear function is shown below on the graph.

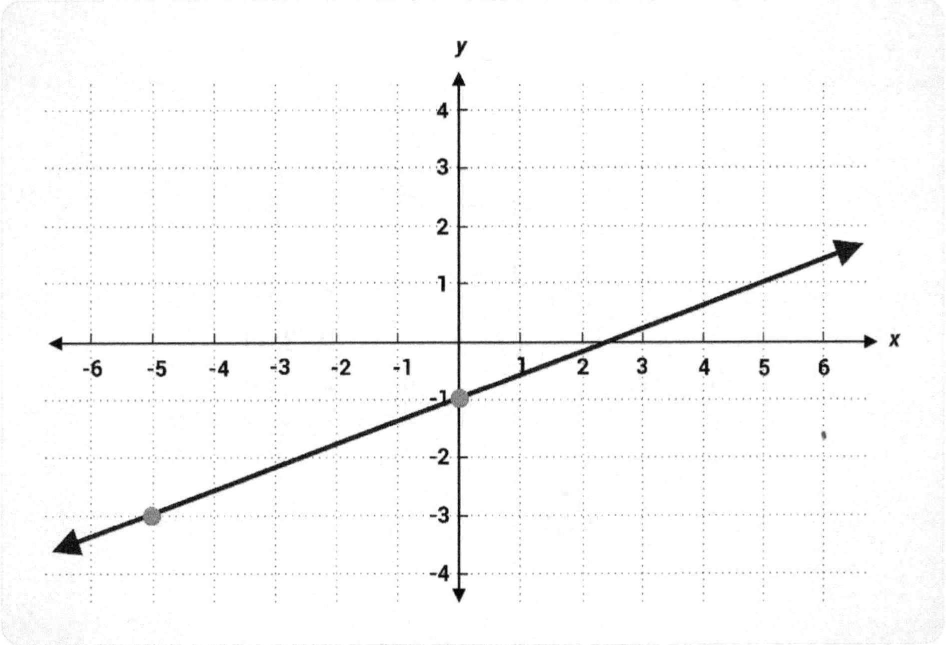

This is a graph of the following function: $y = \frac{2}{5}x - 1$. A table of values that satisfies this function is shown below.

x	y
-5	-3
0	-1
5	1
10	3

These points can be found on the graph using the form (x, y). For more on graphing in the coordinate plane, refer to the Graphing section below.

Graphing Functions and Relations

To graph relations and functions, the Cartesian plane is used. This means to think of the plane as being given a grid of squares, with one direction being the *x*-axis and the other direction the *y*-axis. Generally, the independent variable is placed along the horizontal axis, and the dependent variable is placed along the vertical axis. Any point on the plane can be specified by saying how far to go along the *x*-axis and how far along the *y*-axis with a pair of numbers (x, y). Specific values for these pairs can be given names such as $C = (-1, 3)$. Negative values mean to move left or down; positive values mean to move right or up. The point where the axes cross one another is called the *origin*. The origin has coordinates $(0, 0)$ and is usually called O when given a specific label. An illustration of the Cartesian plane, along with graphs of $(2, 1)$ and $(-1, -1)$, are below.

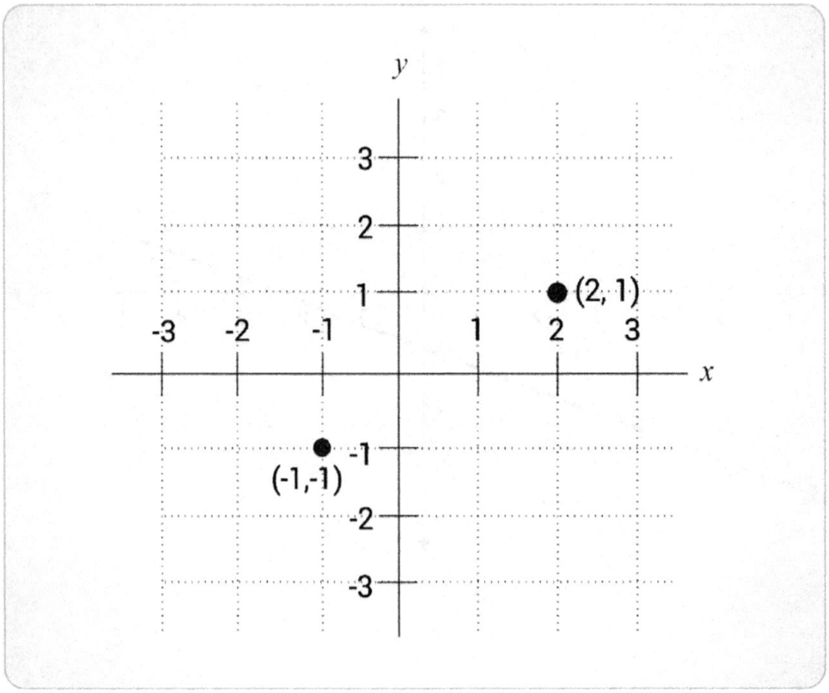

Relations also can be graphed by marking each point whose coordinates satisfy the relation. If the relation is a function, then there is only one value of *y* for any given value of *x*. This leads to the *vertical line test*: if a relation is graphed, then the relation is a function if every vertical line touches the graph at either zero or one point. Conversely, when graphing a function, then every vertical line will touch the graph at no points or just one point.

Forms of Linear Equations

When graphing a linear function, note that the ratio of the change of the *y* coordinate to the change in the *x* coordinate is constant between any two points on the resulting line, no matter which two points are chosen. In other words, in a pair of points on a line, (x_1, y_1) and (x_2, y_2), with $x_1 \neq x_2$ so that the two points are distinct, then the ratio $\frac{y_2-y_1}{x_2-x_1}$ will be the same, regardless of which particular pair of points are chosen. This ratio, $\frac{y_2-y_1}{x_2-x_1}$, is called the *slope* of the line and is frequently denoted with the letter m. If slope *m* is positive, then the line goes upward when moving to the right, while if slope *m* is negative, then the line goes downward when moving to the right. If the slope is 0, then the line is called *horizontal*, and the *y* coordinate is constant along the entire line. In lines where the *x* coordinate is constant along the entire line, *y* is not actually a function of *x*. For such lines, the slope is not defined. These lines are called *vertical* lines.

Linear functions may take forms other than $y = ax + b$. The most common forms of linear equations are explained below:

1. Standard Form: $Ax + By = C$, in which the slope is given by $m = \frac{-A}{B}$, and the *y*-intercept is given by $\frac{C}{B}$.

2. Slope-Intercept Form: $y = mx + b$, where the slope is *m* and the *y* intercept is *b*.

3. Point-Slope Form: $y - y_1 = m(x - x_1)$, where the slope is *m* and (x_1, y_1) is any point on the chosen line.

4. Two-Point Form: $\frac{y-y_1}{x-x_1} = \frac{y_2-y_1}{x_2-x_1}$, where (x_1, y_1) and (x_2, y_2) are any two distinct points on the chosen line. Note that the slope is given by $m = \frac{y_2-y_1}{x_2-x_1}$.

5. Intercept Form: $\frac{x}{x_1} + \frac{y}{y_1} = 1$, in which x_1 is the *x*-intercept and y_1 is the *y*-intercept.

These five ways to write linear equations are all useful in different circumstances. Depending on the given information, it may be easier to write one of the forms over another.

If $y = mx$, *y* is directly proportional to *x*. In this case, changing *x* by a factor changes *y* by that same factor. If $y = \frac{m}{x}$, *y* is inversely proportional to *x*. For example, if *x* is increased by a factor of 3, then *y* will be decreased by the same factor, 3.

Solving Linear Equations

Sometimes, rather than a situation where there's an equation such as $y = ax + b$ and finding *y* for some value of *x* is requested, the result is given and finding *x* is requested.

The key to solving any equation is to remember that from one true equation, another true equation can be found by adding, subtracting, multiplying, or dividing both sides by the same quantity. In this case, it's necessary to manipulate the equation so that one side only contains *x*. Then the other side will show what *x* is equal to.

For example, in solving $3x - 5 = 2$, adding 5 to each side results in $3x = 7$. Next, dividing both sides by 3 results in $x = \frac{7}{3}$. To ensure the value of x is correct, the number can be substituted into the original equation and solved to see if it makes a true statement. For example, $3(\frac{7}{3}) - 5 = 2$ can be simplified by cancelling out the two 3s. This yields $7 - 5 = 2$, which is a true statement.

Sometimes an equation may have more than one *x* term. For example, consider the following equation: $3x + 2 = x - 4$. Moving all of the *x* terms to one side by subtracting *x* from both sides results in $2x + 2 = -4$. Next, subtract 2 from both sides so that there is no constant term on the left side. This yields $2x = -6$. Finally, divide both sides by 2, which leaves $x = -3$.

Solving Linear Inequalities

Solving linear inequalities is very similar to solving equations, except for one rule: when multiplying or dividing an inequality by a negative number, the inequality symbol changes direction. Given the following inequality, solve for x: $-2x + 5 < 13$. The first step in solving this equation is to subtract 5 from both sides. This leaves the inequality: $-2x < 8$. The last step is to divide both sides by -2. By using the rule, the answer to the inequality is $x > -4$.

Since solutions to inequalities include more than one value, number lines are used many times to model the answer. For the previous example, the answer is modelled on the number line below. It shows that any number greater than -4, not including -4, satisfies the inequality.

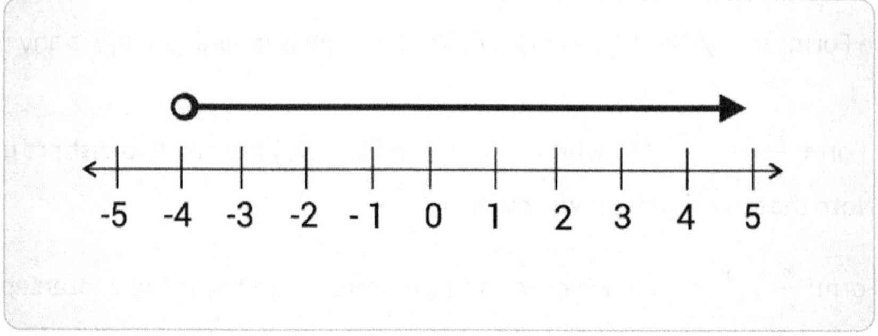

Linear Systems of Equations

A problem sometimes involves multiple variables and multiple equations. These are called *systems of equations*. In this case, try to manipulate them until an expression is found that provides the value of one of the variables. There are a couple of different approaches to this, and some of them can be used together in some cases. The three basic rules to keep in mind are the following.

- *1. Manipulate a set of equations by doing the same operation to both equations, just as is done when working with just one equation.*
- *2. If one of the equations can be changed so that it expresses one variable in terms of the others, then that expression can be substituted into the other equations and the variable can be*

eliminated. This means the other equations will have one less variable in them. This is called the method of substitution.

- *3. If two equations of the form $a = b, c = d$ are included, then a new equation can be formed by adding the left sides and adding the right sides, $a + c = b + d$, or $a - c = b - d$. This enables the elimination of one of the variables from an equation. This is called the method of elimination.*

The simplest case is the case of a *linear* system of equations. Although the equations may be written in more complicated forms, linear systems of equations with two variables can always be written in the form $ax + by = c, dx + ey = f$. The two basic approaches to solving these systems are substitution and elimination.

Consider the system $3x - y = 2$ *and* $2x + 2y = 3$. This can be solved in two ways.

1. By substitution: start by solving the first equation for y. First, subtract $3x$ from both sides to obtain $-y = 2 - 3x$. Next, divide both sides by -1, to obtain $y = 3x - 2$. Then substitute this value for y into the second equation. This yields $2x + 2(3x - 2) = 3$. This can be simplified to $2x + 6x - 4 = 3$, or $8x = 7$, which means $x = \frac{7}{8}$. By plugging in this value for x into $y = 3x - 2$, the result is $y = 3\left(\frac{7}{8}\right) - 2 = \frac{21}{8} - \frac{16}{8} = \frac{5}{8}$. So, this results in $x = \frac{7}{8}, y = \frac{5}{8}$.

2. By elimination: first, multiply the first equation by 2. This results in $-2y$, which could cancel out the $+2y$ in the second equation. Multiplying both sides of the first equation by 2 gives results in $2(3x - y) = 2(2)$, or $6x - 2y = 4$. Adding the left sides and the right sides of the two equations and setting the results equal to one another results in $(6x + 2x) + (-2y + 2y) = 4 + 3$. This simplifies to $8x = 7$, so again $x = \frac{7}{8}$. Plug this back into either of the original equations and the result is $3\left(\frac{7}{8}\right) - y = 2$ or $y = 3\left(\frac{7}{8}\right) - 2 = \frac{21}{8} - \frac{16}{8} = \frac{5}{8}$. This again yields $x = \frac{7}{8}, y = \frac{5}{8}$.

As this shows, both methods will give the same answer. However, one method is sometimes preferred over another simply because of the amount of work required. To check the answer, the values can be substituted into the given system to make sure they form two true statements.

Rate of Change

Rate of change for any line calculates the steepness of the line over a given interval. Rate of change is also known as the slope or rise/run. The rates of change for nonlinear functions vary depending on the interval being used for the function. The rate of change over one interval may be zero, while the next interval may have a positive rate of change.

The equation plotted on the graph below, $y = x^2$, is a quadratic function and non-linear. The average rate of change from points $(0, 0)$ to $(1, 1)$ is 1 because the vertical change is 1 over the horizontal change of 1. For the next interval, $(1, 1)$ to $(2, 4)$, the average rate of change is 3 because the slope is $\frac{3}{1}$.

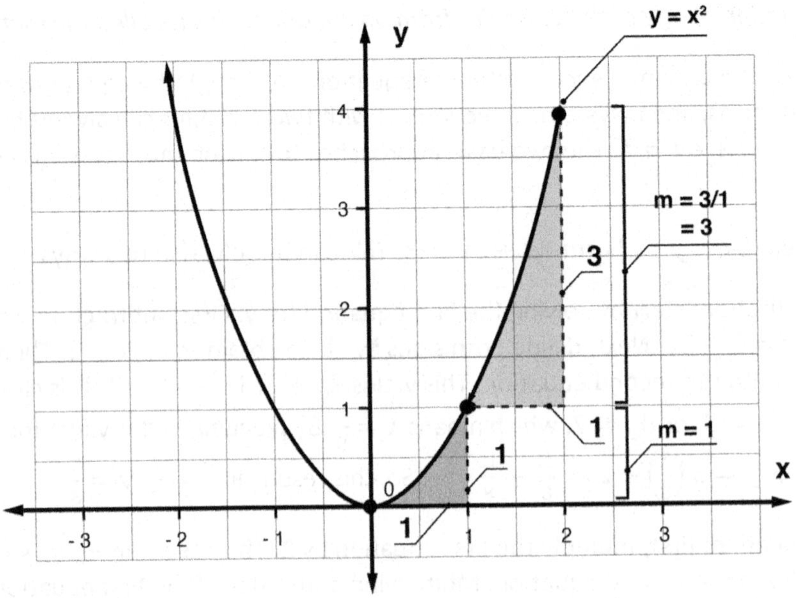

The rate of change for a linear function is constant and can be determined based on a few representations. One method is to place the equation in slope-intercept form: $y = mx + b$. Thus, m is the slope, and b is the y-intercept. In the graph below, the equation is $y = x + 1$, where the slope is 1 and the y-intercept is 1. For every vertical change of 1 unit, there is a horizontal change of 1 unit. The x-intercept is -1, which is the point where the line crosses the x-axis.

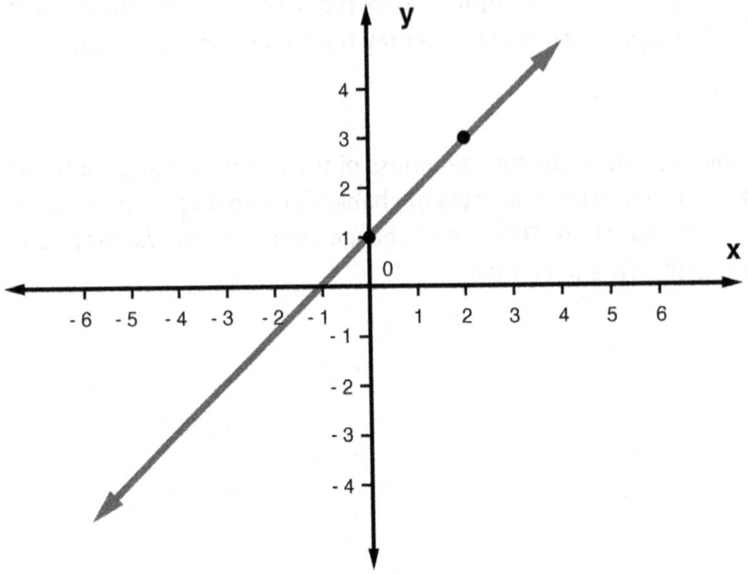

Relations and Functions

First, it's important to understand the definition of a *relation*. Given two variables, *x* and *y*, which stand for unknown numbers, a *relation* between *x* and *y* is an object that splits all of the pairs (*x*, *y*) into those for which the relation is true and those for which it is false. For example, consider the relation of $x^2 = y^2$. This relationship is true for the pair (1, 1) and for the pair (-2, 2), but false for (2, 3). Another example of a relation is $x \leq y$. This is true whenever *x* is less than or equal to *y*.

A *function* is a special kind of relation where, for each value of *x*, there is only a single value of *y* that satisfies the relation. So, $x^2 = y^2$ is *not* a function because in this case, if *x* is 1, *y* can be either 1 or -1: the pair (1, 1) and (1, -1) both satisfy the relation. More generally, for this relation, any pair of the form $(a, \pm a)$ will satisfy it. On the other hand, consider the following relation: $y = x^2 + 1$. This is a function because for each value of *x*, there is a unique value of *y* that satisfies the relation. Notice, however, there are multiple values of *x* that give us the same value of *y*. This is perfectly acceptable for a function. Therefore, *y* is a function of *x*.

To determine if a relation is a function, check to see if every *x* value has a unique corresponding *y* value.

A function can be viewed as an object that has *x* as its input and outputs a unique *y*-value. It is sometimes convenient to express this using *function notation*, where the function itself is given a name, often *f*. To emphasize that *f* takes *x* as its input, the function is written as $f(x)$. In the above example, the equation could be rewritten as $f(x) = x^2 + 1$. To write the value that a function yields for some specific value of *x*, that value is put in place of *x* in the function notation. For example, $f(3)$ means the value that the function outputs when the input value is 3. If $f(x) = x^2 + 1$, then $f(3) = 3^2 + 1 = 10$.

A function can also be viewed as a table of pairs (*x*, *y*), which lists the value for *y* for each possible value of *x*.

The set of all possible values for *x* in $f(x)$ is called the *domain* of the function, and the set of all possible outputs is called the *range* of the function. Note that usually the domain is assumed to be all real numbers, except those for which the expression for $f(x)$ is not defined, unless the problem specifies otherwise. An example of how a function might not be defined is in the case of $f(x) = \frac{1}{x+1}$, which is not defined when $x = -1$ (which would require dividing by zero). Therefore, in this case the domain would be all real numbers except $x = -1$.

If *y* is a function of *x*, then *x* is the *independent variable* and *y* is the *dependent variable*. This is because in many cases, the problem will start with some value of *x* and then see how *y* changes depending on this starting value.

Evaluating Functions

To evaluate functions, plug in the given value everywhere the variable appears in the expression for the function. For example, find $g(-2)$ where $g(x) = 2x^2 - \frac{4}{x}$. To complete the problem, plug in -2 in the following way: $g(-2) = 2(-2)^2 - \frac{4}{-2} = 2 \cdot 4 + 2 = 8 + 2 = 10$.

Finding the Zeros of a Function

The zeros of a function are the points where its graph crosses the x-axis. At these points, $y = 0$. One way to find the zeros is to analyze the graph. If given the graph, the x-coordinates can be found where the line crosses the x-axis. Another way to find the zeros is to set $y = 0$ in the equation and solve for x. Depending on the type of equation, this could be done by using opposite operations, by factoring the equation, by completing the square, or by using the quadratic formula. If a graph does not cross the x-axis, then the function may have complex roots.

Probability, Statistics, and Data Interpretation

Interpretation of Graphs

Data can be represented in many ways including picture graphs, bar graphs, line plots, and tally charts. It is important to be able to organize the data into categories that could be represented using one of these methods. Equally important is the ability to read these types of diagrams and interpret their meaning.

A *picture graph* is a diagram that shows pictorial representation of data being discussed. The symbols used can represent a certain number of objects. Notice how each fruit symbol in the following graph represents a count of two fruits. One drawback of picture graphs is that they can be less accurate if each symbol represents a large number. For example, if each banana symbol represented ten bananas, and students consumed 22 bananas, it may be challenging to draw and interpret two and one-fifth bananas as a frequency count of 22.

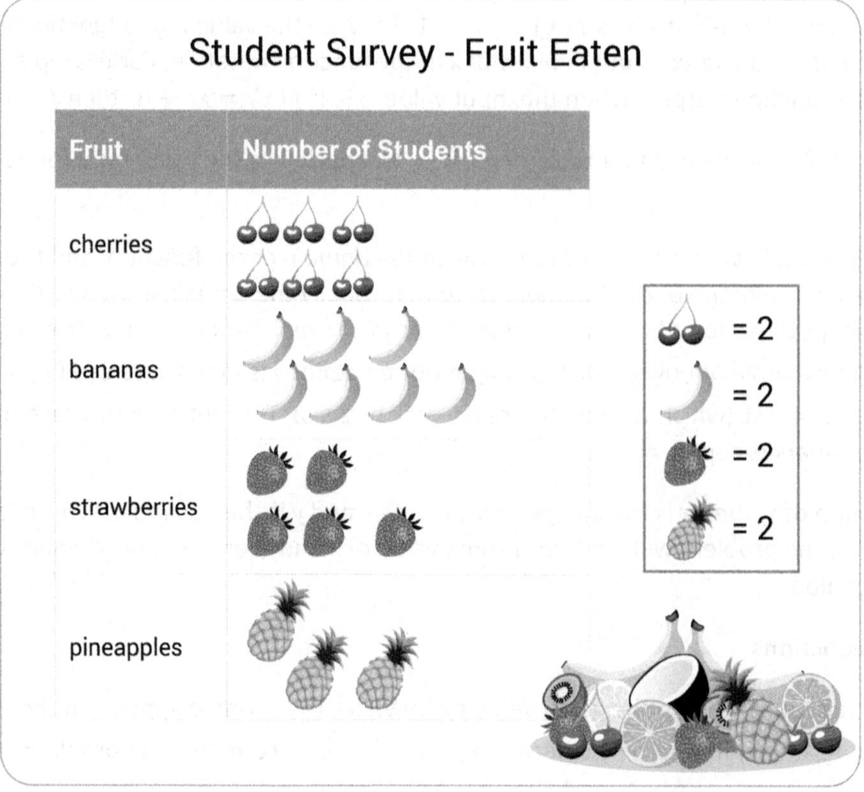

A *bar graph* is a diagram in which the quantity of items within a specific classification is represented by the height of a rectangle. Each type of classification is represented by a rectangle of equal width. Here is an example of a bar graph:

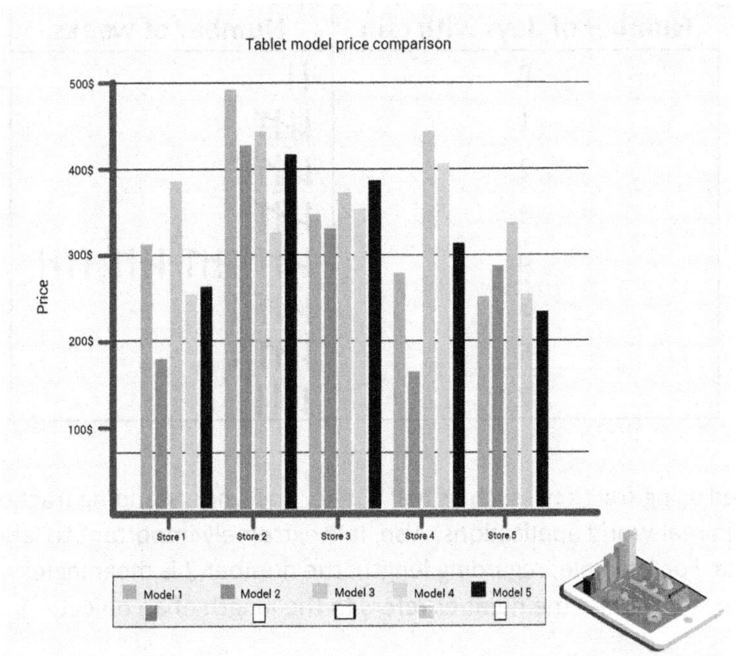

A *line plot* is a diagram that shows quantity of data along a number line. It is a quick way to record data in a structure similar to a bar graph without needing to do the required shading of a bar graph. Here is an example of a line plot:

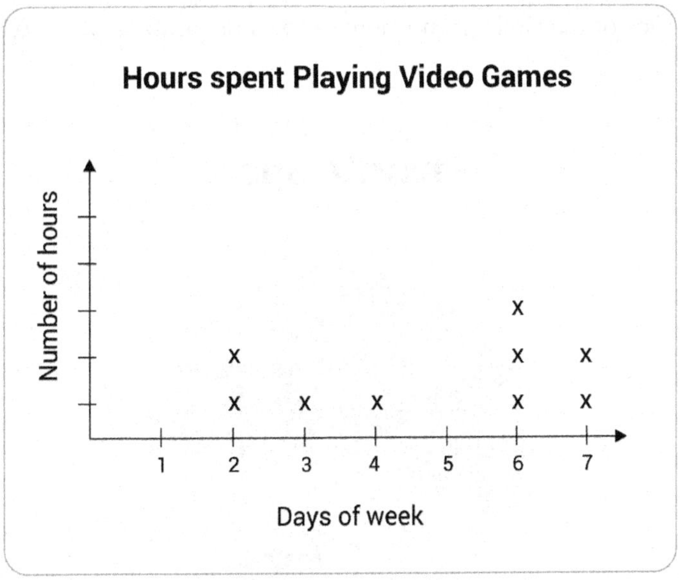

A *tally chart* is a diagram in which tally marks are utilized to represent data. Tally marks are a means of showing a quantity of objects within a specific classification. Here is an example of a tally chart:

Number of days with rain	Number of weeks
0	II
1	𝍸
2	𝍸
3	𝍸
4	𝍸 𝍸 𝍸 IIII
5	𝍸 I
6	𝍸 I
7	IIII

Data is often recorded using fractions, such as half a mile, and understanding fractions is critical because of their popular use in real-world applications. Also, it is extremely important to label values with their units when using data. For example, regarding length, the number 2 is meaningless unless it is attached to a unit. Writing 2 cm shows that the number refers to the length of an object.

A circle graph, also called a pie chart, shows categorical data with each category representing a percentage of the whole data set. To make a circle graph, the percent of the data set for each category must be determined. To do so, the frequency of the category is divided by the total number of data points and converted to a percent. For example, if 80 people were asked what their favorite sport is and 20 responded basketball, basketball makes up 25% of the data ($\frac{20}{80}$ =.25=25%). Each category in a data set is represented by a *slice* of the circle proportionate to its percentage of the whole.

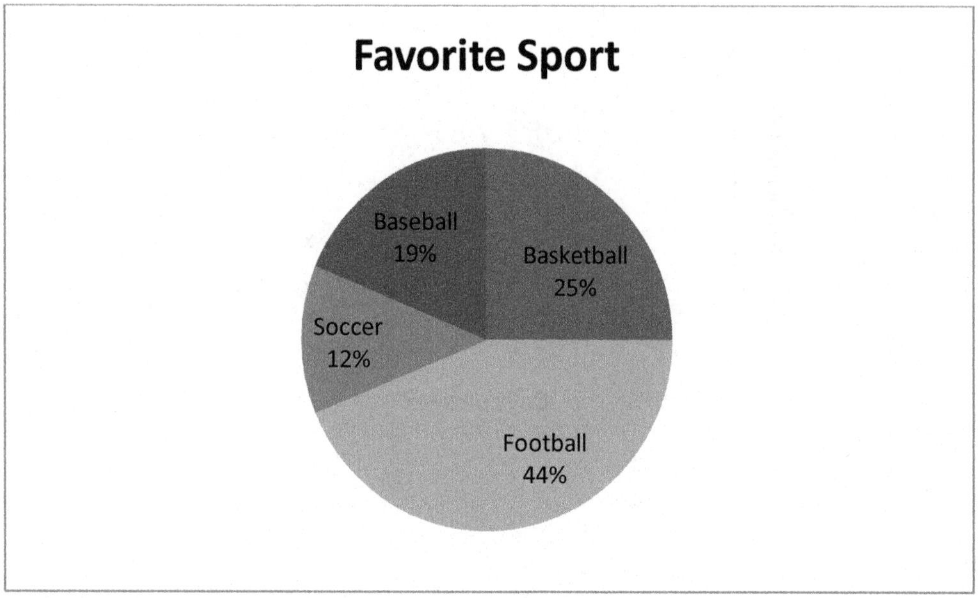

A scatter plot displays the relationship between two variables. Values for the independent variable, typically denoted by *x*, are paired with values for the dependent variable, typically denoted by *y*. Each set of corresponding values are written as an ordered pair (*x*, *y*). To construct the graph, a coordinate grid is labeled with the *x*-axis representing the independent variable and the *y*-axis representing the dependent variable. Each ordered pair is graphed.

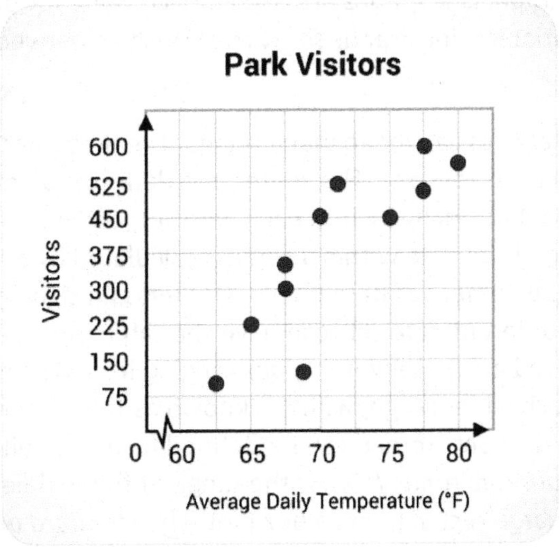

Like a scatter plot, a line graph compares two variables that change continuously, typically over time. Paired data values (ordered pair) are plotted on a coordinate grid with the *x*- and *y*-axis representing the two variables. A line is drawn from each point to the next, going from left to right. A double line graph simply displays two sets of data that contain values for the same two variables. The double line graph below displays the profit for given years (two variables) for Company A and Company B (two data sets).

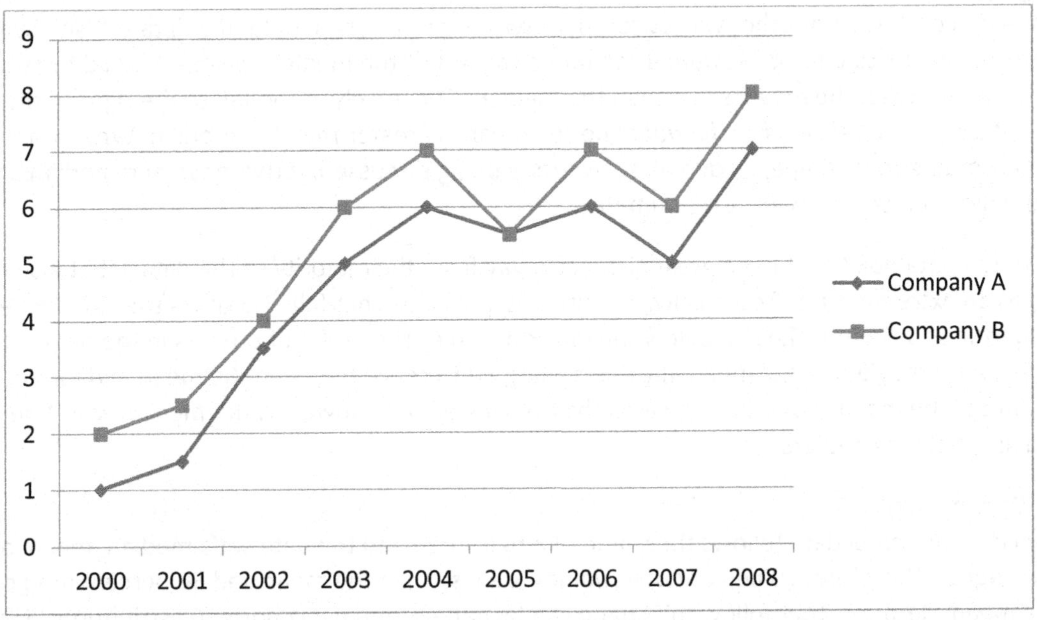

Choosing the appropriate graph to display a data set depends on what type of data is included in the set and what information must be shown. Histograms and box plots can be used for data sets consisting of individual values across a wide range. Examples include test scores and incomes. Histograms and box plots will indicate the center, spread, range, and outliers of a data set. A histogram will show the shape of the data set, while a box plot will divide the set into quartiles (25% increments), allowing for comparison between a given value and the entire set.

Scatter plots and line graphs can be used to display data consisting of two variables. Examples include height and weight, or distance and time. A correlation between the variables is determined by examining the points on the graph. Line graphs are used if each value for one variable pairs with a distinct value for the other variable. Line graphs show relationships between variables.

Comparing Data

Comparing data sets within statistics can mean many things. The first way to compare data sets is by looking at the center and spread of each set. The center of a data set can mean two things: median or mean. The *median* is the value that's halfway into each data set, and it splits the data into two intervals. The *mean* is the average value of the data within a set. It's calculated by adding up all of the data in the set and dividing the total by the number of data points. Outliers can significantly impact the mean. Additionally, two completely different data sets can have the same mean. For example, a data set with values ranging from 0 to 100 and a data set with values ranging from 44 to 56 can both have means of 50. The first data set has a much wider range, which is known as the *spread* of the data. This measures how varied the data is within each set. Spread can be defined further as either interquartile range or standard deviation. The *interquartile range (IQR)* is the range of the middle 50 percent of the data set. This range can be seen in the large rectangle on a box plot. The *standard deviation (σ)* quantifies the amount of variation with respect to the mean. A lower standard deviation shows that the data set doesn't differ greatly from the mean. A larger standard deviation shows that the data set is spread out farther from the mean. The formula for standard deviation is $\sigma = \sqrt{\frac{\Sigma(x-\bar{x})^2}{n-1}}$, where x is each value in the data set, $\bar{x}$ is the mean, and n is the total number of data points in the set.

Interpreting Data

The shape of a data set is another way to compare two or more sets of data. If a data set isn't symmetric around its mean, it's said to be ***skewed.*** If the tail to the left of the mean is longer, it's said to be *skewed to the left*. In this case, the mean is less than the median. Conversely, if the tail to the right of the mean is longer, it's said to be *skewed to the right* and the mean is greater than the median. When classifying a data set according to its shape, its overall *skewness* is being discussed. If the mean and median are equal, the data set isn't skewed; it is *symmetric*.

An *outlier* is a data point that lies a great distance away from the majority of the data set. It also can be labelled as an *extreme value*. Technically, an outlier is any value that falls 1.5 times the IQR above the upper quartile or 1.5 times the IQR below the lower quartile. The effect of outliers in the data set is seen visually because they affect the mean. If there's a large difference between the mean and mode, outliers are the cause. The mean shows bias towards the outlying values. However, the median won't be affected as greatly by outliers.

Normal Distribution

A *normal distribution* of data follows the shape of a bell curve and the data set's median, mean, and mode are equal. Therefore, 50 percent of its values are less than the mean and 50 percent are greater than the mean. Data sets that follow this shape can be generalized using normal distributions. Normal distributions are described as *frequency distributions* in which the data set is plotted as percentages rather than true data points. A *relative frequency distribution* is one where the *y*-axis is between 0 and 1, which is the same as 0% to 100%. Within a standard deviation, 68 percent of the values are within 1 standard deviation of the mean, 95 percent of the values are within 2 standard deviations of the mean, and 99.7 percent of the values are within 3 standard deviations of the mean. The number of standard deviations that a data point falls from the mean is called the *z-score*. The formula for the z-score is $Z = \frac{x-\mu}{\sigma}$, where μ is the mean, σ is the standard deviation, and x is the data point. This formula is used to fit any data set that resembles a normal distribution to a standard normal distribution, in a process known as *standardizing*.

Here is a normal distribution with labelled z-scores:

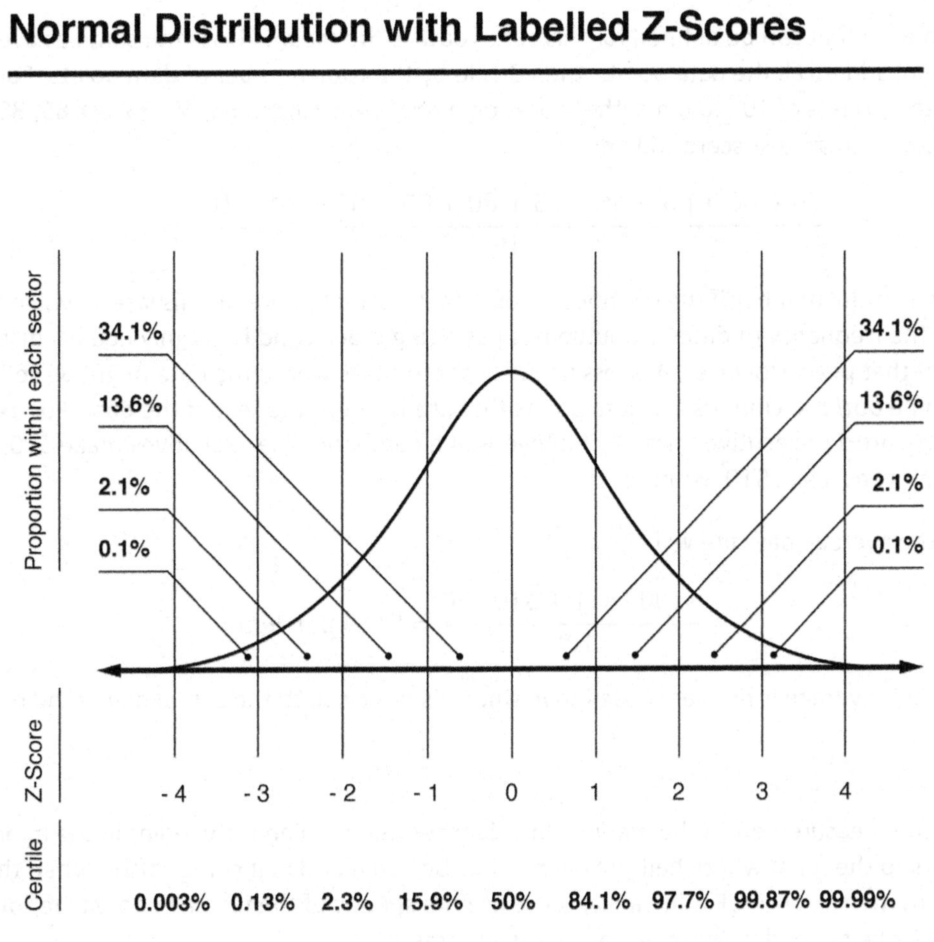

Population percentages can be estimated using normal distributions. For example, the probability that a data point will be less than the mean, or that the z-score will be less than 0, is 50%. Similarly, the probability that a data point will be within 1 standard deviation of the mean, or that the z-score will be between -1 and 1, is about 68.2%. When using a table, the left column states how many standard deviations (to one decimal place) away from the mean the point is, and the row heading states the second decimal place. The entries in the table corresponding to each column and row give the probability, which is equal to the area.

Areas Under the Curve

The area under the curve of a standard normal distribution is equal to 1. Areas under the curve can be estimated using the z-score and a table. The area is equal to the probability that a data point lies in that region in decimal form. For example, the area under the curve from $z = -1$ to $z = 1$ is 0.682.

Mean, Median, and Mode

Mean

Suppose that you have a set of data points and some description of the general properties of this data need to be found.

The first property that can be defined for this set of data is the *mean*. This is the same as average. To find the mean, add up all the data points, then divide by the total number of data points. For example, suppose that in a class of 10 students, the scores on a test were 50, 60, 65, 65, 75, 80, 85, 85, 90, 100. Therefore, the average test score will be:

$$\frac{50 + 60 + 65 + 65 + 75 + 80 + 85 + 85 + 90 + 100}{10} = 75.5$$

The mean is a useful number if the distribution of data is normal (more on this later), which roughly means that the frequency of different outcomes has a single peak and is roughly equally distributed on both sides of that peak. However, it is less useful in some cases where the data might be split or where there are some *outliers*. Outliers are data points that are far from the rest of the data. For example, suppose there are 11 executives and 90 employees at a company. The executives make $1000 per hour, and the employees make $10 per hour.

Therefore, the average pay rate will be:

$$\frac{\$1000 \cdot 11 + \$10 \cdot 90}{100} = \$119 \; per\ hour$$

In this case, this average is not very descriptive since it's not close to the actual pay of the executives *or* the employees.

Median

Another useful measurement is the *median*. In a data set, the median is the point in the middle. The middle refers to the point where half the data comes before it and half comes after, when the data is recorded in numerical order. For instance, these are the speeds of the fastball of a pitcher during the last inning that he pitched (in order from least to greatest):

$$90, 92, 93, 93, 95, 96, 97, 97, 97$$

There are nine total numbers, so the middle or *median* number in the 5th one, which is 95.

In cases where the number of data points is an even number than the average of the two middle points it taken. In the previous example of test scores, the two middle points are 75 and 80. Since there is no single point, the average of these two scores needs to be found. The average is:

$$\frac{75 + 80}{2} = 77.5$$

The median is generally a good value to use if there are a few outliers in the data. It prevents those outliers from affecting the "middle" value as much as when using the mean.

Since an outlier is a data point that is far from most of the other data points in a data set, this means an outlier also is any point that is far from the median of the data set. The outliers can have a substantial effect on the mean of a data set, but usually do not change the median or mode, or do not change them by a large quantity. For example, consider the data set (3, 5, 6, 6, 6, 8). This has a median of 6 and a mode of 6, with a mean of $\frac{34}{6} \approx 5.67$. Now, suppose a new data point of 1000 is added so that the data set is now (3, 5, 6, 6, 6, 8, 1000). This does not change the median or mode, which are both still 6. However, the average is now $\frac{1034}{7}$, which is approximately 147.7. In this case, the median and mode will be better descriptions for most of the data points.

The reason for outliers in a given data set is a complicated problem. It is sometimes the result of an error by the experimenter, but often they are perfectly valid data points that must be taken into consideration.

<u>Mode</u>
One additional measure to define for X is the *mode*. This is the data point that appears most frequently. If two or more data points all tie for the most frequent appearance, then each of them is considered a mode. In the case of the test scores, where the numbers were 50, 60, 65, 65, 75, 80, 85, 85, 90, 100, there are two modes: 65 and 85.

Quartiles and Percentiles

The *first quartile* of a set of data X refers to the largest value from the first ¼ of the data points. In practice, there are sometimes slightly different definitions that can be used, such as the median of the first half of the data points (excluding the median itself if there are an odd number of data points). The term also has a slightly different use: when it is said that a data point lies *in the first quartile*, it means it is less than or equal to the median of the first half of the data points. Conversely, if it lies *at* the first quartile, then it is equal to the first quartile.

When it is said that a data point lies in the *second quartile*, it means it is between the first quartile and the median.

The *third quartile* refers to data that lies between ½ and ¾ of the way through the data set. Again, there are various methods for defining this precisely, but the simplest way is to include all of the data that lie between the median and the median of the top half of the data.

Data that lies in the *fourth quartile* refers to all of the data above the third quartile.

Percentiles may be defined in a similar manner to quartiles. Generally, this is defined in the following manner:

If a data point lies *in the n-th percentile*, this means it lies in the range of the first *n*% of the data.

If a data point lies *at* the *n*-th percentile, then it means that *n*% of the data lies below this data point.

Standard Deviation

Given a data set X consisting of data points $(x_1, x_2, x_3, \ldots x_n)$, the *variance* of X is defined to be $\frac{\sum_{i=1}^{n}(x_i-\bar{X})^2}{n}$. This means that the variance of X is the average of the squares of the differences between each data point and the mean of X.

Given a data set X consisting of data points $(x_1, x_2, x_3, \ldots x_n)$, the *standard deviation* of X is defined to be $s_x = \sqrt{\frac{\sum_{i=1}^{n}(x_i-\bar{X})^2}{n}}$. In other words, the standard deviation is the square root of the variance.

Both the variance and the standard deviation are measures of how much the data tend to be spread out. When the standard deviation is low, the data points are mostly clustered around the mean. When the standard deviation is high, this generally indicates that the data are quite spread out, or else that there are a few substantial outliers.

As a simple example, compute the standard deviation for the data set (1, 3, 3, 5). First, compute the mean, which will be $\frac{1+3+3+5}{4} = \frac{12}{4} = 3$. Now, find the variance of X with the formula: $\sum_{i=1}^{4}(x_i - \bar{X})^2 = (1-3)^2 + (3-3)^2 + (5-3)^2 = -2^2 + 0^2 + 0^2 + 2^2 = 8$. Therefore, the variance is $\frac{8}{4} = 2$. Taking the square root, the standard deviation will be $\sqrt{2}$.

Note that the standard deviation only depends upon the mean, not upon the median or mode(s). Generally, if there are multiple modes that are far apart from one another, the standard deviation will be high. A high standard deviation does not always mean there are multiple modes, however.

Fitting Functions to Data

Sometimes, when data are measured, it is not simply measuring the frequency of a given outcome, but rather measuring a relationship between two different quantities. In these cases, there is usually one variable that is controlled, the *independent variable*, and one that depends on this variable, the *dependent variable*. If there is a relationship between the two variables, then they are said to be *correlated*.

There are two caveats to these terms. First, the independent variable is not necessarily controlled by the experimenters. It is simply the one chosen to organize the data. In other words, the data are divided up based on the value of an independent variable. Second, finding a significant relationship between the dependent variable and the independent variable does not necessarily imply that there is a causal relationship between the two variables. It only means that once the independent variable is known, a fairly accurate prediction of the dependent variable can be made. This is often expressed with the phrase *correlation does not imply causation*. In other words, just because there is a relationship between two variables does not mean that one is the cause of the other. There could be other factors involved that are the real cause.

Consider some examples. An experimenter could do an experiment in which the independent variable is the number of hours that a student studies for a given test, and the dependent variable is the score the student receives when he or she actually takes the test. Such an experiment would attempt to measure whether there is a relationship between the time spent studying and the score a student receives when taking the test. The expectation would be that the larger value of the independent variable would yield a larger value for the dependent variable. Another experimenter might do an experiment with runners, where the independent variable is the length of the runner's leg, and the dependent variable is the time it takes for the runner to run a fixed distance. In this experiment, as the independent variable increases, the dependent variable would be expected to decrease.

As an example of the phenomenon that correlation does not imply causation, consider an experiment where the independent variable is the value of a person's house, and the dependent variable is their income. Although people in more expensive houses are expected to make more money, it is clear that their expensive houses are not the cause of them making more money. This illustrates one example of why it is important for experimenters to be careful when drawing conclusions about causation from their data.

Linear Data Fitting

The simplest type of correlation between two variables is a *linear correlation*. If the independent variable is *x* and the dependent variable is *y*, then a linear correlation means $y = mx + b$. If *m* is positive, then *y* will increase as *x* increases. While if *m* is negative, then *y* decreases while *x* increases. The variable *b* represents the value of *y* when *x* is 0.

As one example of such a correlation, consider a manufacturing plant. Suppose *x* is the number of units produced by the plant, and *y* is the cost to the company. In this example, *b* will be the cost of the plant itself. The plant will cost money even if it is never used, just by buying the machinery. For each unit produced, there will be a cost for the labor and the material. Let *m* represent this cost to produce one unit of the product.

For a more concrete example, suppose a computer factory costs $100,000. It requires $100 of parts and $50 of labor to make one computer. How much will it cost for a company to make 1000 computers? To figure this, let *y* be the amount of money the company spends, and let *x* be the number of computers. The cost of the factory is $100,000, so $b = 100{,}000$. On the other hand, the cost of producing a computer is the parts plus labor, or $150, so $m = 150$. Therefore, $y = 150x + 100{,}000$. Substitute 1000 for *x* and get $y = 150 \cdot 1000 + 100{,}000 = 150{,}000 + 1000 = 250{,}000$. It will cost the company $250,000 to make 1000 computers.

Creating and Interpreting Linear Regression Models

Linear Regression

Regression lines are a way to calculate a relationship between the independent variable and the dependent variable. A straight line means that there's a linear trend in the data. The average daily temperature example above is one in which a straight line represented the data because the shape of the scatterplot resembles a straight line. Technology can be used to find the equation of this line (e.g., a graphing calculator or Microsoft Excel®). In either case, all of the data points are entered and a line is "fit" that best represents the shape of the data. Other functions used to model data sets include quadratic and exponential models.

Estimating Data Points

Regression lines can be used to estimate data points not already given. For example, if an equation of a line is found that fit the temperature and beach visitor data set, its input is the average daily temperature and its output is the projected number of visitors. Thus, the number of beach visitors on a 100-degree day can be estimated. The output is a data point on the regression line, and the number of daily visitors is expected to be greater than on a 96-degree day because the regression line has a positive slope.

Plotting and Analyzing Residuals

Once the function is found that fits the data, its accuracy can be calculated. Therefore, how well the line fits the data can be determined. The difference between the actual dependent variable from the data set and the estimated value located on the regression line is known as a *residual.* Therefore, the residual is known as the predicted value $\hat{y}$ minus the actual value y. A residual is calculated for each data point and can be plotted on the scatterplot. If all the residuals appear to be approximately the same distance from the regression line, the line is a good fit. If the residuals seem to differ greatly across the board, the line isn't a good fit.

Interpreting the Regression Line

The formula for a regression line is $y = mx + b$, where m is the slope and b is the *y*-intercept. Both the slope and *y*-intercept are found in the *Method of Least Squares*, which is the process of finding the equation of the line through minimizing residuals. The slope represents the rate of change in *y* as x gets larger. Therefore, because *y* is the dependent variable, the slope actually provides the predicted values given the independent variable. The *y*-intercept is the predicted value for when the independent variable equals 0. In the temperature example, the *y*-intercept is the expected number of beach visitors for a very cold average daily temperature of 0 degrees.

Correlation Coefficient

The *correlation coefficient (r)* measures the association between two variables. Its value is between -1 and 1, where -1 represents a perfect negative linear relationship, 0 represents no relationship, and 1 represents a perfect positive linear relationship. A *negative linear relationship* means that as x values increase, *y* values decrease. A *positive linear relationship* means that as *x* values increase, *y* values increase. The formula for computing the correlation coefficient is $r = \frac{n\sum xy-(\sum x)(\sum y)}{\sqrt{n(\sum x^2)-(\sum x)^2}\sqrt{n(\sum y^2)-(y)^2}}$, where n is the number of data points. Both Microsoft Excel® and a graphing calculator can evaluate this easily once the data points are entered. A correlation greater than 0.8 or less than -0.8 is classified as "strong" while a correlation between -0.5 and 0.5 is classified as "weak."

Correlation Versus Causation

Correlation and causation have two different meanings. As stated previously, if two values are *correlated*, there is an association between them. However, correlation doesn't necessarily mean that one variable causes the other. *Causation* (or "cause and effect") occurs when one variable causes the other. Average daily temperature and number of beachgoers are correlated and have causation. If the temperature increases, the change in weather causes more people to go to the beach. However, alcoholism and smoking are correlated but don't have causation. The more someone drinks the more likely they are to smoke, but drinking alcohol doesn't cause someone to smoke.

Probabilities

Given a set of possible outcomes *X*, a *probability distribution* on *X* is a function that assigns a probability to each possible outcome. If the outcomes are $(x_1, x_2, x_3, \dots x_n)$, and the probability distribution is *p*, then the following rules are applied.

- $0 \leq p(x_i) \leq 1$, *for any i.*
- $\sum_{i=1}^{n} p(x_i) = 1.$

In other words, the probability of a given outcome must be between zero and 1, while the total probability must be 1.

If $p(x_i)$ is constant, then this is called a *uniform probability distribution*, and $p(x_i) = \frac{1}{n}$. For example, on a six-sided die, the probability of each of the six outcomes will be $\frac{1}{6}$.

If seeking the probability of an outcome occurring in some specific range *A* of possible outcomes, written $P(A)$, add up the probabilities for each outcome in that range. For example, consider a six-sided die, and figure the probability of getting a 3 or lower when it is rolled. The possible rolls are 1, 2, 3, 4, 5, and 6. So, to get a 3 or lower, a roll a 1, 2, or 3 must be completed. The probabilities of each of these is $\frac{1}{6}$, so add these to get $p(1) + p(2) + p(3) = \frac{1}{6} + \frac{1}{6} + \frac{1}{6} = \frac{1}{2}$.

Conditional Probabilities

An outcome occasionally lies within some range of possibilities *B*, and the probability that the outcomes also lie within some set of possibilities *A* needs to be figured. This is called a *conditional probability*. It is written as $P(A|B)$, which is read "the probability of *A* given *B*." The general formula for computing conditional probabilities is $P(A|B) = \frac{P(A \cap B)}{P(B)}$.

However, when dealing with uniform probability distributions, simplify this a bit. Write $|A|$ to indicate the number of outcomes in *A*. Then, for uniform probability distributions, write $P(A|B) = \frac{|A \cap B|}{|B|}$ (recall that $A \cap B$ means "*A* intersect *B*," and consists of all of the outcomes that lie in both *A* and *B*). This means that all possible outcomes do not need to be known. To see why this formula works, suppose that the set of outcomes *X* is $(x_1, x_2, x_3, \dots x_n)$, so that $|X| = n$. Then, for a uniform probability distribution, $P(A) = \frac{|A|}{n}$. However, this means $(A|B) = \frac{P(A \cap B)}{P(B)} = \frac{\frac{|A \cap B|}{n}}{\frac{|B|}{n}} = \frac{|A \cap B|}{|B|}$, since the *n*'s cancel out.

For example, suppose a die is rolled and it is known that it will land between 1 and 4. However, how many sides the die has is unknown. Figure the probability that the die is rolled higher than 2. To figure this, $P(3)$ or $P(4)$ does not need to be determined, or any of the other probabilities, since it is known that a fair die has a uniform probability distribution. Therefore, apply the formula $\frac{|A \cap B|}{|B|}$. So, in this case *B* is (1, 2, 3, 4) and $A \cap B$ is (3, 4). Therefore $\frac{|A \cap B|}{|B|} = \frac{2}{4} = \frac{1}{2}$.

Conditional probability is an important concept because, in many situations, the likelihood of one outcome can differ radically depending on how something else comes out. The probability of passing a test given that one has studied all of the material is generally much higher than the probability of passing a test given that one has not studied at all. The probability of a person having heart trouble is much lower if that person exercises regularly. The probability that a college student will graduate is higher when his or her SAT scores are higher, and so on. For this reason, there are many people who are interested in conditional probabilities.

Note that in some practical situations, changing the order of the conditional probabilities can make the outcome very different. For example, the probability that a person with heart trouble has exercised regularly is quite different than the probability that a person who exercises regularly will have heart trouble. The probability of a person receiving a military-only award, given that he or she is or was a soldier, is generally not very high, but the probability that a person being or having been a soldier, given that he or she received a military-only award, is 1.

However, in some cases, the outcomes do not influence one another this way. If the probability of *A* is the same regardless of whether *B* is given; that is, if $P(A|B) = P(A)$, then *A* and *B* are considered *independent*. In this case, $P(A|B) = \frac{P(A \cap B)}{P(B)} = P(A)$, so $P(A \cap B) = P(A)P(B)$. In fact, if $P(A \cap B) = P(A)P(B)$, it can be determined that $P(A|B) = P(A)$ and $P(A|B) = P(B)$ by working backward. Therefore, *B* is also independent of *A*.

An example of something being independent can be seen in rolling dice. In this case, consider a red die and a green die. It is expected that when the dice are rolled, the outcome of the green die should not depend in any way on the outcome of the red die. Or, to take another example, if the same die is rolled repeatedly, then the next number rolled should not depend on which numbers have been rolled previously. Similarly, if a coin is flipped, then the next flip's outcome does not depend on the outcomes of previous flips.

This can sometimes be counter-intuitive, since when rolling a die or flipping a coin, there can be a streak of surprising results. If, however, it is known that the die or coin is fair, then these results are just the result of the fact that over long periods of time, it is very likely that some unlikely streaks of outcomes will occur. Therefore, avoid making the mistake of thinking that when considering a series of independent outcomes, a particular outcome is "due to happen" simply because a surprising series of outcomes has already been seen.

There is a second type of common mistake that people tend to make when reasoning about statistical outcomes: the idea that when something of low probability happens, this is surprising. It would be surprising that something with low probability happened after just one attempt. However, with so much happening all at once, it is easy to see at least something happen in a way that seems to have a very low probability. In fact, a lottery is a good example. The odds of winning a lottery are very small, but the odds that somebody wins the lottery each week are actually fairly high. Therefore, no one should be surprised when some low probability things happen.

Addition Rule

The *addition rule* for probabilities states that the probability of *A* or *B* happening is $P(A \cup B) = P(A) + P(B) - P(A \cap B)$. Note that the subtraction of $P(A \cap B)$ must be performed, or else it would result in double counting any outcomes that lie in both *A* and in *B*. For example, suppose that a 20-sided die is being rolled. Fred bets that the outcome will be greater than 10, while Helen bets that it will be greater than 4 but less than 15. What is the probability that at least one of them is correct?

We apply the rule $P(A \cup B) = P(A) + P(B) - P(A \cap B)$, where *A* is that outcome *x* is in the range $x > 10$, and *B* is that outcome *x* is in the range $4 < x < 15$. $P(A) = 10 \cdot \frac{1}{20} = \frac{1}{2}$. $P(B) = 10 \cdot \frac{1}{20} = \frac{1}{2}$. $P(A \cap B)$ can be computed by noting that $A \cap B$ means the outcome *x* is in the range $10 < x < 15$, so $P(A \cap B) = 4 \cdot \frac{1}{20} = \frac{1}{5}$. Therefore, $P(A \cup B) = P(A) + P(B) - P(A \cap B) = \frac{1}{2} + \frac{1}{2} - \frac{1}{5} = \frac{4}{5}$.

Note that in this particular example, we could also have directly reasoned about the set of possible outcomes $A \cup B$, by noting that this would mean that *x* must be in the range $5 \leq x$. However, this is not always the case, depending on the given information.

Multiplication Rule

The *multiplication rule* for probabilities states the probability of *A* and *B* both happening is $P(A \cap B) = P(A)P(B|A)$. As an example, suppose that when Jamie wears black pants, there is a ½ probability that she wears a black shirt as well, and that she wears black pants ¾ of the time. What is the probability that she is wearing both a black shirt and black pants?

To figure this, use the above formula, where *A* will be "Jamie is wearing black pants," while *B* will be "Jamie is wearing a black shirt." It is known that $P(A)$ is ¾. It is also known that $P(B|A) = \frac{1}{2}$. Multiplying the two, the probability that she is wearing both black pants and a black shirt is $P(A)P(B|A) = \frac{3}{4} \cdot \frac{1}{2} = \frac{3}{8}$.

What are Statistics?

The field of statistics describes relationships between quantities that are related, but not necessarily in a deterministic manner. For example, a graduating student's salary will often be higher when the student graduates with a higher GPA, but this is not always the case. Likewise, people who smoke tobacco are more likely to develop lung cancer, but, in fact, it is possible for non-smokers to develop the disease as well. *Statistics* describes these kinds of situations, where the likelihood of some outcome depends on the starting data.

Descriptive statistics involves analyzing a collection of data to describe its broad properties such average (or mean), what percent of the data falls within a given range, and other such properties. An example of this would be taking all of the test scores from a given class and calculating the average test score. *Inferential statistics* attempts to use data about a subset of some population to make inferences about the rest of the population. An example of this would be taking a collection of students who received tutoring and comparing their results to a collection of students who did not receive tutoring, then using that comparison to try to predict whether the tutoring program in question is beneficial.

To be sure that inferences have a high probability of being true for the whole population, the subset that is analyzed needs to resemble a miniature version of the population as closely as possible. For this reason, statisticians like to choose random samples from the population to study, rather than picking a specific group of people based on some similarity. For example, studying the incomes of people who live in Portland does not tell anything useful about the incomes of people who live in Tallahassee.

Statistical Processes

Samples and Populations

Statistics involves making decisions and predictions about larger data sets based on smaller data sets. Basically, the information from one part or subset can help predict what happens in the entire data set or population at large. The entire process involves guessing, and the predictions and decisions may not be 100 percent correct all of the time; however, there is some truth to these predictions, and the decisions do have mathematical support. The smaller data set is called a *sample* and the larger data set (in which the decision is being made) is called a *population*. A *random sample* is used as the sample, which is an unbiased collection of data points that represents the population as well as it can. There are many methods of forming a random sample, and all adhere to the fact that every potential data point has a predetermined probability of being chosen.

Goodness of Fit

Goodness of fit tests show how well a statistical model fits a given data set. They allow the differences between the observed and expected quantities to be summarized to determine if the model is consistent with the results. The *Chi-Squared Goodness of Fit Test* (or *Chi-Squared Test* for short) is used with one categorical variable from one population, and it concludes whether or not the sample data is consistent with a hypothesized distribution. Chi-Squared is evaluated using the following formula:

$\chi^2 = \sum \frac{(O-E)^2}{E}$, where O is the observed frequency value and E is the expected frequency value. Also, the *degree of freedom* must be calculated, which is the number of categories in the data set minus one. Then a Chi-Squared table is used to test the data. The *degree of freedom value* and a *significance value,* such as 0.05, are located on the table. The corresponding entry represents a critical value.

If the calculated χ^2 is greater than the critical value, the data set does not work with the statistical model. If the calculated χ^2 is less than the critical value, the statistical model can be used.

Making Inferences and Justifying Conclusions from Samples, Experiments, and Observational Studies

Data Gathering Techniques

The three most common types of data gathering techniques are sample surveys, experiments, and observational studies. *Sample surveys* involve collecting data from a random sample of people from a desired population. The measurement of the variable is only performed on this set of people. To have accurate data, the sampling must be unbiased and random. For example, surveying students in an advanced calculus class on how much they enjoy math classes is not a useful sample if the population should be all college students based on the research question. An *experiment* is the method in which a hypothesis is tested using a trial-and-error process. A cause and the effect of that cause are measured, and the hypothesis is accepted or rejected. Experiments are usually completed in a controlled environment where the results of a control population are compared to the results of a test population. The groups are selected using a randomization process in which each group has a representative mix of the population being tested. Finally, an *observational study* is similar to an experiment. However, this design is used when there cannot be a designed control and test population because of circumstances (e.g., lack of funding or unrealistic expectations). Instead, existing control and test populations must be used, so this method has a lack of randomization.

Population Mean and Proportion

Both the population mean and proportion can be calculated using data from a sample. The *population mean (μ)* is the average value of the parameter for the entire population. Due to size constraints, finding the exact value of μ is impossible, so the mean of the sample population is used as an estimate instead. The larger the sample size, the closer the sample mean gets to the population mean. An alternative to finding μ is to find the *proportion* of the population, which is the part of the population with the given characteristic. The proportion can be expressed as a decimal, a fraction, or a percentage, and can be given as a single value or a range of values. Because the population mean and proportion are both estimates, there's a *margin of error,* which is the difference between the actual value and the expected value.

T-Tests

A *randomized experiment* is used to compare two treatments by using statistics involving a *t-test,* which tests whether two data sets are significantly different from one another. To use a t-test, the test statistic must follow a normal distribution. The first step of the test involves calculating the *t* value, which is given as $t = \frac{\overline{x}_1 - \overline{x}_2}{s_{\bar{x}_1 - \bar{x}_2}}$, where $\bar{x}_1$ and $\bar{x}_2$ are the averages of the two samples. Also, $s_{\bar{x}_1 - \bar{x}_2} = \sqrt{\frac{s_1^2}{n_1} + \frac{s_2^2}{n_2}}$, where $s_1$and s_2 are the standard deviations of each sample and $n_1$and n_2 are their respective sample sizes. The *degrees of freedom* for two samples are calculated as $df = \frac{(n_1-1)+(n_2-1)}{2}$ rounded to the lowest whole number. Also, a significance level α must be chosen, where a typical value is $\alpha = 0.05$. Once everything is compiled, the decision is made to use either a *one-tailed test* or a *two-tailed test.* If there's an assumed difference between the two treatments, a one-tailed test is used. If no difference is assumed, a two-tailed test is used.

Analyzing Test Results

Once the type of test is determined, the t-value, significance level, and degrees of freedom are applied to the published table showing the *t* distribution. The row is associated with degrees of freedom and each column corresponds to the probability. The t-value can be exactly equal to one entry or lie between two entries in a row. For example, consider a t-value of 1.7 with degrees of freedom equal to 30. This *test statistic* falls between the *p* values of 0.05 and 0.025. For a one-tailed test, the corresponding *p* value lies between 0.05 and 0.025. For a two-tailed test, the *p* values need to be doubled so the corresponding *p* value falls between 0.1 and 0.05. Once the probability is known, this range is compared to α. If $p < \alpha$, the hypothesis is rejected. If $p > \alpha$, the hypothesis isn't rejected. In a two-tailed test, this scenario means the hypothesis is accepted that there's no difference in the two treatments. In a one-tailed test, the hypothesis is accepted, indicating that there's a difference in the two treatments.

Evaluating Completed Tests

In addition to applying statistical techniques to actual testing, evaluating completed tests is another important aspect of statistics. Reports can be read that already have conclusions, and the process can be evaluated using learned concepts. For example, deciding if a sample being used is appropriate. Other things that can be evaluated include determining if the samples are randomized or the results are significant. Once statistical concepts are understood, the knowledge can be applied to many applications.

Practice Questions

1. Which of the following numbers has the greatest value?
   a. 1.4378
   b. 1.07548
   c. 1.43592
   d. 0.89409

2. The value of 6 x 12 is the same as:
   a. 2 x 4 x 4 x 2
   b. 7 x 4 x 3
   c. 6 x 6 x 3
   d. 3 x 3 x 4 x 2

3. This chart indicates how many sales of CDs, vinyl records, and MP3 downloads occurred over the last year. Approximately what percentage of the total sales was from CDs?

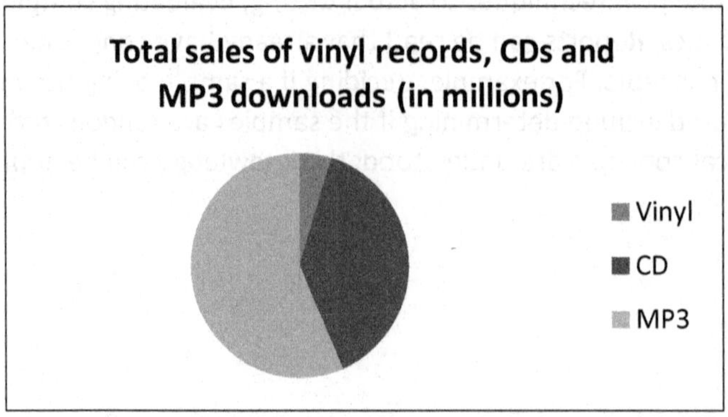

   a. 55%
   b. 25%
   c. 40%
   d. 5%

4. After a 20% sale discount, Frank purchased a new refrigerator for $850. How much did he save from the original price?
   a. $170
   b. $212.50
   c. $105.75
   d. $200

5. A student gets an 85% on a test with 20 questions. How many answers did the student solve correctly?
   a. 16
   b. 17
   c. 18
   d. 19

6. Alan currently weighs 200 pounds, but he wants to lose weight to get down to 175 pounds. What is this difference in kilograms? (1 pound is approximately equal to 0.45 kilograms.)

a. 9 kg
b. 11.25 kg
c. 78.75 kg
d. 90 kg

7. Johnny earns $2334.50 from his job each month. He pays $1437 for monthly expenses. Johnny is planning a vacation in 3 months' time that he estimates will cost $1750 total. How much will Johnny have left over from three months' of saving once he pays for his vacation?

a. $948.50
b. $584.50
c. $852.50
d. $942.50

8. What is $\frac{420}{98}$ rounded to the nearest integer?

a. 3
b. 4
c. 5
d. 6

9. Dwayne has received the following scores on his math tests: 78, 92, 83, 97. What score must Dwayne get on his next math test to have an overall average of at least 90?

a. 89
b. 98
c. 95
d. 100

10. What is the overall median of Dwayne's current scores: 78, 92, 83, 97?

a. 19
b. 85
c. 83
d. 87.5

11. Solve the following:

$$(\sqrt{36} \times \sqrt{16}) - 3^2$$

a. 30
b. 21
c. 15
d. 13

12. In Jim's school, there are 3 girls for every 2 boys. There are 650 students in total. Using this information, how many students are girls?

a. 260
b. 130
c. 65
d. 390

13. Five of six numbers have a sum of 25. The average of all six numbers is 6. What is the sixth number?

a. 8
b. 12
c. 11
d. 10

14. Kimberley earns $10 an hour babysitting, and after 10 p.m., she earns $12 an hour, with the amount paid being rounded to the nearest hour accordingly. On her last job, she worked from 5:30 p.m. to 11 p.m. In total, how much did Kimberley earn on her last job?

a. $45
b. $57
c. $62
d. $42

15. Arrange the following numbers from least to greatest value:

$0.85, \frac{4}{5}, \frac{2}{3}, \frac{91}{100}$

a. $0.85, \frac{4}{5}, \frac{2}{3}, \frac{91}{100}$
b. $\frac{4}{5}, 0.85, \frac{91}{100}, \frac{2}{3}$
c. $\frac{2}{3}, \frac{4}{5}, 0.85, \frac{91}{100}$
d. $0.85, \frac{91}{100}, \frac{4}{5}, \frac{2}{3}$

16. Keith's bakery had 252 customers go through its doors last week. This week, that number increased to 378. Express this increase as a percentage.

a. 26%
b. 50%
c. 35%
d. 12%

17. The following graph compares the various test scores of the top three students in each of these teacher's classes. Based on the graph, which teacher's students had the lowest range of test scores?

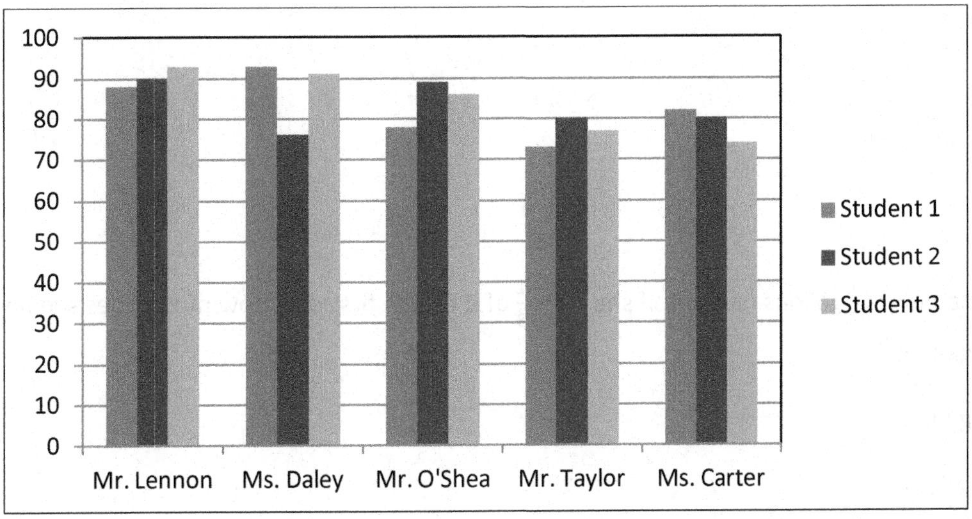

a. Mr. Lennon
b. Mr. O'Shea
c. Mr. Taylor
d. Ms. Daley

18. Four people split a bill. The first person pays for $\frac{1}{5}$, the second person pays for $\frac{1}{4}$, and the third person pays for $\frac{1}{3}$. What fraction of the bill does the fourth person pay?

a. $\frac{13}{60}$

b. $\frac{47}{60}$

c. $\frac{1}{4}$

d. $\frac{4}{15}$

19. How is the expression $4\frac{2}{3} - 3\frac{4}{9}$ simplified?

a. $1\frac{1}{3}$

b. $1\frac{2}{9}$

c. 1

d. $1\frac{2}{3}$

20. A closet is filled with red, blue, and green shirts. If $\frac{1}{3}$ of the shirts are green and $\frac{2}{5}$ are red, what fraction of the shirts are blue?

a. $\frac{4}{15}$

b. $\frac{1}{5}$

c. $\frac{7}{15}$

d. $\frac{1}{2}$

21. Shawna buys $2\frac{1}{2}$ gallons of paint. If she uses $\frac{1}{3}$ of it on the first day, how much does she have left?

a. $1\frac{5}{6}$ gallons

b. $1\frac{1}{2}$ gallons

c. $1\frac{2}{3}$gallons

d. 2 gallons

22. Jessica buys 10 cans of paint. Red paint costs $1 per can and blue paint costs $2 per can. In total, she spends $16. How many red cans did she buy?

a. 2
b. 3
c. 4
d. 5

23. Six people apply to work for Janice's company, but she only needs four workers. How many different groups of four employees can Janice choose?

a. 6
b. 10
c. 15
d. 36

24. Which of the following is equivalent to the value of the digit 3 in the number 792.134?

a. 3×10

b. 3×100

c. $\frac{3}{10}$

d. $\frac{3}{100}$

25. In the following expression, which operation should be completed first? $5 \times 6 + (5 + 4) \div 2 - 1$.

a. Multiplication
b. Addition
c. Division
d. Parentheses

26. How will the number 847.89632 be written if rounded to the nearest hundredth?

a. 847.90
b. 900
c. 847.89
d. 847.896

27. The perimeter of a 6-sided polygon is 56 cm. The length of three of the sides are 9 cm each. The length of two other sides are 8 cm each. What is the length of the missing side?

a. 11 cm
b. 12 cm
c. 13 cm
d. 10 cm

28. Which of the following is a mixed number?

a. $16\frac{1}{2}$
b. 16
c. $\frac{16}{3}$
d. $\frac{1}{4}$

29. If you were showing your friend how to round 245.2678 to the nearest thousandth, which place value would be used to decide whether to round up or round down?

a. Ten-thousandth
b. Thousandth
c. Hundredth
d. Thousands

30. What is the value of *b* in the equation: $5b - 4 = 2b + 17$?

a. 13
b. 24
c. 7
d. 21

31. What is the solution to $\frac{3}{5} \times \frac{7}{10} \div \frac{1}{2}$ in decimal form?

a. 0.042
b. 84%
c. 0.84
d. 0.42

32. What is an equivalent measurement for 1.3 cm?

a. 0.13 m
b. 0.013 m
c. 0.13 mm
d. 0.013 mm

33. Katie works at a clothing company and sold 192 shirts over the weekend. $\frac{1}{3}$ of the shirts that were sold were patterned, and the rest were solid. Which mathematical expression would calculate the number of solid shirts Katie sold over the weekend?

a. $192 \times \frac{1}{3}$
b. $192 \div \frac{1}{3}$
c. $192 \times (1 - \frac{1}{3})$
d. $192 \div 3$

34. Which four-sided shape is always a rectangle?

a. Rhombus
b. Square
c. Parallelogram
d. Quadrilateral

35. A rectangle was formed out of pipe cleaner. Its length was $\frac{1}{2}$ ft, and its width was $\frac{11}{2}$ inches. What is its area in square inches?

a. $\frac{11}{4}$ $inch^2$

b. $\frac{11}{2}$ $inch^2$

c. 22 $inches^2$

d. 33 $inches^2$

36. How will $\frac{4}{5}$ be written as a percent?

a. 40 percent
b. 125 percent
c. 90 percent
d. 80 percent

37. If Danny takes 48 minutes to walk 3 miles, how long should it take him to walk 5 miles maintaining the same speed?

a. 32 min
b. 64 min
c. 80 min
d. 96 min

38. A solution needs 5 ml of saline for every 8 ml of medicine given. How much saline is needed for 45 ml of medicine?

a. $\frac{225}{8}$ ml

b. 72 ml

c. 28 ml

d. $\frac{45}{8}$ ml

39. What unit of volume is used to describe the following 3-dimensional shape?

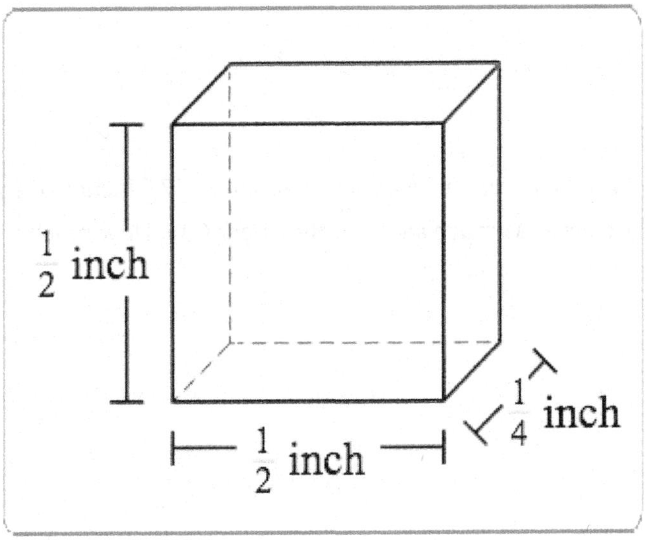

a. Square inches
b. Inches
c. Cubic inches
d. Squares

40. Which common denominator would be used in order to evaluate $\frac{2}{3} + \frac{4}{5}$?
a. 15
b. 3
c. 5
d. 10

41. The diameter of a circle measures 5.75 centimeters. What tool could be used to draw such a circle?
a. Ruler
b. Meter stick
c. Compass
d. Yard stick

42. A piggy bank contains 12 dollars' worth of nickels. A nickel weighs 5 grams, and the empty piggy bank weighs 1050 grams. What is the total weight of the full piggy bank?

a. 1,110 grams
b. 1,200 grams
c. 2,250 grams
d. 2,200 grams

43. Last year, the New York City area received approximately $27\frac{3}{4}$ inches of snow. The Denver area received approximately 3 times as much snow as New York City. How much snow fell in Denver?

a. $71\frac{3}{4}$ inches

b. $27\frac{1}{4}$ inches

c. $89\frac{1}{4}$ inches

d. $83\frac{1}{4}$ inches

44. Which of the following would be an instance in which ordinal numbers are used?

a. Katie scored a 9 out of 10 on her quiz.
b. Matthew finished second in the spelling bee.
c. Jacob missed one day of school last month.
d. Kim was 5 minutes late to school this morning.

45. The graph shows the position of a car over a 10-second time interval. Which of the following is the correct interpretation of the graph for the interval 1 to 3 seconds?

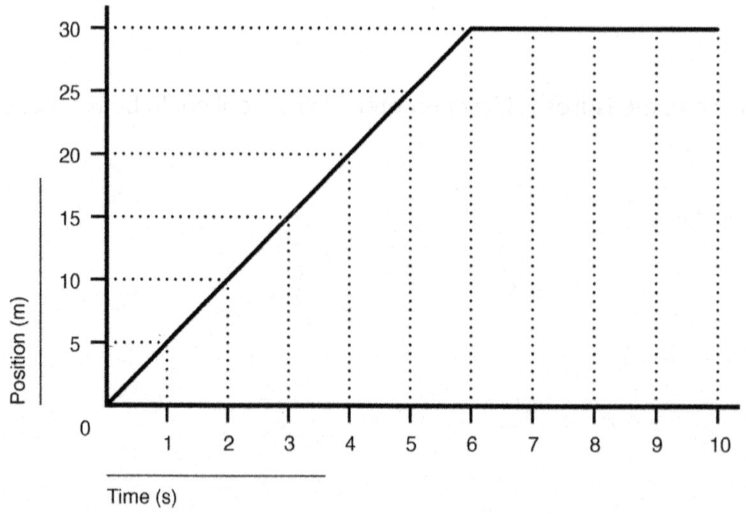

a. The car remains in the same position.
b. The car is traveling at a speed of 5m/s.
c. The car is traveling up a hill.
d. The car is traveling at 5mph.

Answer Explanations

1. A: Compare each numeral after the decimal point to figure out which overall number is greatest. In answers *A* (1.43785) and *C* (1.43592), both have the same tenths (4) and hundredths (3). However, the thousandths is greater in answer *A* (7), so *A* has the greatest value overall.

2. D: By grouping the four numbers in the answer into factors of the two numbers of the question (6 and 12), it can be determined that (3 x 2) x (4 x 3) = 6 x 12. Alternatively, each of the answer choices could be prime factored or multiplied out and compared to the original value. 6×12 has a value of 72 and a prime factorization of $2^3 \times 3^2$. The answer choices respectively have values of 64, 84, 108, and 72 and prime factorizations of 2^6, $2^2 \times 3 \times 7$, $2^2 \times 3^3$, and $2^3 \times 3^2$, so answer *D* is the correct choice.

3. C: The sum total percentage of a pie chart must equal 100%. Since the CD sales take up less than half of the chart and more than a quarter (25%), it can be determined to be 40% overall. This can also be measured with a protractor. The angle of a circle is 360°. Since 25% of 360 would be 90° and 50% would be 180°, the angle percentage of CD sales falls in between; therefore, it would be answer *C*.

4. B: Since \$850 is the price *after* a 20% discount, \$850 represents 80% of the original price. To determine the original price, set up a proportion with the ratio of the sale price (850) to original price (unknown) equal to the ratio of sale percentage:

$$\frac{850}{x} = \frac{80}{100}$$

(where *x* represents the unknown original price)

To solve a proportion, cross multiply the numerators and denominators and set the products equal to each other: (850)(100) = (80)(x). Multiplying each side results in the equation 85,000=80x.

To solve for *x*, divide both sides by 80: $\frac{85{,}000}{80} = \frac{80x}{80}$, resulting in *x*=1062.5. Remember that *x* represents the original price. Subtracting the sale price from the original price (\$1062.50-\$850) indicates that Frank saved \$212.50.

5. B: 85% of a number means that number should be multiplied by 0.85: $0.85 \times 20 = \frac{85}{100} \times \frac{20}{1}$, which can be simplified to $\frac{17}{20} \times \frac{20}{1} = 17$.

6. B: Using the conversion rate, multiply the projected weight loss of 25 lb. by 0.45 $\frac{kg}{lb}$ to get the amount in kilograms (11.25 kg).

7. D: First, subtract \$1437 from \$2334.50 to find Johnny's monthly savings; this equals \$897.50. Then, multiply this amount by 3 to find out how much he will have (in three months) before he pays for his vacation: this equals \$2692.50. Finally, subtract the cost of the vacation (\$1750) from this amount to find how much Johnny will have left: \$942.50.

8. B: Dividing by 98 can be approximated by dividing by 100, which would mean shifting the decimal point of the numerator to the left by 2. The result is 4.2 which rounds to 4.

9. D: To find the average of a set of values, add the values together and then divide by the total number of values. In this case, include the unknown value of what Dwayne needs to score on his next test, in order to solve it.

$$\frac{78 + 92 + 83 + 97 + x}{5} = 90$$

Add the unknown value to the new average total, which is 5. Then multiply each side by 5 to simplify the equation, resulting in:

$78 + 92 + 83 + 97 + x = 450$
$350 + x = 450$
$x = 100$

Dwayne would need to get a perfect score of 100 in order to get an average of at least 90.

Test this answer by substituting back into the original formula.

$$\frac{78 + 92 + 83 + 97 + 100}{5} = 90$$

10. D: For an even number of total values, the *median* is calculated by finding the *mean* or average of the two middle values once all values have been arranged in ascending order from least to greatest. In this case, $(92 \ + 83) \div 2$ would equal the median 87.5, answer *D.*

11. C: Follow the *order of operations* in order to solve this problem. Solve the parentheses first, and then follow the remainder as usual.

$$(6 \times 4) - 9$$

This equals 24 – 9 or 15, answer *C.*

12. D: Three girls for every two boys can be expressed as a ratio: 3:2. This can be visualized as splitting the school into 5 groups: 3 girl groups and 2 boy groups. The number of students which are in each group can be found by dividing the total number of students by 5:

650 divided by 5 equals 1 part, or 130 students per group

To find the total number of girls, multiply the number of students per group (130) by how the number of girl groups in the school (3). This equals 390, answer *D.*

13. C: If the average of all six numbers is 6, that means $\frac{a+b+c+d+e+x}{6} = 6$. The sum of the first five numbers is 25, so this equation can be simplified to $\frac{25+x}{6} = 6$. Multiplying both sides by 6 gives $25 + x = 36$, and *x*, or the sixth number, can be solved to equal 11.

14. C: Kimberley worked 4.5 hours at the rate of \$10/h and 1 hour at the rate of \$12/h. The problem states that her pay is rounded to the nearest hour, so the 4.5 hours would round up to 5 hours at the rate of \$10/h. (5h)(\$10/h) + (1h)(\$12/h) = \$50 + \$12= \$62.

15. C: The first step is to depict each number using decimals. $\frac{91}{100}$ = 0.91

Multiplying both the numerator and denominator of $\frac{4}{5}$ by 20 makes it $\frac{80}{100}$ or 0.80; the closest approximation of $\frac{2}{3}$ would be $\frac{66}{100}$ or 0.66 recurring. Rearrange each expression in ascending order, as found in answer *C*.

16. B: First, calculate the difference between the larger value and the smaller value.

378 – 252 = 126

17. A: To calculate the range in a set of data, subtract the highest value with the lowest value. In this graph, the range of Mr. Lennon's students is 5, which can be seen physically in the graph as having the smallest difference compared with the other teachers between the highest value and the lowest value.

18. A: To find the fraction of the bill that the first three people pay, the fractions need to be added, which means finding common denominator. The common denominator will be 60. $\frac{1}{5}+\frac{1}{4}+\frac{1}{3}=\frac{12}{60}+\frac{15}{60}+\frac{20}{60}=\frac{47}{60}$. The remainder of the bill is $1-\frac{47}{60}=\frac{60}{60}-\frac{47}{60}=\frac{13}{60}$.

19. B: Simplify each mixed number of the problem into a fraction by multiplying the denominator by the whole number and adding the numerator:

$$\frac{14}{3}-\frac{31}{9}$$

Since the first denominator is a multiple of the second, simplify it further by multiplying both the numerator and denominator of the first expression by 3 so that the denominators of the fractions are equal.

$$\frac{42}{9}-\frac{31}{9}=\frac{11}{9}$$

Simplifying this further, divide the numerator 11 by the denominator 9; this leaves 1 with a remainder of 2. To write this as a mixed number, place the remainder over the denominator, resulting in $1\frac{2}{9}$.

20. A: The total fraction taken up by green and red shirts will be $\frac{1}{3}+\frac{2}{5}=\frac{5}{15}+\frac{6}{15}=\frac{11}{15}$. The remaining fraction is $1-\frac{11}{15}=\frac{15}{15}-\frac{11}{15}=\frac{4}{15}$.

21. C: If she has used 1/3 of the paint, she has 2/3 remaining. $2\frac{1}{2}$ gallons are the same as $\frac{5}{2}$ gallons. The calculation is $\frac{2}{3}\times\frac{5}{2}=\frac{5}{3}=1\frac{2}{3}$ gallons.

22. C: Let *r* be the number of red cans and *b* be the number of blue cans. One equation is $r+b=10$. The total price is $16, and the prices for each can means $1r+2b=16$. Multiplying the first equation on both sides by -1 results in $-r-b=-10$. Add this equation to the second equation, leaving $b=6$. So, she bought 6 *blue* cans. From the first equation, this means *r* = 4; thus, she bought 4 *red* cans.

23. C: Janice will be choosing 4 employees out of a set of 6 applicants, so this will be given by the choice function. The following equation shows the choice function worked out: $\binom{6}{4}=\frac{6!}{4!(6-4)!}=\frac{6!}{4!(2)!}=\frac{6\cdot5\cdot4\cdot3\cdot2\cdot1}{4\cdot3\cdot2\cdot1\cdot2\cdot1}=\frac{6\cdot5}{2}=15$.

24. D:$\frac{3}{100}$. Each digit to the left of the decimal point represents a higher multiple of 10 and each digit to the right of the decimal point represents a quotient of a higher multiple of 10 for the divisor. The first digit to the right of the decimal point is equal to the value $\div$ 10. The second digit to the right of the decimal point is equal to the value $\div$ (10×10), or the value $\div$ 100.

25. D: Using the order of operations, multiplication and division are computed first from left to right. Multiplication is on the left; therefore, the teacher should perform multiplication first.

26. A:847.90. The hundredth place value is located two digits to the right of the decimal point (the digit 9). The digit to the right of the place value is examined to decide whether to round up or keep the digit. In this case, the digit 6 is 5 or greater so the hundredth place is rounded up. When rounding up, if the digit to be increased is a 9, the digit to its left is increased by one and the digit in the desired place value is made a zero. Therefore, the number is rounded to 847.90.

27. C: Perimeter is found by calculating the sum of all sides of the polygon. $9 + 9 + 9 + 8 + 8 + s = 56$, where s is the missing side length. Therefore, 43 plus the missing side length is equal to 56. The missing side length is 13 cm.

28. A:$16\frac{1}{2}$. A mixed number contains both a whole number and either a fraction or a decimal. Therefore, the mixed number is $16\frac{1}{2}$.

29. A: The place value to the right of the thousandth place, which would be the ten-thousandth place, is what gets utilized. The value in the thousandth place is 7. The number in the place value to its right is greater than 4, so the 7 gets bumped up to 8. Everything to its right turns to a zero, to get 245.2680. The zero is dropped because it is part of the decimal.

30. C: To solve for the value of b, both sides of the equation need to be equalized.

Start by cancelling out the lower value of -4 by adding 4 to both sides:

$5b - 4 = 2b + 17$
$5b - 4 + 4 = 2b + 17 + 4$
$5b = 2b + 21$

The variable *b* is the same on each side, so subtract the lower 2b from each side:

$5b = 2b + 21$
$5b - 2b = 2b + 21 - 2b$
$3b = 21$

Then divide both sides by 3 to get the value of *b*:

$$3b = 21$$

$$\frac{3b}{3} = \frac{21}{3}$$

$$b = 7$$

31. C: The first step in solving this problem is expressing the result in fraction form. Separate this problem first by solving the division operation of the last two fractions. When dividing one fraction by another, invert or flip the second fraction and then multiply the numerator and denominator.

$$\frac{7}{10} \times \frac{2}{1} = \frac{14}{10}$$

Next, multiply the first fraction with this value:

$$\frac{3}{5} \times \frac{14}{10} = \frac{42}{50}$$

Decimals are expressions of 1 or 100%, so multiply both the numerator and denominator by 2 to get the fraction as an expression of 100.

$$\frac{42}{50} \times \frac{2}{2} = \frac{84}{100}$$

In decimal form, this would be expressed as 0.84.

32. B: 100 cm is equal to 1 m. 1.3 divided by 100 is 0.013. Therefore, 1.3 cm is equal to 0.013 mm. Because 1 cm is equal to 10 mm, 1.3 cm is equal to 13 mm.

33. C: $\frac{1}{3}$ of the shirts sold were patterned. Therefore, $1 - \frac{1}{3} = \frac{2}{3}$ of the shirts sold were solid. Anytime "of" a quantity appears in a word problem, multiplication needs to be used. Therefore, $192 \times \frac{2}{3} = 192 \times \frac{2}{3} = \frac{384}{3} = 128$ solid shirts were sold. The entire expression is $192 \times \left(1 - \frac{1}{3}\right)$.

34. B: A rectangle is a specific type of parallelogram. It has 4 right angles. A square is a rhombus that has 4 right angles. Therefore, a square is always a rectangle because it has two sets of parallel lines and 4 right angles.

35. D: Area = length x width. The answer must be in square inches, so all values must be converted to inches. $\frac{1}{2}$ ft is equal to 6 inches. Therefore, the area of the rectangle is equal to $6 \times \frac{11}{2} = \frac{66}{2} = 33$ square inches.

36. D:80 percent. To convert a fraction to a percent, the fraction is first converted to a decimal. To do so, the numerator is divided by the denominator: $4 \div 5 = 0.8$. To convert a decimal to a percent, the number is multiplied by 100: $0.8 \times 10 = 80\%$.

37. C: 80 min. To solve the problem, a proportion is written consisting of ratios comparing distance and time. One way to set up the proportion is: $\frac{3}{48} = \frac{5}{x}\left(\frac{distance}{time} = \frac{distance}{time}\right)$ where *x* represents the unknown value of time. To solve a proportion, the ratios are cross-multiplied: $(3)(x) = (5)(48) \rightarrow 3x = 240$. The equation is solved by isolating the variable, or dividing by 3 on both sides, to produce $x = 80$.

38. A: Every 8 ml of medicine requires 5 ml. The 45 ml first needs to be split into portions of 8 ml. This results in $\frac{45}{8}$portions. Each portion requires 5 ml. Therefore, $\frac{45}{8} \times 5 = 45 \times \frac{5}{8} = \frac{225}{8}$ml is necessary.

39. C: Volume of this 3-dimensional figure is calculated using length x width x height. Each measure of length is in inches. Therefore, the answer would be labeled in cubic inches.

40. A: A common denominator must be found. The least common denominator is 15 because it has both 5 and 3 as factors. The fractions must be rewritten using 15 as the denominator.

41. C: A compass is a tool that can be used to draw a circle. The compass would be drawn by using the length of the radius, which is half of the diameter.

42. C: A dollar contains 20 nickels. Therefore, if there are 12 dollars' worth of nickels, there are $12 \times 20 = 240$ nickels. Each nickel weighs 5 grams. Therefore, the weight of the nickels is $240 \times 5 = 1{,}200$ grams. Adding in the weight of the empty piggy bank, the filled bank weighs 2,250 grams.

43. D: 3 must be multiplied times $27\frac{3}{4}$. In order to easily do this, the mixed number should be converted into an improper fraction. $27\frac{3}{4} = 27 \times 4 + \frac{3}{4} = \frac{111}{4}$. Therefore, Denver had approximately $3 \times \frac{111}{4} = \frac{333}{4}$ inches of snow. The improper fraction can be converted back into a mixed number through division. $\frac{333}{4} = 83\frac{1}{4}$ inches.

44. B: Ordinal numbers represent a ranking. Placing second in a competition is a ranking among the other participants of the spelling bee.

45. B: The car is traveling at a speed of five meters per second. On the interval from one to three seconds, the position changes by fifteen meters. By making this change in position over time into a rate, the speed becomes ten meters in two seconds or five meters in one second.

Reading

Key Ideas and Details of Text Selections

Topic Versus the Main Idea

It is very important to know the difference between the topic and the main idea of the text. Even though these two are similar because they both present the central point of a text, they have distinctive differences. A *topic* is the subject of the text; it can usually be described in a one- to two-word phrase and appears in the simplest form. On the other hand, the *main idea* is more detailed and provides the author's central point of the text. It can be expressed through a complete sentence and is often found in the beginning, middle, or end of a paragraph. In most nonfiction books, the first sentence of the passage usually (but not always) states the main idea. Review the passage below to explore the topic versus the main idea.

Cheetahs

> *Cheetahs are one of the fastest mammals on the land, reaching up to 70 miles an hour over short distances. Even though cheetahs can run as fast as 70 miles an hour, they usually only have to run half that speed to catch up with their choice of prey. Cheetahs cannot maintain a fast pace over long periods of time because their bodies will overheat. After a chase, cheetahs need to rest for approximately 30 minutes prior to eating or returning to any other activity.*

In the example above, the topic of the passage is "Cheetahs" simply because that is the subject of the text. The main idea of the text is "Cheetahs are one of the fastest mammals on the land but can only maintain a fast pace for shorter distances." While it covers the topic, it is more detailed and refers to the text in its entirety. The text continues to provide additional details called *supporting details,* which will be discussed in the next section.

Supporting Details

Supporting details help readers better develop and understand the main idea. Supporting details answer questions like *who, what, where, when, why,* and *how*. Different types of supporting details include examples, facts and statistics, anecdotes, and sensory details.

Persuasive and informative texts often use supporting details. In persuasive texts, authors attempt to make readers agree with their points of view, and supporting details are often used as "selling points." If authors make a statement, they need to support the statement with evidence in order to adequately persuade readers. Informative texts use supporting details such as examples and facts to inform readers. Review the previous "Cheetahs" passage to find examples of supporting details.

Cheetahs

> *Cheetahs are one of the fastest mammals on the land, reaching up to 70 miles an hour over short distances. Even though cheetahs can run as fast as 70 miles an hour, they usually only have to run half that speed to catch up with their choice of prey. Cheetahs cannot maintain a fast pace over long periods of time because their bodies will overheat.*

After a chase, cheetahs need to rest for approximately 30 minutes prior to eating or returning to any other activity.

In the example, supporting details include:

- Cheetahs reach up to 70 miles per hour over short distances.
- They usually only have to run half that speed to catch up with their prey.
- Cheetahs will overheat if they exert a high speed over longer distances.
- Cheetahs need to rest for 30 minutes after a chase.

Look at the diagram below (applying the cheetah example) to help determine the hierarchy of topic, main idea, and supporting details.

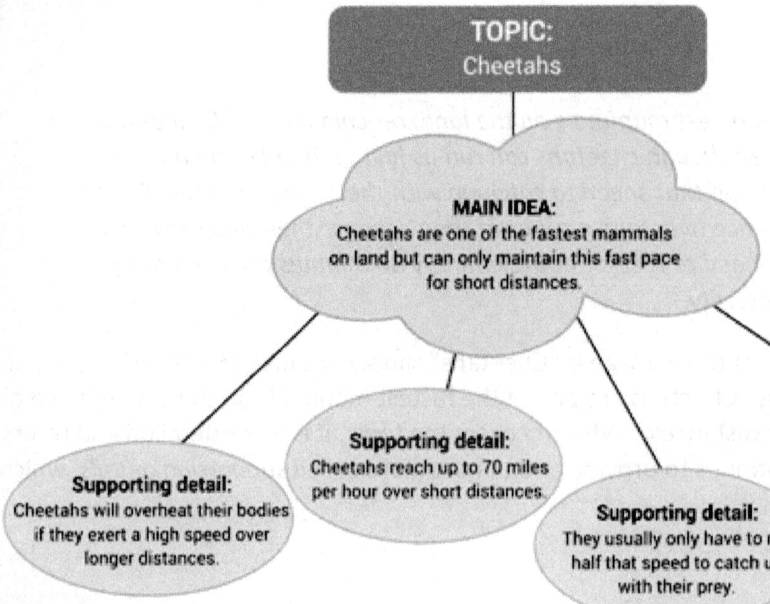

Inferences in a Text

Readers should be able to make *inferences*. Making an inference requires the reader to read between the lines and look for what is *implied* rather than what is directly stated. That is, using information that is known from the text, the reader is able to make a logical assumption about information that is *not* directly stated but is probably true. Read the following passage:

"Hey, do you wanna meet my new puppy?" Jonathan asked.

"Oh, I'm sorry but please don't—" Jacinta began to protest, but before she could finish, Jonathan had already opened the passenger side door of his car and a perfect white ball of fur came bouncing towards Jacinta.

"Isn't he the cutest?" beamed Jonathan.

> "Yes—achoo!—he's pretty—aaaachooo!!—adora—aaa—aaaachoo!" Jacinta managed to say in between sneezes. "But if you don't mind, I—I—achoo!—need to go inside."

Which of the following can be inferred from Jacinta's reaction to the puppy?

a. she hates animals
b. she is allergic to dogs
c. she prefers cats to dogs
d. she is angry at Jonathan

An inference requires the reader to consider the information presented and then form their own idea about what is probably true. Based on the details in the passage, what is the best answer to the question? Important details to pay attention to include the tone of Jacinta's dialogue, which is overall polite and apologetic, as well as her reaction itself, which is a long string of sneezes. Answer choices (a) and (d) both express strong emotions ("hates" and "angry") that are not evident in Jacinta's speech or actions. Answer choice (c) mentions cats, but there is nothing in the passage to indicate Jacinta's feelings about cats. Answer choice (b), "she is allergic to dogs," is the most logical choice—based on the fact that she began sneezing as soon as a fluffy dog approached her, it makes sense to guess that Jacinta might be allergic to dogs. So even though Jacinta never directly states, "Sorry, I'm allergic to dogs!" using the clues in the passage, it is still reasonable to guess that this is true.

Making inferences is crucial for readers of literature, because literary texts often avoid presenting complete and direct information to readers about characters' thoughts or feelings, or they present this information in an unclear way, leaving it up to the reader to interpret clues given in the text. In order to make inferences while reading, readers should ask themselves:

- What details are being presented in the text?
- Is there any important information that seems to be missing?
- Based on the information that the author does include, what else is probably true?
- Is this inference reasonable based on what is already known?

Apply Information

A natural extension of being able to make an inference from a given set of information is also being able to apply that information to a new context. This is especially useful in non-fiction or informative writing. Considering the facts and details presented in the text, readers should consider how the same information might be relevant in a different situation. The following is an example of applying an inferential conclusion to a different context:

> Often, individuals behave differently in large groups than they do as individuals. One example of this is the psychological phenomenon known as the bystander effect. According to the bystander effect, the more people who witness an accident or crime occur, the less likely each individual bystander is to respond or offer assistance to the victim. A classic example of this is the murder of Kitty Genovese in New York City in the 1960s. Although there were over thirty witnesses to her killing by a stabber, none of them intervened to help Kitty or contact the police.

Considering the phenomenon of the bystander effect, what would probably happen if somebody tripped on the stairs in a crowded subway station?

a. Everybody would stop to help the person who tripped
b. Bystanders would point and laugh at the person who tripped
c. Someone would call the police after walking away from the station
d. Few if any bystanders would offer assistance to the person who tripped

This question asks readers to apply the information they learned from the passage, which is an informative paragraph about the bystander effect. According to the passage, this is a concept in psychology that describes the way people in groups respond to an accident—the more people are present, the less likely any one person is to intervene. While the passage illustrates this effect with the example of a woman's murder, the question asks readers to apply it to a different context—in this case, someone falling down the stairs in front of many subway passengers. Although this specific situation is not discussed in the passage, readers should be able to apply the general concepts described in the paragraph. The definition of the bystander effect includes any instance of an accident or crime in front of a large group of people. The question asks about a situation that falls within the same definition, so the general concept should still hold true: in the midst of a large crowd, few individuals are likely to actually respond to an accident. In this case, answer choice (d) is the best response.

Understanding Literary Interpretation

Literary interpretation is an interpretation and analysis of a literary work, based on the textual evidence in the work. It is often subjective as critical readers may discern different meanings in the details. A Praxis test taker needs to be prepared for questions that will test how well he or she can read a passage, make an analysis, and then provide evidence to support that analysis.

Literal and Figurative Meanings

When analyzing and interpreting fiction, readers must be active participants in the experience. Some authors make their messages clearer than others, but the onus is on the reader to add layers to what is read through interpretation. In literary interpretation, the goal is not to offer an opinion as to the inherent value of the work. Rather, the goal is to determine what the text means by analyzing the *literal and figurative meanings* of the text through critical reading.

Critical reading is close reading that elicits questions as the reader progresses. Many authors of fiction use literary elements and devices to further theme and to speak to their audience. These elements often utilize language that has an alternate or figurative meaning in addition to their actual or literal meaning. Readers should be asking questions about these and other important details as a passage is analyzed. What unfamiliar words are there? What is their contextual definition? How do they contribute to the overall feel of the work? How do they contribute to the mood and general message? Literal and figurative meanings are discussed further in the informational texts and rhetoric section.

Drawing Inferences

An *inference* refers to a point that is implied (as opposed to directly-stated) by the evidence presented. It's necessary to use inference in order to draw conclusions about the meaning of a passage. Authors make implications through character dialogue, thoughts, effects on others, actions, and looks.

When making an inference about a passage, it's important to rely only on the information that is provided in the text itself. This helps readers ensure that their conclusions are valid. Drawing inferences is also discussed in the informational texts and rhetoric section.

Textual Evidence

It's helpful to read a passage a few times, noting details that seem important to the piece. Textual evidence within the details helps readers draw a conclusion about a passage. *Textual evidence* refers to information—facts and examples that support the main idea. Textual evidence will likely come from outside sources and can be in the form of quoted or paraphrased material. In order to draw a conclusion from evidence, it's important to examine the credibility and validity of that evidence as well as how (and if) it relates to the main idea. Effective use of textual evidence should connect to the main idea and support a specific point. Textual evidence is examined further in the informational texts and rhetoric section.

Directly Stated Information Versus Implications

Engaged readers should constantly self-question while reviewing texts to help them form conclusions. Self-questioning is when readers review a paragraph, page, passage, or chapter and ask themselves, "Did I understand what I read?," "What was the main event in this section?," "Where is this taking place?," and so on. Authors can provide clues or pieces of evidence throughout a text or passage to guide readers toward a conclusion. This is why active and engaged readers should read the text or passage in its entirety before forming a definitive conclusion. If readers do not gather all the pieces of evidence needed, then they may jump to an illogical conclusion.

At times, authors directly state conclusions while others simply imply them. Of course, it is easier if authors outwardly provide conclusions to readers, because it does not leave any information open to interpretation. On the other hand, implications are things that authors do not directly state but can be assumed based off of information they provided. If authors only imply what may have happened, readers can form a menagerie of ideas for conclusions. For example, look at the following statement: "Once we heard the sirens, we hunkered down in the storm shelter." In this statement, the author does not directly state that there was a tornado, but clues such as "sirens" and "storm shelter" provide insight to the readers to help form that conclusion.

Understanding the Development of Themes

Identifying Theme or Central Message

The *theme* is the central message of a fictional work, whether that work is structured as prose, drama, or poetry. It is the heart of what an author is trying to say to readers through the writing, and theme is largely conveyed through literary elements and techniques.

In literature, a theme can be often be determined by considering the over-arching narrative conflict with the work. Though there are several types of conflicts and several potential themes within them, the following are the most common:

- Individual against the self—relevant to themes of self-awareness, internal struggles, pride, coming of age, facing reality, fate, free will, vanity, loss of innocence, loneliness, isolation, fulfillment, failure, and disillusionment
- Individual against nature— relevant to themes of knowledge vs. ignorance, nature as beauty, quest for discovery, self-preservation, chaos and order, circle of life, death, and destruction of beauty

- Individual against society— relevant to themes of power, beauty, good, evil, war, class struggle, totalitarianism, role of men/women, wealth, corruption, change vs. tradition, capitalism, destruction, heroism, injustice, and racism
- Individual against another individual— relevant to themes of hope, loss of love or hope, sacrifice, power, revenge, betrayal, and honor

For example, in Hawthorne's *The Scarlet Letter*, one possible narrative conflict could be the individual against the self, with a relevant theme of internal struggles. This theme is alluded to through characterization—Dimmesdale's moral struggle with his love for Hester and Hester's internal struggles with the truth and her daughter, Pearl. It's also alluded to through plot—Dimmesdale's suicide and Hester helping the very townspeople who initially condemned her.

Sometimes, a text can convey a *message* or *universal lesson*—a truth or insight that the reader infers from the text, based on analysis of the literary and/or poetic elements. This message is often presented as a statement. For example, a potential message in Shakespeare's *Hamlet* could be "Revenge is what ultimately drives the human soul." This message can be immediately determined through plot and characterization in numerous ways, but it can also be determined through the setting of Norway, which is bordering on war.

<u>How Authors Develop Theme</u>

Authors employ a variety of techniques to present a theme. They may compare or contrast characters, events, places, ideas, or historical or invented settings to speak thematically. They may use analogies, metaphors, similes, allusions, or other literary devices to convey the theme. An author's use of diction, syntax, and tone can also help convey the theme. Authors will often develop themes through the development of characters, use of the setting, repetition of ideas, use of symbols, and through contrasting value systems. Authors of both fiction and nonfiction genres will use a variety of these techniques to develop one or more themes.

Regardless of the literary genre, there are commonalities in how authors, playwrights, and poets develop themes or central ideas.

Authors often do research, the results of which contributes to theme. In prose fiction and drama, this research may include real historical information about the setting the author has chosen or include elements that make fictional characters, settings, and plots seem realistic to the reader. In nonfiction, research is critical since the information contained within this literature must be accurate and, moreover, accurately represented.

In fiction, authors present a narrative conflict that will contribute to the overall theme. In fiction, this conflict may involve the storyline itself and some trouble within characters that needs resolution. In nonfiction, this conflict may be an explanation or commentary on factual people and events.

Authors will sometimes use character motivation to convey theme, such as in the example from *Hamlet* regarding revenge. In fiction, the characters an author creates will think, speak, and act in ways that effectively convey the theme to readers. In nonfiction, the characters are factual, as in a biography, but authors pay particular attention to presenting those motivations to make them clear to readers.

Authors also use literary devices as a means of conveying theme. For example, the use of moon symbolism in Shelley's *Frankenstein* is significant as its phases can be compared to the phases that the Creature undergoes as he struggles with his identity.

The selected point of view can also contribute to a work's theme. The use of first person point of view in a fiction or non-fiction work engages the reader's response differently than third person point of view. The central idea or theme from a first person narrative may differ from a third-person limited text.

In literary nonfiction, authors usually identify the purpose of their writing, which differs from fiction, where the general purpose is to entertain. The purpose of nonfiction is usually to inform, persuade, or entertain the audience. The stated purpose of a non-fiction text will drive how the central message or theme, if applicable, is presented.

Authors identify an audience for their writing, which is critical in shaping the theme of the work. For example, the audience for J.K. Rowling's *Harry Potter* series would be different than the audience for a biography of George Washington. The audience an author chooses to address is closely tied to the purpose of the work. The choice of an audience also drives the choice of language and level of diction an author uses. Ultimately, the intended audience determines the level to which that subject matter is presented and the complexity of the theme.

Summarizing and Paraphrasing a Passage

Creating an outline that identifies the main ideas of a passage as well as the supporting details is a helpful tool in effectively summarizing a text. Most outlines will include a title that reveals the topic of the text, and is usually a single phrase or word, such as "whales." If the passage is divided up into paragraphs, or the paragraphs into sections, each paragraph or section will have its own main idea. These "main ideas" are usually depicted in outlines as roman numerals. Next, writers use supporting details in order to support or prove the main ideas. The supporting details should be listed underneath each main idea in the outline. For example:

Title: Whales
I. Killer whales
    a. Highly social
    b. Apex predator
II. Humpback whales
    a. Males produce "song"
    b. Targeted for whaling industry
III. Beluga whales
    a. Complex sense of hearing
    b. Slow swimmers

Making an outline is a useful method of summarization because it forces the reader to deconstruct the text as a whole and to identify only the most important parts of the text.

Ideas from a text can also be organized using graphic organizers. A graphic organizer is a way to simplify information and take key points from the text. A graphic organizer such as a timeline may have an event listed for a corresponding date on the timeline while an outline may have an event listed under a key point that occurs in the text. Each reader needs to create the type of graphic organizer that works the best for him or her in terms of being able to recall information from a story. Examples include a *spider-map,* which takes a main idea from the story and places it in a bubble with supporting points branching off the main idea. An *outline* is useful for diagramming the main and supporting points of the entire story, and a *Venn diagram* classifies information as separate or overlapping.

Writing a summary is similar to creating an outline. In both instances, the reader wants to relay the most important parts of the text without being too verbose. A summary of a text should begin with stating the main idea of that text. Then, the reader must decide which supporting details are absolutely essential to the main idea of the text and leave any irrelevant information out of the summary. A summary shouldn't be too brief—readers should include important details depicted in the text--, but it also shouldn't be too long either. The appeal of a summary to an audience is that they are able to receive the message of the text without being distracted by the style or detours of the author.

Another effective reading comprehension strategy is paraphrasing. Paraphrasing is usually longer than a summary. Paraphrasing is taking the author's text and rewriting, or "translating," it into their own words. A tip for paraphrasing is to read a passage over three times. Once you've read the passage and understand what the author is saying, cover the original passage and begin to write everything you remember from that passage into your own words. Usually, if you understand the content well enough, you will have translated the main idea of the author into your own words with your own writing style. An effective paraphrase will be as long as the original passage but will have a different writing structure.

<u>Outlining</u>

As mentioned, an *outline* is a system used to organize writing. When reading texts, outlining is important because it helps readers organize important information in a logical pattern using Roman numerals. Usually, outlines start out with the main idea(s) and then branch out into subgroups or subsidiary thoughts or subjects. Not only do outlines provide a visual tool for readers to reflect on how events, characters, settings, or other key parts of the text or passage relate to one another, but they can also lead readers to a stronger conclusion. The sample below demonstrates what a general outline looks like.

I. Main Topic 1
    a. Subtopic 1
    b. Subtopic 2
        1. Detail 1
        2. Detail 2
II. Main Topic 2
    a. Subtopic 1
    b. Subtopic 2
        1. Detail 1
        2. Detail 2

Summarizing

At the end of a text or passage, it is important to summarize what the readers read. *Summarizing* is a strategy in which readers determine what is important throughout the text or passage, shorten those ideas, and rewrite or retell it in their own words. A summary should identify the main idea of the text or passage. Important details or supportive evidence should also be accurately reported in the summary. If writers provide irrelevant details in the summary, it may cloud the greater meaning of the text or passage. When summarizing, writers should not include their opinions, quotes, or what they thought the author should have said. A clear summary provides clarity of the text or passage to the readers. The following checklist lists items that writers should include in a summary:

<u>Summary Checklist</u>

- Title of the story
- Someone: Who is or are the main character(s)?

- Wanted: What did the character(s) want?
- But: What was the problem?
- So: How did the character(s) solve the problem?
- Then: How did the story end? What was the resolution?

Identifying Logical Conclusions

Determining conclusions requires being an active reader, as a reader must make a prediction and analyze facts to identify a conclusion. A reader should identify key words in a passage to determine the logical conclusion or determination that flows from the information presented. Consider the passage below:

> Lindsay, covered in flour, moved around the kitchen frantically. Her mom yelled from another room, "Lindsay, we're going to be late!

You can conclude that Lindsay's next steps are to finish baking, clean herself up, and head off somewhere with her baked goods. Notice that the conclusion cannot be verified factually. Many conclusions are not spelled out specifically in the text, thus they have to be identified and drawn out by the reader.

Interpreting Textual Evidence in Informational Text

Literal and Figurative Meanings
It is important when evaluating informational texts to consider the use of both *literal and figurative meanings*. The words and phrases an author chooses to include in a text must be evaluated. How does the word choice affect the meaning and tone? By recognizing the use of literal and figurative language, a reader can more readily ascertain the message or purpose of a text. Literal word choice is the easiest to analyze as it represents the usual and intended way a word or phrase is used. It is also more common in informational texts because it is used to state facts and definitions. While figurative language is typically associated with fiction and poetry, it can be found in informational texts as well. The reader must determine not only what is meant by the figurative language in context, but also how the author intended it to shape the overall text.

Inference in Informational Text
Inference refers to the reader's ability to understand the unwritten text, i.e., "read between the lines" in terms of an author's intent or message. The strategy asks that a reader not take everything he or she reads at face value but instead, add his or her own interpretation of what the author seems to be trying to convey. A reader's ability to make inferences relies on his or her ability to think clearly and logically about the text. It does not ask that the reader make wild speculation or guess about the material but demands that he or she be able to come to a sound conclusion about the material.

An author's use of less literal words and phrases requires readers to make more inference when they read. Since inference involves *deduction*—deriving conclusions from ideas assumed to be true—there's more room for interpretation. Still, critical readers who employ inference, if careful in their thinking, can still arrive at the logical, sound conclusions the author intends.

Textual Evidence in Informational Text
Once a reader has determined an author's thesis or main idea, he or she will need to understand how textual evidence supports interpretation of that thesis or main idea. Test takers will be asked direct questions regarding an author's main idea and may be asked to identify evidence that would support

those ideas. This will require test takers to comprehend literal and figurative meanings within the text passage, be able to draw inferences from provided information, and be able to separate important evidence from minor supporting detail. It's often helpful to skim test questions and answer options prior to critically reading informational text; however, test takers should avoid the temptation to solely look for the correct answers. Just trying to find the "right answer" may cause test takers to miss important supporting textual evidence. Making mental note of test questions is only helpful as a guide when reading.

After identifying an author's thesis or main idea, a test taker should look at the supporting details that the author provides to back up his or her assertions, identifying those additional pieces of information that help expand the thesis. From there, test takers should examine that additional information and related details for credibility, the author's use of outside sources, and be able to point to direct evidence that supports the author's claims. It's also imperative that test takers be able to identify what is strong support and what is merely additional information that is nice to know but not necessary. Being able to make this differentiation will help test takers effectively answer questions regarding an author's use of supporting evidence within informational text.

Understanding Organizational Patterns and Structures

Organizational Structure within Informational Text

Informational text is specifically designed to relate factual information, and although it is open to a reader's interpretation and application of the facts, the structure of the presentation is carefully designed to lead the reader to a particular conclusion or central idea. When reading informational text, it is important that readers are able to understand its organizational structure as the structure often directly relates to an author's intent to inform and/or persuade the reader.

The first step in identifying the text's structure is to determine the thesis or main idea. The thesis statement and organization of a work are closely intertwined. *A thesis statement* indicates the writer's purpose and may include the scope and direction of the text. It may be presented at the beginning of a text or at the end, and it may be explicit or implicit.

Once a reader has a grasp of the thesis or main idea of the text, he or she can better determine its organizational structure. Test takers are advised to read informational text passages more than once in order to comprehend the material fully. It is also helpful to examine any text features present in the text including the table of contents, index, glossary, headings, footnotes, and visuals. The analysis of these features and the information presented within them, can offer additional clues about the central idea and structure of a text. The following questions should be asked when considering structure:

- How does the author assemble the parts to make an effective whole argument?
- Is the passage linear in nature and if so, what is the timeline or thread of logic?
- What is the presented order of events, facts, or arguments? Are these effective in contributing to the author's thesis?
- How can the passage be divided into sections? How are they related to each other and to the main idea or thesis?
- What key terms are used to indicate the organization?

Next, test takers should skim the passage, noting the first line or two of each body paragraph—the *topic sentences*—and the conclusion. Key *transitional terms*, such as *on the other hand, also, because, however, therefore, most importantly*, and *first*, within the text can also signal organizational structure.

Based on these clues, readers should then be able to identify what type of organizational structure is being used.

The following organizational structures are most common:

- *Problem/solution—organized by an analysis/overview of a problem, followed by potential solution(s)*
- *Cause/effect—organized by the effects resulting from a cause or the cause(s) of a particular effect*
- *Spatial order—organized by points that suggest location or direction—e.g., top to bottom, right to left, outside to inside*
- *Chronological/sequence order—organized by points presented to indicate a passage of time or through purposeful steps/stages*
- *Comparison/Contrast—organized by points that indicate similarities and/or differences between two things or concepts*
- *Order of importance—organized by priority of points, often most significant to least significant or vice versa*

Craft and Structure of Text Selections

Understanding the Use of Affixes, Context, and Syntax

Paraphrasing

Another strategy readers can use to help them fully comprehend a text or passage is *paraphrasing.* Paraphrasing is when readers take the author's words and put them into their own words. When readers and writers paraphrase, they need to avoid copying the text—that is plagiarism. It is also important to include as many details as possible when restating the facts. Not only will this help readers and writers recall information, but by putting the information into their own words, they demonstrate if they fully comprehend the text or passage. The example below shows an original text and how to paraphrase it.

> *Original Text: Fenway Park is home to the beloved Boston Red Sox. The stadium opened on April 20, 1912. The stadium currently seats over 37,000 fans, many of whom travel from all over the country to experience the iconic team and nostalgia of Fenway Park.*
>
> *Paraphrased: On April 20, 1912, Fenway Park opened. Home to the Boston Red Sox, the stadium now seats over 37,000 fans. Many spectators travel to watch the Red Sox and experience the spirit of Fenway Park.*

Paraphrasing, summarizing, and quoting can often cross paths with one another. The chart below shows the similarities and differences between the three strategies:

PARAPHRASING	**SUMMARIZING**	**QUOTING**
Uses own words	Puts main ideas into own words	Uses words that are identical to text
References original source	References original source	Requires quotation marks
Uses own sentences	Shows important ideas of source	Uses author's words and ideas

Affixes

Individual words are constructed from building blocks of meaning. An *affix* is an element that is added to a root or stem word that can change the word's meaning.

For example, the stem word *fix* is a verb meaning *to repair*. When the ending *–able* is added, it becomes the adjective *fixable*, meaning "capable of being repaired." Adding *un–* to the beginning changes the word to *unfixable*, meaning "incapable of being repaired." In this way, affixes attach to the word stem to create a new word and a new meaning. Knowledge of affixes can assist in deciphering the meaning of unfamiliar words.

Affixes are also related to inflection. *Inflection* is the modification of a base word to express a different grammatical or syntactical function. For example, countable nouns such as *car* and *airport* become plural with the addition of *–s* at the end: *cars* and *airports*.

Verb tense is also expressed through inflection. *Regular verbs*—those that follow a standard inflection pattern—can be changed to past tense using the affixes *–ed*, *–d*, or *–ied*, as in *cooked* and *studied*. Verbs can also be modified for continuous tenses by using *–ing*, as in *working* or *exploring*. Thus, affixes are used not only to express meaning but also to reflect a word's grammatical purpose.

A *prefix* is an affix attached to the beginning of a word. The meanings of English prefixes mainly come from Greek and Latin origins. The chart below contains a few of the most commonly used English prefixes.

Prefix	**Meaning**	**Example**
a-	Not	amoral, asymptomatic
anti-	Against	antidote, antifreeze
auto-	Self	automobile, automatic
circum-	Around	circumference, circumspect
co-, com-, con-	Together	coworker, companion
contra-	Against	contradict, contrary
de-	negation or reversal	deflate, deodorant
extra-	outside, beyond	extraterrestrial, extracurricular
in-, im-, il-, ir-	Not	impossible, irregular
inter-	Between	international, intervene
intra-	Within	intramural, intranet
mis-	Wrongly	mistake, misunderstand
mono-	One	monolith, monopoly
non-	Not	nonpartisan, nonsense
pre-	Before	preview, prediction
re-	Again	review, renew
semi-	Half	semicircle, semicolon
sub-	Under	subway, submarine
super-	Above	superhuman, superintendent
trans-	across, beyond, through	trans-Siberian, transform
un-	Not	unwelcome, unfriendly

While the addition of a prefix alters the meaning of the base word, the addition of a *suffix* may also affect a word's part of speech. For example, adding a suffix can change the noun *material* into the verb *materialize* and back to a noun again in *materialization*.

Suffix	Part of Speech	Meaning	Example
-able, -ible	adjective	having the ability to	honorable, flexible
-acy, -cy	noun	state or quality	intimacy, dependency
-al, -ical	adjective	having the quality of	historical, tribal
-en	verb	to cause to become	strengthen, embolden
-er, -ier	adjective	comparative	happier, longer
-est, -iest	adjective	superlative	sunniest, hottest
-ess	noun	female	waitress, actress
-ful	adjective	full of, characterized by	beautiful, thankful
-fy, -ify	verb	to cause, to come to be	liquefy, intensify
-ism	noun	doctrine, belief, action	Communism, Buddhism
-ive, -ative, -itive	adjective	having the quality of	creative, innovative
-ize	verb	to convert into, to subject to	Americanize, dramatize
-less	adjective	without, missing	emotionless, hopeless
-ly	adverb	in the manner of	quickly, energetically
-ness	noun	quality or state	goodness, darkness
-ous, -ious, -eous	adjective	having the quality of	spontaneous, pious
-ship	noun	status or condition	partnership, ownership
-tion	noun	action or state	renovation, promotion
-y	adjective	characterized by	smoky, dreamy

Through knowledge of prefixes and suffixes, a student's vocabulary can be instantly expanded with an understanding of *etymology*—the origin of words. This, in turn, can be used to add sentence structure variety to academic writing.

<u>Context Clues</u>

Familiarity with common prefixes, suffixes, and root words assists tremendously in unraveling the meaning of an unfamiliar word and making an educated guess as to its meaning. However, some words do not contain many easily-identifiable clues that point to their meaning. In this case, rather than looking at the elements within the word, it is useful to consider elements around the word—i.e., its context. *Context* refers to the other words and information within the sentence or surrounding sentences that indicate the unknown word's probable meaning. The following sentences provide context for the potentially-unfamiliar word *quixotic*:

> Rebecca had never been one to settle into a predictable, ordinary life. Her quixotic personality led her to leave behind a job with a prestigious law firm in Manhattan and move halfway around the world to pursue her dream of becoming a sushi chef in Tokyo.

A reader unfamiliar with the word *quixotic* doesn't have many clues to use in terms of affixes or root meaning. The suffix *–ic* indicates that the word is an adjective, but that is it. In this case, then, a reader would need to look at surrounding information to obtain some clues about the word. Other adjectives in the passage include *predictable* and *ordinary*, things that Rebecca was definitely not, as indicated by

"Rebecca had never been one to settle." Thus, a first clue might be that *quixotic* means the opposite of predictable.

The second sentence doesn't offer any other modifier of *personality* other than *quixotic*, but it does include a story that reveals further information about her personality. She had a stable, respectable job, but she decided to give it up to follow her dream. Combining these two ideas together, then—unpredictable and dream-seeking—gives the reader a general idea of what *quixotic* probably means. In fact, the root of the word is the character Don Quixote, a romantic dreamer who goes on an impulsive adventure.

While context clues are useful for making an approximate definition for newly-encountered words, these types of clues also come in handy when encountering common words that have multiple meanings. The word *reservation* is used differently in each the following sentences:

- That restaurant is booked solid for the next month; it's impossible to make a reservation unless you know somebody.
- The hospital plans to open a branch office inside the reservation to better serve Native American patients who cannot easily travel to the main hospital fifty miles away.
- Janet Clark is a dependable, knowledgeable worker, and I recommend her for the position of team leader without reservation.

All three sentences use the word to express different meanings. In fact, most words in English have more than one meaning—sometimes meanings that are completely different from one another. Thus, context can provide clues as to which meaning is appropriate in a given situation. A quick search in the dictionary reveals several possible meanings for *reservation*:

4. 1. An exception or qualification
5. 2. A tract of public land set aside, such as for the use of American Indian tribes
6. 3. An arrangement for accommodations, such as in a hotel, on a plane, or at a restaurant

Sentence A mentions a restaurant, making the third definition the correct one in this case. In sentence B, some context clues include Native Americans, as well as the implication that a reservation is a place—"inside the reservation," both of which indicate that the second definition should be used here. Finally, sentence C uses *without reservation* to mean "completely" or "without exception," so the first definition can be applied here.

Using context clues in this way can be especially useful for words that have multiple, widely varying meanings. If a word has more than one definition and two of those definitions are the opposite of each other, it is known as an *auto-antonym*—a word that can also be its own antonym. In the case of auto-antonyms, context clues are crucial to determine which definition to employ in a given sentence. For example, the word *sanction* can either mean "to approve or allow" or "a penalty." Approving and penalizing have opposite meanings, so *sanction* is an example of an auto-antonym. The following sentences reflect the distinction in meaning:

- In response to North Korea's latest nuclear weapons test, world leaders have called for harsher sanctions to punish the country for its actions.
- The general has sanctioned a withdrawal of troops from the area.

A context clue can be found in sentence A, which mentions "to punish." A punishment is similar to a penalty, so sentence A is using the word *sanction* according to this definition.

Other examples of auto-antonyms include *oversight*—"to supervise something" or "a missed detail"), *resign*—"to quit" or "to sign again, as a contract," and *screen*—"to show" or "to conceal." For these types of words, recognizing context clues is an important way to avoid misinterpreting the sentence's meaning.

Syntax

Syntax refers to the arrangement of words, phrases, and clauses to form a sentence. Knowledge of syntax can also give insight into a word's meaning. The section above considered several examples using the word *reservation* and applied context clues to determine the word's appropriate meaning in each sentence. Here is an example of how the placement of a word can impact its meaning and grammatical function:

> The development team has reserved the conference room for today.
>
> Her quiet and reserved nature is sometimes misinterpreted as unfriendliness when people first meet her.

In addition to using *reserved* to mean different things, each sentence also uses the word to serve a different grammatical function. In sentence A, *reserved* is part of the verb phrase *has reserved,* indicating the meaning "to set aside for a particular use." In sentence B, *reserved* acts as a modifier within the noun phrase "her quiet and reserved nature." Because the word is being used as an adjective to describe a personality characteristic, it calls up a different definition of the word—"restrained or lacking familiarity with others." As this example shows, the function of a word within the overall sentence structure can allude to its meaning. It is also useful to refer to the earlier chart about suffixes and parts of speech as another clue into what grammatical function a word is serving in a sentence.

Analyzing Nuances of Word Meaning and Figures of Speech

By now, it should be apparent that language is not as simple as one word directly correlated to one meaning. Rather, one word can express a vast array of diverse meanings, and similar meanings can be expressed through different words. However, there are very few words that express exactly the same meaning. For this reason, it is important to be able to pick up on the nuances of word meaning.

Many words contain two levels of meaning: connotation and denotation as discussed previously in the informational texts and rhetoric section. A word's *denotation* is its most literal meaning—the definition that can readily be found in the dictionary. A word's *connotation* includes all of its emotional and cultural associations.

In literary writing, authors rely heavily on connotative meaning to create mood and characterization. The following are two descriptions of a rainstorm:

> A. The rain slammed against the windowpane and the wind howled through the fireplace. A pair of hulking oaks next to the house cast eerie shadows as their branches trembled in the wind.
>
> B. The rain pattered against the windowpane and the wind whistled through the fireplace. A pair of stately oaks next to the house cast curious shadows as their branches swayed in the wind.

Description *A* paints a creepy picture for readers with strongly emotional words like *slammed*, connoting force and violence. *Howled* connotes pain or wildness, and *eerie* and *trembled* connote fear. Overall, the connotative language in this description serves to inspire fear and anxiety.

However, as can be seen in description B, swapping out a few key words for those with different connotations completely changes the feeling of the passage. *Slammed* is replaced with the more cheerful *pattered*, and *hulking* has been swapped out for *stately*. Both words imply something large, but *hulking* is more intimidating whereas *stately* is more respectable. *Curious* and *swayed* seem more playful than the language used in the earlier description. Although both descriptions represent roughly the same situation, the nuances of the emotional language used throughout the passages create a very different sense for readers.

Selective choice of connotative language can also be extremely impactful in other forms of writing, such as editorials or persuasive texts. Through connotative language, writers reveal their biases and opinions while trying to inspire feelings and actions in readers:

7. 1. Parents won't stop complaining about standardized tests.
8. 2. Parents continue to raise concerns about standardized tests.

Readers should be able to identify the nuance in meaning between these two sentences. The first one carries a more negative feeling, implying that parents are being bothersome or whiny. Readers of the second sentence, though, might come away with the feeling that parents are concerned and involved in their children's education. Again, the aggregate of even subtle cues can combine to give a specific emotional impression to readers, so from an early age, students should be aware of how language can be used to influence readers' opinions.

Another form of non-literal expression can be found in *figures of speech*. As with connotative language, figures of speech tend to be shared within a cultural group and may be difficult to pick up on for learners outside of that group. In some cases, a figure of speech may be based on the literal denotation of the words it contains, but in other cases, a figure of speech is far removed from its literal meaning. A case in point is *irony*, where what is said is the exact opposite of what is meant:

> The new tax plan is poorly planned, based on faulty economic data, and unable to address the financial struggles of middle class families. Yet legislators remain committed to passing this brilliant proposal.

When the writer refers to the proposal as brilliant, the opposite is implied—the plan is "faulty" and "poorly planned." By using irony, the writer means that the proposal is anything but brilliant by using the word in a non-literal sense.

Another figure of speech is *hyperbole*—extreme exaggeration or overstatement. Statements like, "I love you to the moon and back" or "Let's be friends for a million years" utilize hyperbole to convey a greater depth of emotion, without literally committing oneself to space travel or a life of immortality.

Figures of speech may sometimes use one word in place of another. *Synecdoche*, for example, uses a part of something to refer to its whole. The expression "Don't hurt a hair on her head!" implies protecting more than just an individual hair, but rather her entire body. "The art teacher is training a class of Picassos" uses Picasso, one individual notable artist, to stand in for the entire category of talented artists. Another figure of speech using word replacement is *metonymy*, where a word is replaced with something closely associated to it. For example, news reports may use the word "Washington" to refer to the American government or "the crown" to refer to the British monarch.

Understanding the Effect of Word Choice

An author's choice of words—also referred to as *diction*—helps to convey his or her meaning in a particular way. Through diction, an author can convey a particular tone—e.g., a humorous tone, a serious tone—in order to support the thesis in a meaningful way to the reader.

<u>Connotation and Denotation</u>
Connotation is when an author chooses words or phrases that invoke ideas or feelings other than their literal meaning. An example of the use of connotation is the word *cheap*, which suggests something is poor in value or negatively describes a person as reluctant to spend money. When something or someone is described this way, the reader is more inclined to have a particular image or feeling about it or him/her. Thus, connotation can be a very effective language tool in creating emotion and swaying opinion. However, connotations are sometimes hard to pin down because varying emotions can be associated with a word. Generally, though, connotative meanings tend to be fairly consistent within a specific cultural group.

Denotation refers to words or phrases that mean exactly what they say. It is helpful when a writer wants to present hard facts or vocabulary terms with which readers may be unfamiliar. Some examples of denotation are the words *inexpensive* and *frugal*. *Inexpensive* refers to the cost of something, not its value, and *frugal* indicates that a person is conscientiously watching his or her spending. These terms do not elicit the same emotions that *cheap* does.

Authors sometimes choose to use both, but what they choose and when they use it is what critical readers need to differentiate. One method isn't inherently better than the other; however, one may create a better effect, depending upon an author's intent. If, for example, an author's purpose is to inform, to instruct, and to familiarize readers with a difficult subject, his or her use of connotation may be helpful. However, it may also undermine credibility and confuse readers. An author who wants to create a credible, scholarly effect in his or her text would most likely use denotation, which emphasizes literal, factual meaning and examples.

<u>Technical Language</u>
Test takers and critical readers alike should be very aware of technical language used within informational text. *Technical language* refers to terminology that is specific to a particular industry and is best understood by those specializing in that industry. This language is fairly easy to differentiate, since it will most likely be unfamiliar to readers. It's critical to be able to define technical language either by the author's written definition, through the use of an included glossary—if offered—or through context clues that help readers clarify word meaning.

Figurative Language

Literary texts also employ rhetorical devices. Figurative language like simile and metaphor is a type of rhetorical device commonly found in literature. In addition to rhetorical devices that play on the *meanings* of words, there are also rhetorical devices that use the *sounds* of words. These devices are most often found in poetry, but may also be found in other types of literature and in non-fiction writing like speech texts.

Alliteration and *assonance* are both varieties of sound repetition. Other types of sound repetition include: anaphora, repetition that occurs at the beginning of the sentences; epiphora, repetition occurring at the end of phrases; antimetabole, repetition of words in reverse order; and antiphrasis, a form of denial of an assertion in a text.

Alliteration refers to the repetition of the first sound of each word. Recall Robert Burns' opening line:

> My love is like a red, red rose

This line includes two instances of alliteration: "love" and "like" (repeated *L* sound), as well as "red" and "rose" (repeated *R* sound). Next, assonance refers to the repetition of vowel sounds, and can occur anywhere within a word (not just the opening sound). Here is the opening of a poem by John Keats:

> When I have fears that I may cease to be
> Before my pen has glean'd my teeming brain

Assonance can be found in the words "fears," "cease," "be," "glean'd," and "teeming," all of which stress the long *E* sound. Both alliteration and assonance create a harmony that unifies the writer's language.

Another sound device is *onomatopoeia*, or words whose spelling mimics the sound they describe. Words like "crash," "bang," and "sizzle" are all examples of onomatopoeia. Use of onomatopoetic language adds auditory imagery to the text.

Readers are probably most familiar with the technique of *pun*. A pun is a play on words, taking advantage of two words that have the same or similar pronunciation. Puns can be found throughout Shakespeare's plays, for instance:

> Now is the winter of our discontent
> Made glorious summer by this son of York

These lines from *Richard III* contain a play on words. Richard III refers to his brother, the newly crowned King Edward IV, as the "son of York," referencing their family heritage from the house of York. However, while drawing a comparison between the political climate and the weather (times of political trouble were the "winter," but now the new king brings "glorious summer"), Richard's use of the word "son" also implies another word with the same pronunciation, "sun"—so Edward IV is also like the sun, bringing light, warmth, and hope to England. Puns are a clever way for writers to suggest two meanings at once.

Some examples of figurative language are included in the following graphic.

Term	Definition	Example
Simile	Compares two things using "like" or "as"	Her hair was like gold.
Metaphor	Compares two things as if they are the same	He was a giant teddy bear.
Idiom	Using words with predictable meanings to create a phrase with a different meaning	The world is your oyster.
Alliteration	Repeating the same beginning sound or letter in a phrase for emphasis	The busy baby babbled.
Personification	Attributing human characteristics to an object or an animal	The house glowered menacingly with a dark smile.
Foreshadowing	Giving an indication that something is going to happen later in the story	I wasn't aware at the time, but I would come to regret those words.
Symbolism	Using symbols to represent ideas and provide a different meaning	The ring represented the bond between us.
Onomatopoeia	Using words that imitate sound	The tire went off with a bang and a crunch.
Imagery	Appealing to the senses by using descriptive language	The sky was painted with red and pink and streaked with orange.
Hyperbole	Using exaggeration not meant to be taken literally	The girl weighed less than a feather.

Figurative language can be used to give additional insight into the theme or message of a text by moving beyond the usual and literal meaning of words and phrases. It can also be used to appeal to the senses of readers and create a more in-depth story.

Style, Tone, and Mood

Style, tone, and mood are often thought to be the same thing. Though they're closely related, there are important differences to keep in mind. The easiest way to do this is to remember that style "creates and affects" tone and mood. More specifically, style is how the writer uses words to create the desired tone and mood for their writing.

Style

Style can include any number of technical writing choices. A few examples of style choices include:

- Sentence Construction: When presenting facts, does the writer use shorter sentences to create a quicker sense of the supporting evidence, or do they use longer sentences to elaborate and explain the information?
- Technical Language: Does the writer use jargon to demonstrate their expertise in the subject, or do they use ordinary language to help the reader understand things in simple terms?
- Formal Language: Does the writer refrain from using contractions such as won't or can't to create a more formal tone, or do they use a colloquial, conversational style to connect to the reader?
- Formatting: Does the writer use a series of shorter paragraphs to help the reader follow a line of argument, or do they use longer paragraphs to examine an issue in great detail and demonstrate their knowledge of the topic?

On the test, examine the writer's style and how their writing choices affect the way the text comes across.

Tone

Tone refers to the writer's attitude toward the subject matter. Tone is usually explained in terms of a work of fiction. For example, the tone conveys how the writer feels about their characters and the situations in which they're involved. Nonfiction writing is sometimes thought to have no tone at all; however, this is incorrect.

A lot of nonfiction writing has a neutral tone, which is an important tone for the writer to take. A neutral tone demonstrates that the writer is presenting a topic impartially and letting the information speak for itself. On the other hand, nonfiction writing can be just as effective and appropriate if the tone isn't neutral. For instance, take this example involving seat belts:

> Seat belts save more lives than any other automobile safety feature. Many studies show that airbags save lives as well; however, not all cars have airbags. For instance, some older cars don't. Furthermore, air bags aren't entirely reliable. For example, studies show that in 15% of accidents airbags don't deploy as designed, but, on the other hand, seat belt malfunctions are extremely rare. The number of highway fatalities has plummeted since laws requiring seat belt usage were enacted.

In this passage, the writer mostly chooses to retain a neutral tone when presenting information. If the writer would instead include their own personal experience of losing a friend or family member in a car accident, the tone would change dramatically. The tone would no longer be neutral and would show that the writer has a personal stake in the content, allowing them to interpret the information in a different way. When analyzing tone, consider what the writer is trying to achieve in the text and how they *create* the tone using style.

Mood

Mood refers to the feelings and atmosphere that the writer's words create for the reader. Like tone, many nonfiction texts can have a neutral mood. To return to the previous example, if the writer would choose to include information about a person they know being killed in a car accident, the text would suddenly carry an emotional component that is absent in the previous example. Depending on how they present the information, the writer can create a sad, angry, or even hopeful mood. When analyzing the mood, consider what the writer wants to accomplish and whether the best choice was made to achieve that end.

Point of View

Point of view is an important writing device to consider. In fiction writing, point of view refers to who tells the story or from whose perspective readers are observing as they read. In non-fiction writing, the *point of view* refers to whether the author refers to himself/herself, his/her readers, or chooses not to refer to either. Whether fiction or nonfiction, the author will carefully consider the impact the perspective will have on the purpose and main point of the writing.

- First-person point of view: The story is told from the writer's perspective. In fiction, this would mean that the main character is also the narrator. First-person point of view is easily recognized by the use of personal pronouns such as I, me, we, us, our, my, and myself.
- Third-person point of view: In a more formal essay, this would be an appropriate perspective because the focus should be on the subject matter, not the writer or the reader. Third-person point of view is recognized using the pronouns he, she, they, and it. In fiction writing, third person point of view has a few variations.
- Third-person limited point of view refers to a story told by a narrator who has access to the thoughts and feelings of just one character.
- In third-person omniscient point of view, the narrator has access to the thoughts and feelings of all the characters.
- In third-person objective point of view, the narrator is like a fly on the wall and can see and hear what the characters do and say, but does not have access to their thoughts and feelings.
- Second-person point of view: This point of view isn't commonly used in fiction or non-fiction writing because it directly addresses the reader using the pronouns you, your, and yourself. Second-person perspective is more appropriate in direct communication, such as business letters or emails.

Point of View	Pronouns Used
First person	I, me, we, us, our, my, myself
Second person	You, your, yourself
Third person	He, she, it, they

Consistency

Whatever style, tone, point of view, and mood the writer uses, good writing should remain consistent throughout. If the writer chooses to include the tragic, personal experience above, it would affect the style, tone, and mood of the entire text. It would seem out of place for such an example to be used in the middle of a neutral, measured, and analytical text. To adjust the rest of the text, the writer needs to make additional choices to remain consistent. For example, the writer might decide to use the word *tragedy* in place of the more neutral *fatality*, or they could describe a series of car-related deaths as an *epidemic*. Adverbs and adjectives such as *devastating* or *horribly* could be included to maintain this consistent attitude toward the content. When analyzing writing, look for sudden shifts in style, tone, and mood, and consider whether the writer would be wiser to maintain the prevailing strategy.

Text Structure

Depending on what the author is attempting to accomplish, certain formats or text structures work better than others. For example, a sequence structure might work for narration but not when identifying similarities and differences between dissimilar concepts. Similarly, a comparison-contrast structure is not useful for narration. It's the author's job to put the right information in the correct format.

Readers should be familiar with the five main literary structures:

1. *Sequence* structure (sometimes referred to as the order structure) is when the order of events proceed in a predictable order. In many cases, this means the text goes through the plot elements: exposition, rising action, climax, falling action, and resolution. Readers are introduced to characters, setting, and conflict in the exposition. In the rising action, there's an increase in tension and suspense. The climax is the height of tension and the point of no return. Tension decreases during the falling action. In the resolution, any conflicts presented in the exposition are solved, and the story concludes. An informative text that is structured sequentially will often go in order from one step to the next.

2. In the *problem-solution* structure, authors identify a potential problem and suggest a solution. This form of writing is usually divided into two paragraphs and can be found in informational texts. For example, cell phone, cable and satellite providers use this structure in manuals to help customers troubleshoot or identify problems with services or products.

3. When authors want to discuss similarities and differences between separate concepts, they arrange thoughts in a *comparison-contrast* paragraph structure. Venn diagrams are an effective graphic organizer for comparison-contrast structures, because they feature two overlapping circles that can be used to organize similarities and differences. A comparison-contrast essay organizes one paragraph based on similarities and another based on differences. A comparison-contrast essay can also be arranged with the similarities and differences of individual traits addressed within individual paragraphs. Words such as *however*, *but*, and *nevertheless* help signal a contrast in ideas.

4. *Descriptive* writing structure is designed to appeal to your senses. Much like an artist who constructs a painting, good descriptive writing builds an image in the reader's mind by appealing to the five senses: sight, hearing, taste, touch, and smell. However, overly descriptive writing can become tedious; sparse descriptions can make settings and characters seem flat. Good authors strike a balance by applying descriptions only to passages, characters, and settings that are integral to the plot.

5. Passages that use the *cause and effect* structure are simply asking *why* by demonstrating some type of connection between ideas. Words such as *if*, *since*, *because*, *then*, or *consequently* indicate relationship. By switching the order of a complex sentence, the writer can rearrange the emphasis on different clauses. Saying *If Sheryl is late, we'll miss the dance* is different from saying *We'll miss the dance if Sheryl is late*. One emphasizes Sheryl's tardiness while the other emphasizes missing the dance. Paragraphs can also be arranged in a cause and effect format. Since the format — before and after — is sequential, it is useful when authors wish to discuss the impact of choices. Researchers often apply this paragraph structure to the scientific method.

Identifying Information in an Index or Table of Contents

An index is an alphabetical listing of topics, such as people, works, or concepts that appear at the end of expository materials like textbooks, cookbooks, and repair manuals. When these key words are used in paragraphs, they sometimes appear in bold writing to indicate their importance and let the reader know that they're found in the index as well.

Index listings often discard articles like *a*, *an*, and *the*. Additionally, authors will be listed by their last names, not first. Topics may be further divided into subtopics. If you start by looking for the most basic topics first, you can quickly acquire information. For example, when looking for a cookie recipe in a cookbook, first find the word *cookie* in the index and then examine the indented list of cookie-related topics located directly beneath the original heading.

Some textbooks have multiple indexes arranged by different subjects. If, for instance, you're dealing with a weighty literature textbook, you might find one index that lists authors and another devoted to concepts. The lengthier the book, the more likely you are to find this format.

While an index is typically found at the end of a book, a table of contents is found at the beginning to help readers quickly locate information. A table of contents is arranged differently, however, because it provides a chronological listing of each chapter and a corresponding page number. Each entry may also include a description, summary statement, or objective.

When students first receive a textbook, they should take time to preview the table of contents to create a framework for mentally organizing information. By classifying the contents, the reader creates mental schemas and becomes more likely to retain the information longer.

Analyzing Headings and Subheadings

Headings and subheadings are used in writing to organize discussions and allow the reader to find information quickly. Headings show a complete change in thought. Subheadings, which fall below headings, show different aspects of the same topic. For instance, if you saw the title *Government* and the heading *Forms of Government*, you might see the subheadings *Monarchy*, *Oligarchy*, *Democracy*, *Socialism*, and *Totalitarianism*.

As well as providing organization and structure, headings and subheadings also put more white space on a page, which places less strain on the reader's eyes. It's a good idea to skim a document and get familiar with headings and subheadings. Write down the title, headings, and subheadings before you begin reading to provide structure to your notes and thoughts.

Analyzing and Using Text Features

Text features are used to bring clarity or to affect the meaning of it. Bolding, italics, and underlining are all used to make words stand out.

Bolded words are often key concepts and can usually be found in summary statements at the end of chapters and in indexes.

Italics can be used to identify words of another language or to add extra emphasis to a word or phrase. Writers will sometime place words in italics when the word is being referred to as the word itself. Quotation marks or italics can be used for this, as long as there is consistency.

Italics are also used to represent a character's thoughts.

Entering Jessica's room, Jessica's mom stepped over a pile of laundry, a stack of magazines, and a pile of dishes. *My messy daughter*, she thought, shaking her head.

In addition, formatting—such as indentation or bullet points—helps to clearly present content. Writers can come up with their own uses for text features based on what they feel is best. It's important to catch on to the purpose of the text features that the writer uses.

Transitional Words and Phrases

There are approximately 200 transitional words and phrases that are commonly used in the English language. Below are lists of common transition words and phrases used throughout transitions.

Time

- after
- before
- during
- in the middle

Example about to be Given

- for example
- in fact
- for instance

Compare

- likewise
- also

Contrast

- however
- yet
- but

Addition

- and
- also
- furthermore
- moreover

Logical Relationships

- if
- then
- therefore
- as a result
- since

Steps in a Process

- first
- second

- last

Transitional words and phrases are important writing devices because they connect sentences and paragraphs. Transitional words and phrases present logical order to writing and provide more coherent meaning to readers.

Transition words can be categorized based on the relationships they create between ideas:

- General order: signaling elaboration of an idea to emphasize a point—e.g., for example, for instance, to demonstrate, including, such as, in other words, that is, in fact, also, furthermore, likewise, and, truly, so, surely, certainly, obviously, doubtless

- Chronological order: referencing the time frame in which main event or idea occurs—e.g., before, after, first, while, soon, shortly thereafter, meanwhile

- Numerical order/order of importance: indicating that related ideas, supporting details, or events will be described in a sequence, possibly in order of importance—e.g., first, second, also, finally, another, in addition, equally important, less importantly, most significantly, the main reason, last but not least

- Spatial order: referring to the space and location of something or where things are located in relation to each other—e.g., inside, outside, above, below, within, close, under, over, far, next to, adjacent to

- Cause and effect order: signaling a causal relationship between events or ideas—e.g., thus, therefore, since, resulted in, for this reason, as a result, consequently, hence, for, so

- Compare and contrast order: identifying the similarities and differences between two or more objects, ideas, or lines of thought—e.g., like, as, similarly, equally, just as, unlike, however, but, although, conversely, on the other hand, on the contrary

- Summary order: indicating that a particular idea is coming to a close—e.g., in conclusion, to sum up, in other words, ultimately, above all.

Identifying the Position and Purpose

When it comes to authors' writings, readers should always identify a position or stance. No matter how objective a piece may seem, assume the author has preconceived beliefs. Reduce the likelihood of accepting an invalid argument by looking for multiple articles on the topic, including those with varying opinions. If several opinions point in the same direction, and are backed by reputable peer-reviewed sources, it's more likely the author has a valid argument. Positions that run contrary to widely held beliefs and existing data should invite scrutiny. There are exceptions to the rule, so be a careful consumer of information.

Though themes, symbols, and motifs are buried deep within the text and can sometimes be difficult to infer, an author's purpose is usually obvious from the beginning. There are four purposes of writing: to inform, to persuade, to describe, and to entertain. Informative writings present facts in an accessible way. Persuasive writing is appeals to emotions and logic to inspire the reader to adopt a specific stance. Be wary of this type of writing, as it often lacks objectivity. Descriptive writing is designed to paint a picture in the reader's mind, while writings that entertain are often narratives designed to engage and delight the reader.

The various writing styles are usually blended, with one purpose dominating the rest. For example, a persuasive piece might begin with a humorous tale to make readers more receptive to the persuasive message, or a recipe in a cookbook designed to inform might be preceded by an entertaining anecdote that makes the recipe more appealing.

Writing Devices

Authors use a variety of writing devices throughout texts. Below is a list of some writing devices authors use in their writing.

- Comparison and Contrast
- Cause and Effect
- Analogy
- Point of View
- Transitional Words and Phrases

Each device will be considered individually.

<u>Comparison and Contrast</u>
One writing device authors use is comparison and contrast. Comparison is when authors take objects and show how they are the same. Contrast is when authors take objects and show how they differ. Comparison and contrast essays are mostly written in nonfiction form. There are common words used when authors compare or contrast. The list below will show you some of these words:

Comparison Words:

- Similar to
- Alike
- As well as
- Both

Contrast Words:

- Although
- On the other hand
- Different from
- However
- As opposed to
- More than
- Less than
- On the contrary

<u>Cause and Effect</u>
Cause and effect is a common writing device. A cause is why something happens. An effect is something that happens because of the cause. Many times, authors use key words to show cause and effect, such as *because, so, therefore, without, now, then,* and *since*. For example: "Because of the sun shower, a

rainbow appeared." In this sentence, due to the sun shower (the cause), a rainbow appeared (the effect).

Analogy
An analogyis a comparison between two things. Sometimes the two things are very different from one another. Authors often use analogiesto add meaning and make ideas relatable in texts. There are two types of analogies: metaphors and similes. Metaphors compare two things that are not similar. Similes also compare two unlike things but use the words *like* or *as*. For example, "In the library, students are asked to be as quiet as a mouse." Clearly, students and mice are very different. However, when students are asked to be as quiet as a mouse, readers understand that they are being asked to be absolutely silent.

Point of View
Point of view is the viewpoint in which authors tell stories. Authors can tell stories in either the first or third person. If an author writes in the first person, they are a character within a story telling about their own experiences. The pronouns *I* and *we* are used when writing in the first person. If an author writes in the third person, the narrator is telling the story from an outside perspective. The author is not a character in the story, but rather tells about the characters' actions and dialogues. Pronouns such as *he, she, it,* and *they* are used in texts written in the third person.

Transitional Words and Phrases
There are approximately 200 transitional words and phrases that are commonly used in the English language. Below are lists of common transition words and phrases.

Time	**Example**	**Compare**	**Contrast**	**Addition**	**Logical Relationships**	**Steps**
After	for example	likewise	however	And	if	first
before	in fact	also	yet	Also	then	second
during	for instance		but	furthermore	therefore	last
in the middle				Moreover	as a result	
					since	

Transitional words and phrases are important writing devices. They connect sentences and paragraphs. Transitional words and phrases help writing to make more sense. They provide clearer meaning to readers.

Identifying Rhetorical Strategies

Rhetoric refers to an author's use of particular strategies, appeals, and devices to persuade an intended audience. The more effective the use of rhetoric, the more likely the audience will be persuaded.

Determining an Author's Point of View
A *rhetorical strategy*—also referred to as a *rhetorical mode*—is the structural way an author chooses to present his/her argument. Though the terms noted below are similar to the organizational structures noted earlier, these strategies do not imply that the entire text follows the approach. For example, a cause and effect organizational structure is solely that, nothing more. A persuasive text may use cause and effect as a strategy to convey a singular point. Thus, an argument may include several of the strategies as the author strives to convince his or her audience to take action or accept a different point

of view. It's important that readers are able to identify an author's thesis and position on the topic in order to be able to identify the careful construction through which the author speaks to the reader. The following are some of the more common rhetorical strategies:

- Cause and effect—establishing a logical correlation or causation between two ideas
- Classification/division—the grouping of similar items together or division of something into parts
- Comparison/contrast—the distinguishing of similarities/differences to expand on an idea
- Definition—used to clarify abstract ideas, unfamiliar concepts, or to distinguish one idea from another
- Description—use of vivid imagery, active verbs, and clear adjectives to explain ideas
- Exemplification—the use of examples to explain an idea
- Narration—anecdotes or personal experience to present or expand on a concept
- Problem/Solution—presentation of a problem or problems, followed by proposed solution(s)

Rhetorical Strategies and Devices

A *rhetorical device* is the phrasing and presentation of an idea that reinforces and emphasizes a point in an argument. A rhetorical device is often quite memorable. One of the more famous uses of a rhetorical device is in John F. Kennedy's 1961 inaugural address: "Ask not what your country can do for you, ask what you can do for your country." The contrast of ideas presented in the phrasing is an example of the rhetorical device of antimetabole. Some other common examples are provided below, but test takers should be aware that this is not a complete list.

Device	**Definition**	**Example**
Allusion	A reference to a famous person, event, or significant literary text as a form of significant comparison	"We are apt to shut our eyes against a painful truth, and listen to the song of that siren till she transforms us into beasts." Patrick Henry
Anaphora	The repetition of the same words at the beginning of successive words, phrases, or clauses, designed to emphasize an idea	"We shall not flag or fail. We shall go on to the end. We shall fight in France, we shall fight on the seas and oceans, we shall fight with growing confidence ... we shall fight in the fields and in the streets, we shall fight in the hills. We shall never surrender." Winston Churchill
Understatement	A statement meant to portray a situation as less important than it actually is to create an ironic effect	"The war in the Pacific has not necessarily developed in Japan's favor." Emperor Hirohito, surrendering Japan in World War II
Parallelism	A syntactical similarity in a structure or series of structures used for impact of an idea, making it memorable	"A penny saved is a penny earned." Ben Franklin
Rhetorical question	A question posed that is not answered by the writer though there is a desired response, most often designed to emphasize a point	"Can anyone look at our reduced standing in the world today and say, 'Let's have four more years of this?'" Ronald Reagan

Understanding Methods Used to Appeal to a Specific Audience

Rhetorical Appeals

In an argument or persuasive text, an author will strive to sway readers to an opinion or conclusion. To be effective, an author must consider his or her intended audience. Although an author may write text for a general audience, he or she will use methods of appeal or persuasion to convince that audience. Aristotle asserted that there were three methods or modes by which a person could be persuaded. These are referred to as *rhetorical appeals*.

The three main types of rhetorical appeals are shown in the following graphic.

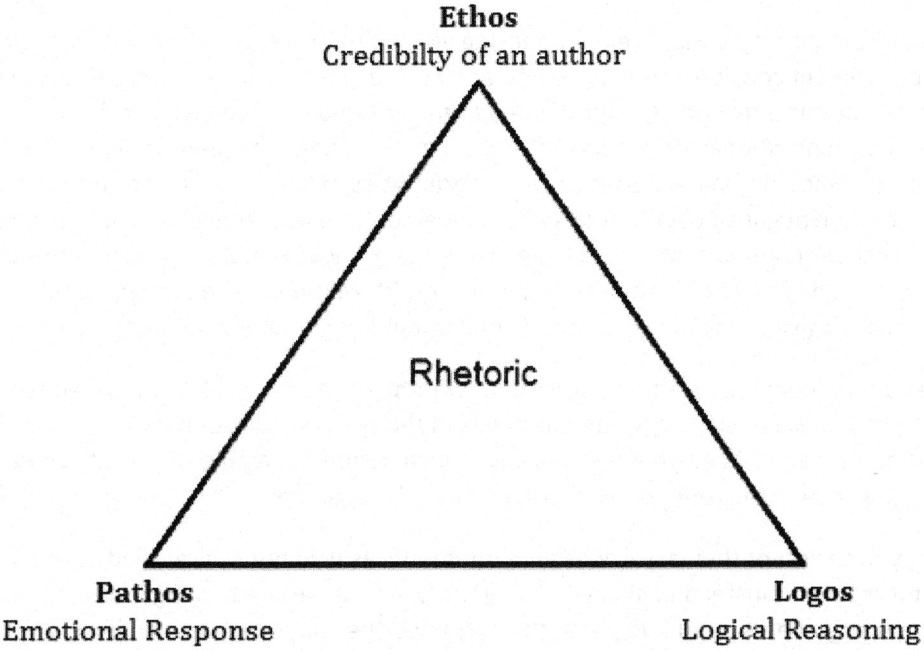

Ethos, also referred to as an *ethical appeal*, is an appeal to the audience's perception of the writer as credible (or not), based on their examination of their ethics and who the writer is, his/her experience or incorporation of relevant information, or his/her argument. For example, authors may present testimonials to bolster their arguments. The reader who critically examines the veracity of the testimonials and the credibility of those giving the testimony will be able to determine if the author's use of testimony is valid to his or her argument. In turn, this will help the reader determine if the author's thesis is valid. An author's careful and appropriate use of technical language can create an overall knowledgeable effect and, in turn, act as a convincing vehicle when it comes to credibility. Overuse of technical language, however, may create confusion in readers and obscure an author's overall intent.

Pathos, also referred to as a *pathetic* or *emotional appeal*, is an appeal to the audience's sense of identity, self-interest, or emotions. A critical reader will notice when the author is appealing to pathos through anecdotes and descriptions that elicit an emotion such as anger or pity. Readers should also beware of factual information that uses generalization to appeal to the emotions. While it's tempting to believe an author is the source of truth in his or her text, an author who presents factual information as universally true, consistent throughout time, and common to all groups is using *generalization*. Authors who exclusively use generalizations without specific facts and credible sourcing are attempting to sway readers solely through emotion.

Logos, also referred to as a *logical appeal*, is an appeal to the audience's ability to see and understand the logic in a claim offered by the writer. A critical reader has to be able to evaluate an author's arguments for validity of reasoning and for sufficiency when it comes to argument.

Counterarguments and Evaluating Arguments

If an author presents a differing opinion or a counterargument in order to refute it, the reader should consider how and why this information is being presented. It is meant to strengthen the original argument and shouldn't be confused with the author's intended conclusion, but it should also be considered in the reader's final evaluation.

Authors can also use bias if they ignore the opposing viewpoint or present their side in an unbalanced way. A strong argument considers the opposition and finds a way to refute it. Critical readers should look for an unfair or one-sided presentation of the argument and be skeptical, as a bias may be present. Even if this bias is unintentional, if it exists in the writing, the reader should be wary of the validity of the argument. Readers should also look for the use of stereotypes, which refer to specific groups. Stereotypes are often negative connotations about a person or place, and should always be avoided. When a critical reader finds stereotypes in a piece of writing, they should be critical of the argument, and consider the validity of anything the author presents. Stereotypes reveal a flaw in the writer's thinking and may suggest a lack of knowledge or understanding about the subject.

In general, readers should always heed attention to whether an author's ideas or stated facts are relevant to the argument or counterargument posed in the reading. Those that are irrelevant can cloud the argument or weaken it. In much the same way, critical readers are able to identify whether statements in a reading strengthen or weaken the author's argument.

Authors want you to accept their assertions and arguments as true but critical readers evaluate the strength of the argument instead of simply taking it at face value and accepting it as the truth or only point of view. All arguments need two parts: the claim and the supporting evidence or rationale. The claim *is* the argument. It asserts an opinion, idea, point of view, or conclusion. The supporting evidence is the rationale, assumptions, beliefs, as well as the factual evidence in support of the stated claim. The supporting evidence is what gives readers the information necessary to accept or reject the stated claim. Critical readers should assess the argument in its entirety by evaluating the claims and conclusions themselves, the process of reasoning, and the accuracy of the evidence. For example, arguments are weaker and should be skeptically considered when the supporting evidence is highly opinionated, biased, or derived from sources that are not credible. Authors should cite where statistics and other stated facts were found. Lastly, the support for a claim should be pertinent to it and consistent with the other statements and evidence.

Opinions, Facts, and Fallacies

As mentioned previously, authors write with a purpose. They adjust their writing for an intended audience. It is the readers' responsibility to comprehend the writing style or purpose of the author. When readers understand a writer's purpose, they can then form their own thoughts about the text(s) regardless of whether their thoughts are the same as or different from the author's. The following section will examine different writing tactics that authors use, such as facts versus opinions, bias and stereotypes, appealing to the readers' emotions, and fallacies (including false analogies, circular reasoning, false dichotomy, and overgeneralization).

<u>Facts Versus Opinions</u>
Readers need to be aware of the writer's purpose to help discern facts and opinions within texts. A *fact* is a piece of information that is true. It can either prove or disprove claims or arguments presented in texts. Facts cannot be changed or altered. For example, the statement: *Abraham Lincoln was assassinated on April 15, 1865*, is a fact. The date and related events cannot be altered.

Authors not only present facts in their writing to support or disprove their claim(s), but they may also express their opinions. Authors may use factsto support their own opinions, especially in a persuasive text; however, that does not make their opinions facts. An *opinion* is a belief or view formed about something that is not necessarily based on the truth. Opinions often express authors' personal feelings about a subject and use words like *believe, think,* or *feel.* For example, the statement: *Abraham Lincoln was the best president who has ever lived*, expresses the writer's opinion. Not all writers or readers agree or disagree with the statement. Therefore, the statement can be altered or adjusted to express opposing or supporting beliefs, such as "Abraham Lincoln was the worst president who has ever lived" or "I also think Abraham Lincoln was a great president."

When authors include facts and opinions in their writing, readers may be less influenced by the text(s). Readers need to be conscious of the distinction between facts and opinions while going through texts. Not only should the intended audience be vigilant in following authors' thoughts versus valid information, readers need to check the source of the facts presented. Facts should have reliable sources derived from credible outlets like almanacs, encyclopedias, medical journals, and so on.

<u>Bias and Stereotypes</u>

Not only can authors state facts or opinions in their writing, they sometimes intentionally or unintentionally show bias or portray a stereotype. A *bias* is when someone demonstrates a prejudice in favor of or against something or someone in an unfair manner. When an author is biased in his or her writing, readers should be skeptical despite the fact that the author's bias may be correct. For example, two athletes competed for the same position. One athlete is related to the coach and is a mediocre athlete, while the other player excels and deserves the position. The coach chose the less talented player who is related to him for the position. This is a biased decision because it favors someone in an unfair way.

Similar to a bias, a *stereotype* shows favoritism or opposition but toward a specific group or place. Stereotypes create an oversimplified or overgeneralized idea about a certain group, person, or place. For example,

> Women are horrible drivers.

This statement basically labels *all* women as horrible drivers. While there may be some terrible female drivers, the stereotype implies that *all* women are bad drivers when, in fact, not *all* women are. While many readers are aware of several vile ethnic, religious, and cultural stereotypes, audiences should be cautious of authors' flawed assumptions because they can be less obvious than the despicable examples that are unfortunately pervasive in society.

Appealing to the Readers' Emotions

Authors write to captivate the attention of their readers. Oftentimes, authors will appeal to their readers' emotions to convince or persuade their audience, especially in when trying to win weak arguments that lack factual evidence. Authors may tell sob stories or use bandwagon approaches in their writing to tap into the readers' emotions. For example, "Everyone is voting yes" or "He only has two months to live" are statements that can tug at the heartstrings of readers. Authors may use other tactics, such as name-calling or advertising, to lead their readers into believing something is true or false. These emotional pleas are clear signs that the authors do not have a favorable point and that they are trying to distract the readers from the fact that their argument is factually weak.

Fallacies

A fallacy is a mistaken belief or faulty reasoning, otherwise known as a *logical fallacy.* It is important for readers to recognize logical fallacies because they discredit the author's message. Readers should continuously self-question as they go through a text to identify logical fallacies. Readers cannot simply complacently take information at face value. There are six common types of logical *fallacies:*

9. 1. False analogy
10. 2. Circular reasoning
11. 3. False dichotomy
12. 4. Overgeneralization
13. 5. Slippery slope
14. 6.Hasty generalization

Each of the six logical fallacies are reviewed individually.

False Analogy
A *false analogy* is when the author assumes two objects or events are alike in all aspects despite the fact that they may be vastly different. Authors intend on making unfamiliar objects relatable to convince readers of something. For example, the letters *A* and *E* are both vowels; therefore, *A = E*. Readers cannot assume that because *A* and *E* are both vowels that they perform the same function in words or independently. If authors tell readers, *A = E*, then that is a false analogy. While this is a simple example, other false analogies may be less obvious.

Circular reasoning
Circular reasoning is when the reasoning is decided based upon the outcome or conclusion and then vice versa. Basically, those who use circular reasoning start out with the argument and then use false logic to try to prove it, and then, in turn, the reasoning supports the conclusion in one big circular pattern. For example, consider the two thoughts, "I don't have time to get organized" and "My disorganization is costing me time." Which is the argument? What is the conclusion? If there is not time to get organized, will more time be spent later trying to find whatever is needed? In turn, if so much time is spent looking for things, there is not time to get organized. The cycle keeps going in an endless series. One problem affects the other; therefore, there is a circular pattern of reasoning.

False dichotomy
A *false dichotomy,* also known as a false dilemma, is when the author tries to make readers believe that there are only two options to choose from when, in fact, there are more. The author creates a false sense of the situation because he or she wants the readers to believe that his or her claim is the most logical choice. If the author does not present the readers with options, then the author is purposefully limiting what readers may believe. In turn, the author hopes that readers will believe that his or her point of view is the most sensible choice. For example, in the statement: *you either love running, or you are lazy,* the fallacy lies in the options of loving to run or being lazy. Even though both statements do not necessarily have to be true, the author tries to make one option seem more appealing than the other.

Overgeneralization

An *overgeneralization* is a logical fallacy that occurs when authors write something so extreme that it cannot be proved or disproved. Words like *all, never, most,* and *few* are commonly used when an overgeneralization is being made. For example,

> All kids are crazy when they eat sugar; therefore, my son will not have a cupcake at the birthday party.

Not *all* kids are crazy when they eat sugar, but the extreme statement can influence the readers' points of view on the subject. Readers need to be wary of overgeneralizations in texts because authors may try to sneak them in to sway the readers' opinions.

Slippery slope

A *slippery slope* is when an author implies that something will inevitably happen as a result of another action. A slippery slope may or may not be true, even though the order of events or gradations may seem logical. For example, in the children's book *If You Give a Mouse a Cookie*, the author goes off on tangents such as "If you give a mouse a cookie, he will ask for some milk. When you give him the milk, he'll probably ask you for a straw." The mouse in the story follows a series of logical events as a result of a previous action. The slippery slope continues on and on throughout the story. Even though the mouse made logical decisions, it very well could have made a different choice, changing the direction of the story.

Hasty generalization

A *hasty generalization* is when the reader comes to a conclusion without reviewing or analyzing all the evidence. It is never a good idea to make a decision without all the information, which is why hasty generalizations are considered fallacies. For example, if two friends go to a hairdresser and give the hairdresser a positive recommendation, that does not necessarily mean that a new client will have the same experience. Two referrals is not quite enough information to form an educated and well-formed conclusion.

Overall, readers should carefully review and analyze authors' arguments to identify logical fallacies and come to sensible conclusions.

Drawing Conclusions

When drawing conclusions about texts or passages, readers should do two main things: 1) Use the information that they already know and 2) Use the information they have learned from the text or passage. Authors write with an intended purpose, and it is the readers' responsibility to understand and form logical conclusions of authors' ideas. It is important to remember that the readers' conclusions should be supported by information directly from the text. Readers cannot simply form conclusions based off of only information they already know.

There are several ways readers can draw conclusions from authors' ideas and points to consider when doing so, such as text evidence, text credibility, and directly stated information versus implications.

Text Evidence

Text evidence is the information readers find in a text or passage that supports the main idea or point(s) in a story. In turn, text evidence can help readers draw conclusions about the text or passage. The information should be taken directly from the text or passage and placed in quotation marks. Text evidence provides readers with information to support ideas about the text or passage so that they simply do not just rely on their own thoughts. Details should be precise, descriptive, and factual. Statistics are a great piece of text evidencebecause it provides readers with exact numbers and not just a generalization. For example, instead of saying "Asia has a larger population than Europe," authors could provide detailed information such as "In Asia there are over 7 billion people, whereas in Europe there are a little over 750 million." More definitive information provides better evidence to readers to help support their conclusions about texts or passages.

Text Credibility

Credible sources are important when drawing conclusions because readers need to be able to trust what they are reading. Authors should always use credible sources to help gain the trust of their readers. A text is *credible* when it is believable and the author is objective and unbiased. If readers do not trust authors' words, they may simply dismiss the text completely. For example, if an author writes a persuasive essay, he or she is outwardly trying to sway readers' opinions to align with his or her own, providing readers with the liberty to do what they please with the text. Readers may agree or disagree with the author, which may, in turn, lead them to believe that the author is credible or not credible. Also, readers should keep in mind the source of the text. If readers review a journal about astronomy, would a more reliable source be a NASA employee or a plumber? Overall, text credibility is important when drawing conclusions because readers want reliable sources that support the decisions they have made about the author's ideas.

Directly Stated Information Versus Implications

Engaged readers should constantly self-question while reviewing texts to help them form conclusions. Self-questioning is when readers review a paragraph, page, passage, or chapter and ask themselves, "Did I understand what I read?," "What was the main event in this section?," "Where is this taking place?," and so on. Authors can provide clues or pieces of evidence throughout a text or passage to guide readers toward a conclusion. This is why active and engaged readers should read the text or passage in its entirety before forming a definitive conclusion. If readers do not gather all the necessary pieces of evidence, then they may jump to an illogical conclusion.

At times, authors directly state conclusions while others simply imply them. Of course, it is easier if authors outwardly provide conclusions to readers because this does not leave any information open to interpretation. However, implications are things that authors do not directly state but can be assumed based off of information they provided. If authors only imply what may have happened, readers can form a menagerie of ideas for conclusions. For example, in the statement: *Once we heard the sirens, we hunkered down in the storm shelter*, the author does not directly state that there was a tornado, but clues such as "sirens" and "storm shelter" provide insight to the readers to help form that conclusion.

Integration of Information and Ideas from Text Selections

Evaluating and Relating Content Presented in Diverse Formats

Evaluating an Author's Purpose

A reader must be able to evaluate the argument or point the author is trying to make and determine if it is adequately supported. The first step is to determine the main idea. The main idea is what the author wants to say about a specific topic. The next step is to locate the supporting details. An author uses supporting details to illustrate the main idea. These are the details that provide evidence or examples to help make a point. Supporting details often appear in the form of quotations, paraphrasing, or analysis. Test takers should then examine the text to make sure the author connects details and analysis to the main point. These steps are crucial to understanding the text and evaluating how well the author presents his or her argument and evidence.

The following graphic demonstrates the connection between the main idea and the supporting details:

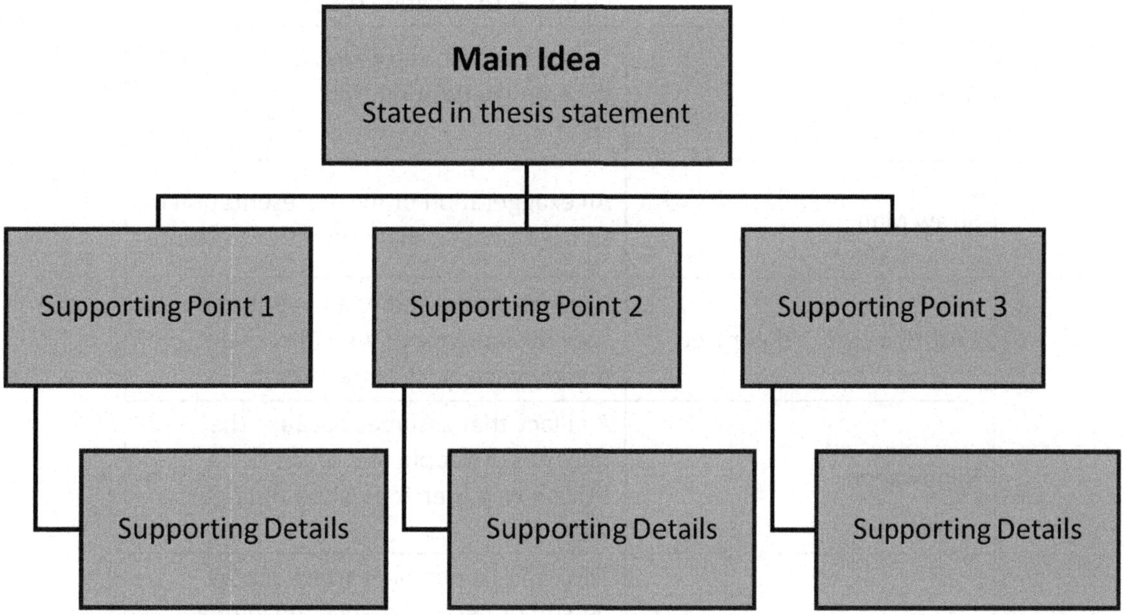

<u>Evaluating Evidence</u>

It is important to evaluate the author's supporting details to be sure that they are credible, provide evidence of the author's point, and directly support the main idea. Critical readers examine the facts used to support an author's argument and check those facts against other sources to be sure the facts are correct. They also check the validity of the sources used to be sure those sources are credible, academic, and/or peer- reviewed. A strong argument uses valid, measurable facts to support ideas.

<u>Identifying False Statements</u>

A reader must also be able to identify any *logical fallacies*—logically-flawed statements—that an author may make as those fallacies impact the validity and veracity of the author's claims.

Some of the more common fallacies are shown in the following chart.

Fallacy	Definition
Slippery Slope	A fallacy that is built on the idea that a particular action will lead to a series of events with negative results
Red Herring	The use of an observation or distraction to remove attention from the actual issue
Straw Man	An exaggeration or misrepresentation of an argument so that it is easier to refute
Post Hoc Ergo Propter Hoc	A fallacy that assumes an event to be the consequence of an earlier event merely because it came after it
Bandwagon	A fallacy that assumes because the majority of people feel or believe a certain way then it must be the right way
Ad Hominem	The use of a personal attack on the person or persons associated with a certain argument rather than focusing on the actual argument itself

Readers who are aware of the types of fallacious reasoning are able to weigh the credibility of the author's statements in terms of effective argument. Rhetorical text that contains a myriad of fallacious statements should be considered ineffectual and suspect.

Interpreting Media and Non-Print Text

In the 21st century, rhetoric is evident in a variety of formats. Blogs, vlogs, videos, news footage, advertisements, and live video fill informational feeds, and readers see many shortened images and snapshot texts a day. It's important to note that the majority of these formats use images to appeal to emotion over factual information. Online visuals spread more quickly and are more easily adopted by consumers as fact than printed formats.

Critical readers should be aware that media and non-print text carries some societal weight to the population. In being inundated with pictures and live footage, readers often feel compelled to skip the task of critical reading analysis and accept truth at literal face value. Authors of non-print media are aware of this fact and frequently capitalize on it.

To critically address non-print media requires that the consumer address additional sources and not exclude printed text in order to reach sound conclusions. While it's tempting for consumers to get swept away in the latest viral media, it's important to remember that creators of such have an agenda, and unless the non-print media in question is backed up with sound supporting evidence, any thesis or message cannot be considered valid or factual. Memes, gifs, and looped video cannot tell the whole, truthful story although they may appeal to opinions with which readers already agree. Sharing such non-print media online can precipitate widespread misunderstanding and invariably does.

When presented with non-print media, critical readers should consider these bits of information as teasers to be investigated for accuracy and veracity. Of course, certain non-print media exists solely for entertainment, but the critical reader should be able to separate out what's generalized for entertainment's sake and what's presented for further verification, before blindly accepting the message. Increasingly, this has become more difficult for readers to do, only because of the onslaught of information to which they are exposed.

If a reader is not to fall prey to strong imagery and non-print media, he or she will need to fact-check. This, of course, requires time and attention on the reader's part, and in current culture, taking the time to fact-check seems counterproductive. However, in order to maintain credibility themselves, readers must be able to evaluate multiple sources of information across media formats and be able to identify the emotional appeal used in the smaller sound bites of non-print media. Readers must view with a discerning eye, listen with a questioning ear, and think with a critical mind.

Understanding the Characteristics of Literary Genres

Classifying literature involves an understanding of the concept of genre. A *genre* is a category of literature that possesses similarities in style and in characteristics. Based on form and structure, there are four basic genres.

Fictional Prose

Fictional prose consists of fictional works written in standard form with a natural flow of speech and without poetic structure. Fictional prose primarily utilizes grammatically complete sentences and a paragraph structure to convey its message.

Drama

Drama is fiction that is written to be performed in a variety of media, intended to be performed for an audience, and structured for that purpose. It might be composed using poetry or prose, often straddling the elements of both in what actors are expected to present. Action and dialogue are the tools used in drama to tell the story.

Poetry

Poetry is fiction in verse that has a unique focus on the rhythm of language and focuses on intensity of feeling. It is not an entire story, though it may tell one; it is compact in form and in function. Poetry can be considered as a poet's brief word picture for a reader. Poetic structure is primarily composed of lines and stanzas. Together, poetic structure and devices are the methods that poets use to lead readers to feeling an effect and, ultimately, to the interpretive message.

Literary Nonfiction

Literary nonfiction is prose writing that is based on current or past real events or real people and includes straightforward accounts as well as those that offer opinions on facts or factual events. The Praxis exam distinguishes between *literary nonfiction*—a form of writing that incorporates literary styles and techniques to create factually-based narratives—and informational texts, which will be addressed in the next section.

Identifying Characteristics of Major Forms Within Each Genre

Fictional Prose

Fiction written in prose can be further broken down into *fiction genres*—types of fiction. Some of the more common genres of fiction are as follows:

- Classical Fiction—a work of fiction considered timeless in its message or theme, remaining noteworthy and meaningful over decades or centuries—e.g., Charlotte *Brontë's* Jane Eyre, Mark Twain's Adventures of Huckleberry Finn

- Fables— short fiction that generally features animals, fantastic creatures, or other forces within nature that assume human-like characters and has a moral lesson for the reader—e.g., Aesop's Fables

- Fairy tales—children's stories with magical characters in imaginary, enchanted lands, usually depicting a struggle between good and evil, a sub-genre of folklore—e.g., Hans Christian Anderson's The Little Mermaid, Cinderella by the Brothers Grimm

- Fantasy—fiction with magic or supernatural elements and plot that cannot occur in the real world, sometimes involving medieval elements in language, usually includes some form of sorcery or witchcraft and sometimes set on a different world—e.g., J.R.R. Tolkien's The Hobbit, J.K. Rowling's Harry Potter and the Sorcerer's Stone, George R.R. Martin's A Game of Thrones

- Folklore—types of fiction passed down from oral tradition, stories indigenous to a particular region or culture, with a local flavor in tone, designed to help humans cope with their condition in life and validate cultural traditions, beliefs, and customs—e.g., William Laughead's Paul Bunyan and The Blue Ox, the Buddhist story of "The Banyan Deer"

- Mythology—closely related to folklore but more widespread, features mystical, otherworldly characters and addresses the basic question of why and how humans exist, relies heavily on allegory and features gods or heroes captured in some sort of struggle—e.g., Greek myths, Genesis I and II in the Bible, Arthurian legends

- Science fiction—fiction that uses the principle of extrapolation—loosely defined as a form of prediction—to imagine future realities and problems of the human experience—e.g., Robert Heinlein's Stranger in a Strange Land, Ayn Rand's Anthem, Isaac Asimov's I, Robot, Philip K. Dick's Do Androids Dream of Electric Sheep?

- Short stories—short works of prose fiction with fully-developed themes and characters, focused on mood, generally developed with a single plot, with a short period of time for settings—e.g., Edgar Allan Poe's "Fall of the House of Usher," Shirley Jackson's "The Lottery," Isaac Bashevis Singer's "Gimpel the Fool"

Drama

Drama refers to a form of literature written for the purpose of performance for an audience. Like prose fiction, drama has several genres. The following are the most common ones:

Comedy—a humorous play designed to amuse and entertain, often with an emphasis on the common person's experience, generally resolved in a positive way—e.g., Richard Sheridan's School for Scandal, Shakespeare's Taming of the Shrew, Neil Simon's The Odd Couple

History—a play based on recorded history where the fate of a nation or kingdom is at the core of the conflict—e.g., Christopher Marlowe's *Edward II*, Shakespeare's *King Richard III*, Arthur Miller's *The Crucible*

Tragedy—a serious play that often involves the downfall of the protagonist, in modern tragedies, the protagonist is not necessarily in a position of power or authority—e.g., Jean Racine's Phèdre, Arthur Miller's *Death of a Salesman*, John Steinbeck's *Of Mice and Men*

Melodrama—a play that is emphasizes heightened emotion and sensationalism, generally with stereotypical characters in exaggerated or realistic situations and with moral polarization—e.g., Jean-Jacques Rousseau's *Pygmalion*

Tragi-comedy—a play that has elements of both tragedy—a character experiencing a tragic loss—and comedy—the resolution is often positive with no clear distinctive mood for either—e.g., Shakespeare's *The Merchant of Venice*, Anton Chekhov's *The Cherry Orchard*

Poetry

The genre of *poetry* refers to literary works that focus on the expression of feelings and ideas through the use of structure and linguistic rhythm to create a desired effect.

Different poetic structures and devices are used to create the various major forms of poetry. Some of the most common forms are discussed in the following chart.

Type	**Poetic Structure**	**Example**
Ballad	A poem or song passed down orally which tells a story and in English tradition usually uses an ABAB or ABCB rhyme scheme	William Butler Yeats' "The Ballad Of Father O'Hart"
Epic	A long poem from ancient oral tradition which narrates the story of a legendary or heroic protagonist	Homer's The Odyssey Virgil's The Aeneid
Haiku	A Japanese poem of three unrhymed lines with five, seven, and five syllables (in English) with nature as a common subject matter	Matsuo Bashō An old silent pond... A frog jumps into the pond, splash! Silence again.
Limerick	A five-line poem written in an AABBA rhyme scheme, with a witty focus	From Edward Lear's Book of Nonsense— "There was a Young Person of Smyrna Whose grandmother threatened to burn her..."
Ode	A formal lyric poem that addresses and praises a person, place, thing, or idea	Edna St. Vincent Millay's "Ode To Silence"
Sonnet	A fourteen-line poem written in iambic pentameter	Shakespeare's Sonnets 18 and 130

Literary nonfiction

Nonfiction works are best characterized by their subject matter, which must be factual and real, describing true life experiences. There are several common types of literary non-fiction.

Biography

A *biography* is a work written about a real person (historical or currently living). It involves factual accounts of the person's life, often in a re-telling of those events based on available, researched factual information. The re-telling and dialogue, especially if related within quotes, must be accurate and reflect reliable sources. A biography reflects the time and place in which the person lived, with the goal of creating an understanding of the person and his/her human experience. Examples of well-known biographies include *The Life of Samuel Johnson* by James Boswell and *Steve Jobs* by Walter Isaacson.

Autobiography

An *autobiography* is a factual account of a person's life written by that person. It may contain some or all of the same elements as a biography, but the author is the subject matter. An autobiography will be told in first person narrative. Examples of well-known autobiographies in literature include *Night* by Elie Wiesel and *Margaret Thatcher: The Autobiography* by Margaret Thatcher.

Memoir
A *memoir* is a historical account of a person's life and experiences written by one who has personal, intimate knowledge of the information. The line between memoir, autobiography, and biography is often muddled, but generally speaking, a memoir covers a specific timeline of events as opposed to the other forms of nonfiction. A memoir is less all-encompassing. It is also less formal in tone and tends to focus on the emotional aspect of the presented timeline of events. Some examples of memoirs in literature include *Angela's Ashes* by Frank McCourt and *All Creatures Great and Small* by James Herriot.

Journalism
Some forms of *journalism* can fall into the category of literary non-fiction—e.g., travel writing, nature writing, sports writing, the interview, and sometimes, the essay. Some examples include Elizabeth Kolbert's "The Lost World, in the Annals of Extinction series for *The New Yorker* and Gary Smith's "Ali and His Entourage" for *Sports Illustrated.*

Identifying Literary Contexts

Understanding that works of literature emerged either because of a particular context—or perhaps despite a context—is key to analyzing them effectively.

<u>Historical Context</u>
The *historical context* of a piece of literature can refer to the time period, setting, or conditions of living at the time it was written as well as the context of the work. For example, Hawthorne's *The Scarlet Letter* was published in 1850, though the setting of the story is 1642-1649. Historically, then, when Hawthorne wrote his novel, the United States found itself at odds as the beginnings of a potential Civil War were in view. Thus, the historical context is potentially significant as it pertains to the ideas of traditions and values, which Hawthorne addresses in his story of Hester Prynne in the era of Puritanism.

<u>Cultural Context</u>
The *cultural context* of a piece of literature refers to cultural factors, such as the beliefs, religions, and customs that surround and are in a work of literature. The Puritan's beliefs, religion, and customs in Hawthorne's novel would be significant as they are at the core of the plot—the reason Hester wears the A and why Arthur kills himself. The customs of people in the Antebellum Period, though not quite as restrictive, were still somewhat similar. This would impact how the audience of the time received the novel.

<u>Literary Context</u>
Literary context refers to the consideration of the genre, potentially at the time the work was written. In 1850, Realism and Romanticism were the driving forces in literature in the U.S., with depictions of life as it was at the time in which the work was written or the time it was written *about* as well as some works celebrating the beauty of nature. Thus, an audience in Hawthorne's time would have been well satisfied with the elements of both offered in the text. They would have been looking for details about everyday things and people (Realism), but they also would appreciate his approach to description of nature and the focus on the individual (American Romanticism). The contexts would be significant as they would pertain to evaluating the work against those criteria.

Here are some questions to use when considering context:

When was the text written?
What was society like at the time the text was written, or what was it like, given the work's identified time period?
Who or what influenced the writer?
What political or social influences might there have been?
What influences may there have been in the genre that may have affected the writer?

Additionally, test takers should familiarize themselves with literary periods such as Old and Middle English, American Colonial, American Renaissance, American Naturalistic, and British and American Modernist and Post-Modernist movements. Most students of literature will have had extensive exposure to these literary periods in history, and while it is not necessary to recognize every major literary work on sight and associate that work to its corresponding movement or cultural context, the test taker should be familiar enough with the historical and cultural significance of each test passage in order to be able to address test questions correctly.

The following brief description of some literary contexts and their associated literary examples follows. It is not an all-inclusive list. The test taker should read each description, then follow up with independent study to clarify each movement, its context, its most familiar authors, and their works.

Metaphysical Poetry
Metaphysical poetry is the descriptor applied to 17th century poets whose poetry emphasized the lyrical quality of their work. These works contain highly creative poetic conceits or metaphoric comparisons between two highly dissimilar things or ideas. Metaphysical poetry is characterized by highly prosaic language and complicated, often layered, metaphor.

Poems such as John Donne's "The Flea," Andrew Marvell's "To His Coy Mistress," George Herbert's "The Collar," Henry Vaughan's "The World," and Richard Crashaw's "A Song" are associated with this type of poetry.

British Romanticism
British Romanticism was a cultural and literary movement within Europe that developed at the end of the 18th century and extended into the 19th century. It occurred partly in response to aristocratic, political, and social norms and partly in response to the Industrial Revolution of the day. Characterized by intense emotion, major literary works of British Romanticism embrace the idea of aestheticism and the beauty of nature. Literary works exalted folk customs and historical art and encouraged spontaneity of artistic endeavor. The movement embraced the heroic ideal and the concept that heroes would raise the quality of society.

Authors who are classified as British Romantics include Samuel Taylor Coleridge, John Keats, George Byron, Mary Shelley, Percy Bysshe Shelley, and William Blake. Well-known works include Samuel Taylor Coleridge's "Kubla Khan," John Keats' "Ode on a Grecian Urn," George Byron's "Childe Harold's Pilgrimage," Mary Shelley's *Frankenstein*, Percy Bysshe Shelley's "Ode to the West Wind," and William Blake's "The Tyger."

American Romanticism

American Romanticism occurred within the American literary scene beginning early in the 19th century. While many aspects were similar to British Romanticism, it is further characterized as having gothic aspects and the idea that individualism was to be encouraged. It also embraced the concept of the *noble savage*—the idea that indigenous culture uncorrupted by civilization is better than advanced society.

Well-known authors and works include Nathanial Hawthorne's *The House of the Seven Gables*, Edgar Allan Poe's "The Raven" and "The Cask of Amontillado," Emily Dickinson's "I Felt a Funeral in My Brain" and James Fenimore Cooper's *The Last of the Mohicans.*

Transcendentalism

Transcendentalism was a movement that applied to a way of thinking that developed within the United States, specifically New England, around 1836. While this way of thinking originally employed philosophical aspects, transcendentalism spread to all forms of art, literature, and even to the ways people chose to live. It was born out of a reaction to traditional rationalism and purported concepts such as a higher divinity, feminism, humanitarianism, and communal living. Transcendentalism valued intuition, self-reliance, and the idea that human nature was inherently good.

Well-known authors include Ralph Waldo Emerson, Henry David Thoreau, Louisa May Alcott, and Ellen Sturgis Hooper. Works include Ralph Waldo Emerson's "Self-Reliance" and "Uriel," Henry David Thoreau's *Walden* and *Civil Disobedience*, Louisa May Alcott's *Little Women*, and Ellen Sturgis Hooper's "I Slept, and Dreamed that Life was Beauty."

The Harlem Renaissance

The Harlem Renaissance is the descriptor given to the cultural, artistic, and social boom that developed in Harlem, New York, at the beginning of the 20th century, spanning the 1920s and 1930s. Originally termed *The New Negro Movement*, it emphasized African-American urban cultural expression and migration across the United States. It had strong roots in African-American Christianity, discourse, and intellectualism. The Harlem Renaissance heavily influenced the development of music and fashion as well. Its singular characteristic was to embrace Pan-American culturalisms; however, strong themes of the slavery experience and African-American folk traditions also emerged. A hallmark of the Harlem Renaissance was that it laid the foundation for the future Civil Rights Movement in the United States.

Well-known authors and works include Zora Neale Hurston's *Their Eyes Were Watching God*, Richard Wright's *Native Son*, Langston Hughes' "I, Too," and James Weldon Johnson's "God's Trombones: Seven Negro Sermons in Verse" and *The Book of American Negro Poetry.*

Practice Questions

The next four questions are based on the following passage.

Smoking is Terrible

Smoking tobacco products is terribly destructive. A single cigarette contains over 4,000 chemicals, including 43 known carcinogens and 400 deadly toxins. Some of the most dangerous ingredients include tar, carbon monoxide, formaldehyde, ammonia, arsenic, and DDT. Smoking can cause numerous types of cancer including throat, mouth, nasal cavity, esophagus, stomach, pancreas, kidney, bladder, and cervical.

Cigarettes contain a drug called nicotine, one of the most addictive substances known to man. Addiction is defined as a compulsion to seek the substance despite negative consequences. According to the National Institute of Drug Abuse, nearly 35 million smokers expressed a desire to quit smoking in 2015; however, more than 85 percent of those addicts will not achieve their goal. Almost all smokers regret picking up that first cigarette. You would be wise to learn from their mistake if you have not yet started smoking.

According to the U.S. Department of Health and Human Services, 16 million people in the United States presently suffer from a smoking-related condition and nearly nine million suffer from a serious smoking-related illness. According to the Centers for Disease Control and Prevention (CDC), tobacco products cause nearly six million deaths per year. This number is projected to rise to over eight million deaths by 2030. Smokers, on average, die ten years earlier than their nonsmoking peers.

In the United States, local, state, and federal governments typically tax tobacco products, which leads to high prices. Nicotine addicts sometimes pay more for a pack of cigarettes than for a few gallons of gas. Additionally, smokers tend to stink. The smell of smoke is all-consuming and creates a pervasive nastiness. Smokers also risk staining their teeth and fingers with yellow residue from the tar.

Smoking is deadly, expensive, and socially unappealing. Clearly, smoking is not worth the risks.

1. Which of the following best describes the passage?
   a. Narrative
   b. Persuasive
   c. Expository
   d. Technical

2. Which of the following statements most accurately summarizes the passage?
   a. Almost all smokers regret picking up that first cigarette.
   b. Tobacco is deadly, expensive, and socially unappealing, and smokers would be much better off kicking the addiction.
   c. In the United States, local, state, and federal governments typically tax tobacco products, which leads to high prices.
   d. Tobacco products shorten smokers' lives by ten years and kill more than six million people per year.

3. The author would be most likely to agree with which of the following statements?

a. Smokers should only quit cold turkey and avoid all nicotine cessation devices.

b. Other substances are more addictive than tobacco.

c. Smokers should quit for whatever reason that gets them to stop smoking.

d. People who want to continue smoking should advocate for a reduction in tobacco product taxes.

4. Which of the following represents an opinion statement on the part of the author?

a. According to the Centers for Disease Control and Prevention (CDC), tobacco products cause nearly six million deaths per year.

b. Nicotine addicts sometimes pay more for a pack of cigarettes than a few gallons of gas.

c. They also risk staining their teeth and fingers with yellow residue from the tar.

d. Additionally, smokers tend to stink. The smell of smoke is all-consuming and creates a pervasive nastiness.

The next three questions are based on the following passage.

George Washington emerged out of the American Revolution as an unlikely champion of liberty. On June 14, 1775, the Second Continental Congress created the Continental Army, and John Adams, serving in the Congress, nominated Washington to be its first commander. Washington fought under the British during the French and Indian War, and his experience and prestige proved instrumental to the American war effort. Washington provided invaluable leadership, training, and strategy during the Revolutionary War. He emerged from the war as the embodiment of liberty and freedom from tyranny.

After vanquishing the heavily favored British forces, Washington could have pronounced himself as the autocratic leader of the former colonies without any opposition, but he famously refused and returned to his Mount Vernon plantation. His restraint proved his commitment to the fledgling state's republicanism. Washington was later unanimously elected as the first American president. But it is Washington's farewell address that cemented his legacy as a visionary worthy of study.

In 1796, President Washington issued his farewell address by public letter. Washington enlisted his good friend, Alexander Hamilton, in drafting his most famous address. The letter expressed Washington's faith in the Constitution and rule of law. He encouraged his fellow Americans to put aside partisan differences and establish a national union. Washington warned Americans against meddling in foreign affairs and entering military alliances. Additionally, he stated his opposition to national political parties, which he considered partisan and counterproductive.

Americans would be wise to remember Washington's farewell, especially during presidential elections when politics hits a fever pitch. They might want to question the political institutions that were not planned by the Founding Fathers, such as the nomination process and political parties themselves.

5. Which of the following statements is logically based on the information contained in the passage above?

a. George Washington's background as a wealthy landholder directly led to his faith in equality, liberty, and democracy.

b. George Washington would have opposed America's involvement in the Second World War.

c. George Washington would not have been able to write as great a farewell address without the assistance of Alexander Hamilton.

d. George Washington would probably not approve of modern political parties.

6. Which of the following statements is the best description of the author's purpose in writing this passage about George Washington?

   a. To caution American voters about being too political during election times because George Washington would not have agreed with holding elections.

   b. To introduce George Washington to readers as a historical figure worthy of study

   c. To inform American voters about a Founding Father's sage advice on a contemporary issue and explain its applicability to modern times

   d. To convince readers that George Washington is a hero of republicanism and liberty

7. In which of the following materials would the author be the most likely to include this passage?

   a. A history textbook

   b. An obituary

   c. A fictional story

   d. A newspaper editorial

The next five questions are based on the following passage.

Christopher Columbus is often credited for discovering America. This is incorrect. First, it is impossible to "discover" something where people already live; however, Christopher Columbus did explore places in the New World that were previously untouched by Europe, so the term “explorer” would be more accurate. Another correction must be made, as well: Christopher Columbus was not the first European explorer to reach the present day Americas! Rather, it was Leif Erikson who first came to the New World and contacted the natives, nearly five hundred years before Christopher Columbus.

Leif Erikson, the son of Erik the Red (a famous Viking outlaw and explorer in his own right), was born in either 970 or 980, depending on which historian you seek. His own family, though, did not raise Leif, which was a Viking tradition. Instead, one of Erik's prisoners taught Leif reading and writing, languages, sailing, and weaponry. At age 12, Leif was considered a man and returned to his family. He killed a man during a dispute shortly after his return, and the council banished the Erikson clan to Greenland.

In 999, Leif left Greenland and traveled to Norway where he would serve as a guard to King Olaf Tryggvason. It was there that he became a convert to Christianity. Leif later tried to return home with the intention of taking supplies and spreading Christianity to Greenland, however his ship was blown off course and he arrived in a strange new land: present day Newfoundland, Canada.

When he finally returned to his adopted homeland Greenland, Leif consulted with a merchant who had also seen the shores of this previously unknown land we now know as Canada. The son of the legendary Viking explorer then gathered a crew of 35 men and set sail. Leif became the first European to touch foot in the New World as he explored present-day Baffin Island and Labrador, Canada. His crew called the land Vinland since it was plentiful with grapes.

During their time in present-day Newfoundland, Leif's expedition made contact with the natives whom they referred to as Skraelings (which translates to "wretched ones" in Norse). There are several secondhand accounts of their meetings. Some contemporaries described trade between the peoples. Other accounts describe clashes where the Skraelings defeated the Viking explorers with long spears, while still others claim the Vikings dominated the natives. Regardless of the circumstances, it seems that the Vikings made contact of some kind. This happened around 1000, nearly five hundred years before Columbus famously sailed the ocean blue.

Eventually, in 1003, Leif set sail for home and arrived at Greenland with a ship full of timber.

In 1020, seventeen years later, the legendary Viking died. Many believe that Leif Erikson should receive more credit for his contributions in exploring the New World.

8. Which of the following best describes how the author generally presents the information?
    a. Chronological order
    b. Comparison-contrast
    c. Cause-effect
    d. Conclusion-premises

9. Which of the following is an opinion, rather than historical fact, expressed by the author?
    a. Leif Erikson was definitely the son of Erik the Red; however, historians debate the year of his birth.
    b. Leif Erikson's crew called the land Vinland since it was plentiful with grapes.
    c. Leif Erikson deserves more credit for his contributions in exploring the New World.
    d. Leif Erikson explored the Americas nearly five hundred years before Christopher Columbus.

10. Which of the following most accurately describes the author's main conclusion?
    a. Leif Erikson is a legendary Viking explorer.
    b. Leif Erikson deserves more credit for exploring America hundreds of years before Columbus.
    c. Spreading Christianity motivated Leif Erikson's expeditions more than any other factor.
    d. Leif Erikson contacted the natives nearly five hundred years before Columbus.

11. Which of the following best describes the author's intent in the passage?
    a. To entertain
    b. To inform
    c. To alert
    d. To suggest

12. Which of the following can be logically inferred from the passage?
    a. The Vikings disliked exploring the New World.
    b. Leif Erikson's banishment from Iceland led to his exploration of present-day Canada.
    c. Leif Erikson never shared his stories of exploration with the King of Norway.
    d. Historians have difficulty definitively pinpointing events in the Vikings' history.

The next five questions are based on the chart following a brief introduction to the topic.

The American Civil War was fought from 1861 to 1865. It is the only civil war in American history. While the South's secession was the initiating event of the war, the conflict grew out of several issues like slavery and differing interpretations of individual state rights. General Robert E. Lee led the Confederate Army for the South for the duration of the conflict (although other generals held command positions over individual battles, as you will see below). The North employed a variety of lead generals, but Ulysses S. Grant finished the war as the victorious general. There were more American casualties in the Civil War than any other military conflict in American history.

Civil War Casualties by Battle (approximate)					
Battle	**Date**	**Union General**	**Confederate General**	**Union Casualties**	**Confederate Casualties**
Gettysburg	July 1863	George Meade	Robert E. Lee	23,049	28,063
Chancellorsville	May 1863	Joseph Hooker	Robert E. Lee	17,304	13,460
Shiloh	April 1862	Ulysses S. Grant	Albert Sydney Johnston	13,047	10,669
Cold Harbor	May 1864	Ulysses S. Grant	Robert E. Lee	12,737	4,595
Atlanta	July 1864	William T. Sherman	John Bell Hood	3,722	5,500

13. In which of the following battles were there more Confederate casualties than Union casualties?
    a. The one in May 1864
    b. Chancellorsville
    c. The one in April 1862
    d. Atlanta

14. Which one of the following battles occurred first?
    a. Cold Harbor
    b. Chancellorsville
    c. Atlanta
    d. Shiloh

15. Robert E. Lee did not lead the Confederate forces in which one of the following battles?
    a. Atlanta
    b. The one in May 1863
    c. Cold Harbor
    d. Gettysburg

16. In which of the following battles did the Union casualties exceed the Confederate casualties by the greatest number?
    a. Cold Harbor
    b. Chancellorsville
    c. Atlanta
    d. Shiloh

17. The total number of American casualties suffered at the battle of Gettysburg is about double the total number of casualties suffered at which one of the following battles?

a. Cold Harbor
b. Chancellorsville
c. Atlanta
d. Shiloh

The next two questions are based on the graphic that follows a brief introduction to the topic.

The United States Constitution directs Congress to conduct a census of the population to determine the country's population and demographic information. The United States Census Bureau carries out the survey. In 1790, then Secretary of State Thomas Jefferson conducted the first census, and the most recent U.S. census was in 2010. The next U.S. census will be the first to be issued primarily through the Internet.

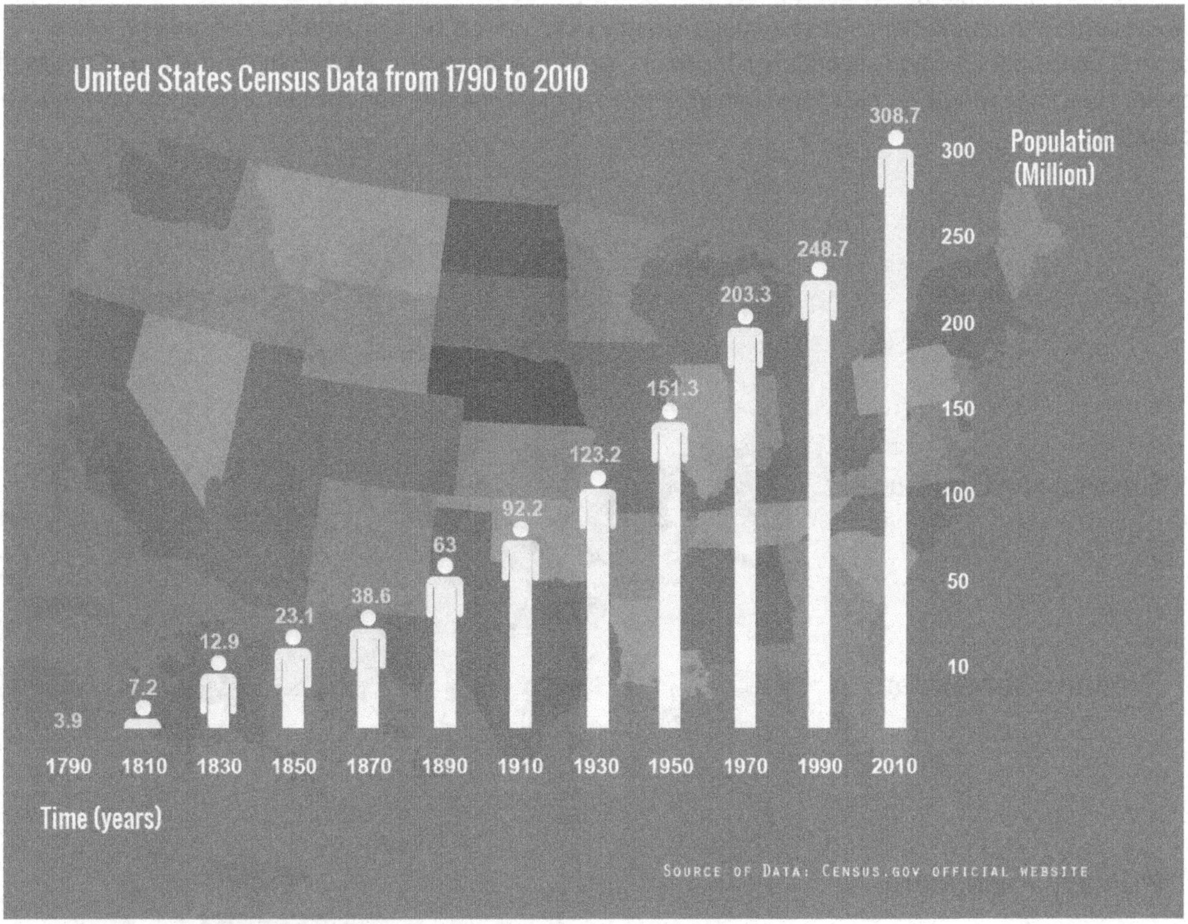

18. In which of the following years was the United States population less than it was in 1930?

a. 1950
b. 1970
c. 1910
d. 1990

19. In what year did the population increase the most during a twenty-year interval?
   a. From 1930 to 1950
   b. From 1950 to 1970
   c. From 1970 to 1990
   d. From 1990 to 2010

The next three questions are based on the graphic following a brief introduction to the topic.

A food chain is a diagram used by biologists to better understand ecosystems. It represents the interrelationships between different plants and animals. The energy is derived from the sun and converted into stored energy by plants through photosynthesis, which travels up the food chain. The energy returns to the ecosystem after the organisms die and decompose back into the Earth. This process is an endless cycle.

In food chains, living organisms are grouped into categories called primary producers and consumers, which come in multiple tiers. For example, secondary consumers feed on primary consumers, while tertiary consumers feed on secondary consumers. Apex predators are the animals at the top of the food chain. They are the highest category consumer in an ecosystem, and apex predators do not have natural predators.

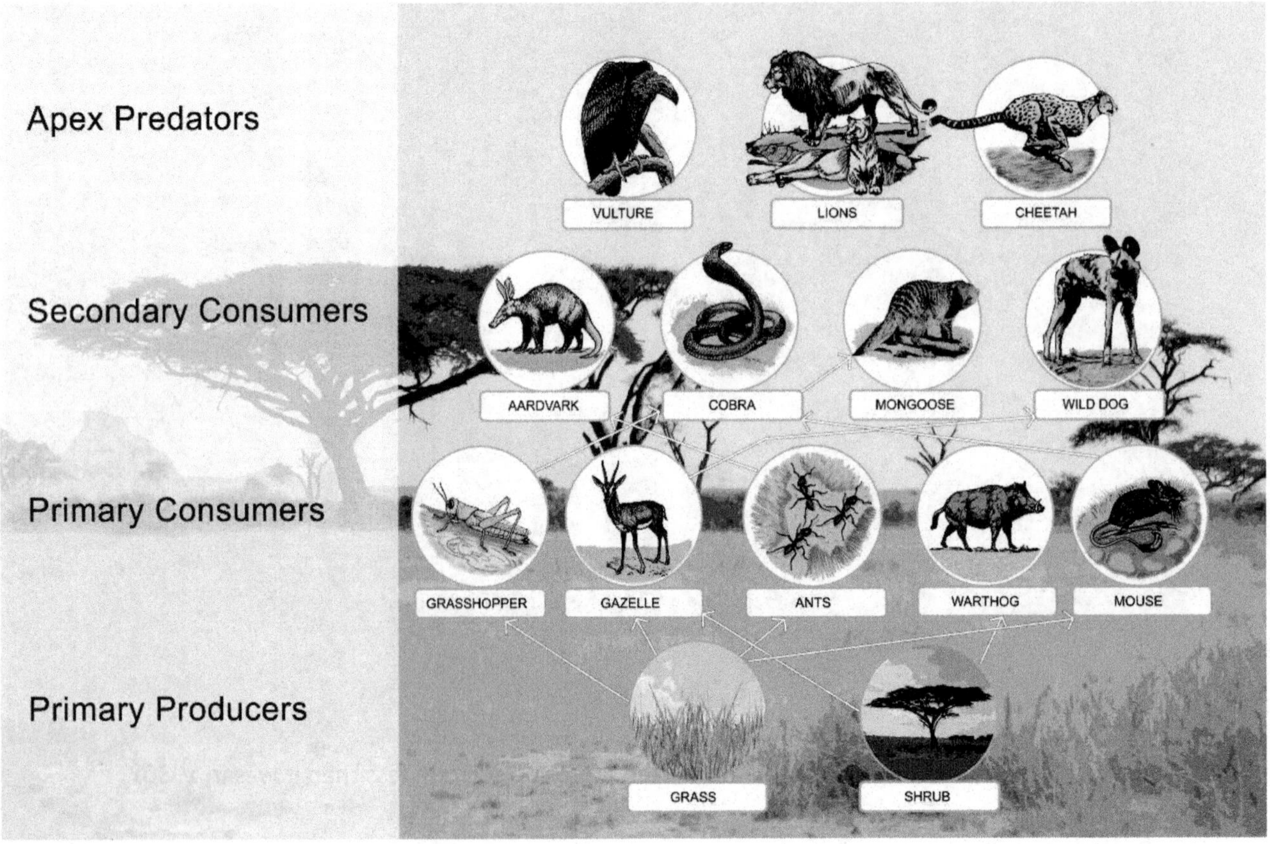

20. Which of the following eats primary producers according to the food chain diagram?
    a. Cobra
    b. Gazelle
    c. Wild dog
    d. Aardvark

21. Which of the following animals has no natural predators according to the food chain diagram?
    a. Vulture
    b. Cobra
    c. Mongoose
    d. Aardvark

22. Which of the following is something that the mongoose would eat?
    a. Shrub
    b. Aardvark
    c. Vulture
    d. Mouse

The next four questions are based on the timeline of the life of Alexander Graham Bell.

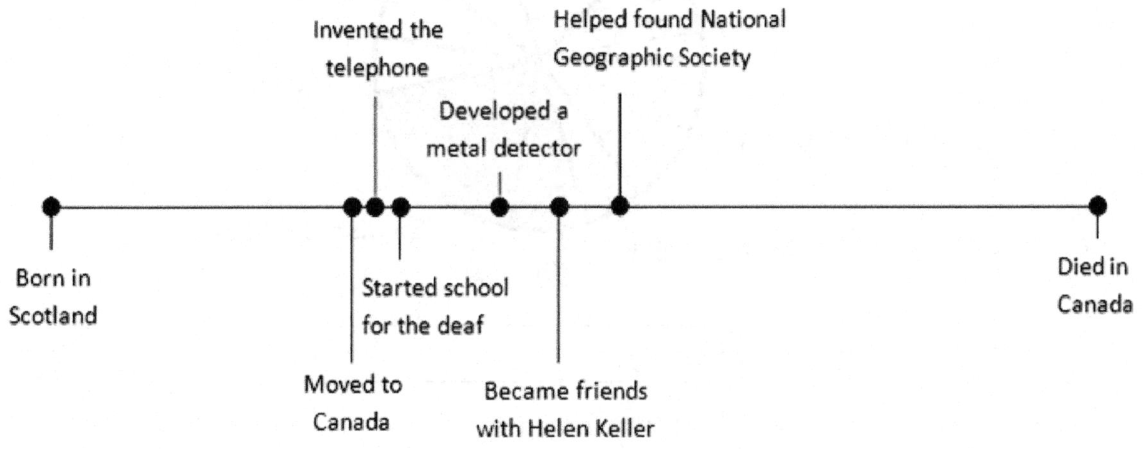

23. Which of the following is the event that occurred fourth on the timeline?
    a. Helped found National Geographic Society
    b. Developed a metal detector
    c. Moved to Canada
    d. Started a school for the deaf

24. Of the pairings in the answer choices, which has the longest gap between the two events?
    a. Moved to Canada and Became friends with Helen Keller
    b. Became friends with Helen Keller and Died in Canada
    c. Started school for the deaf and Developed a metal detector
    d. Born in Scotland and Started school for the deaf

25. Which one of the following statements is accurate based on the timeline?
    a. Bell did nothing significant after he helped found the National Geographic Society.
    b. Bell started a school for the deaf in Canada.
    c. Bell lived in at least two countries.
    d. Developing a metal detector allowed Bell to meet Helen Keller.

26. Which one of the following events occurred most recently?
    a. Bell's invention of the telephone
    b. Bell's founding the National Geographic Society
    c. Bell's birth
    d. Bell's move to Canada

The next two questions are based on the following graph of high school students.

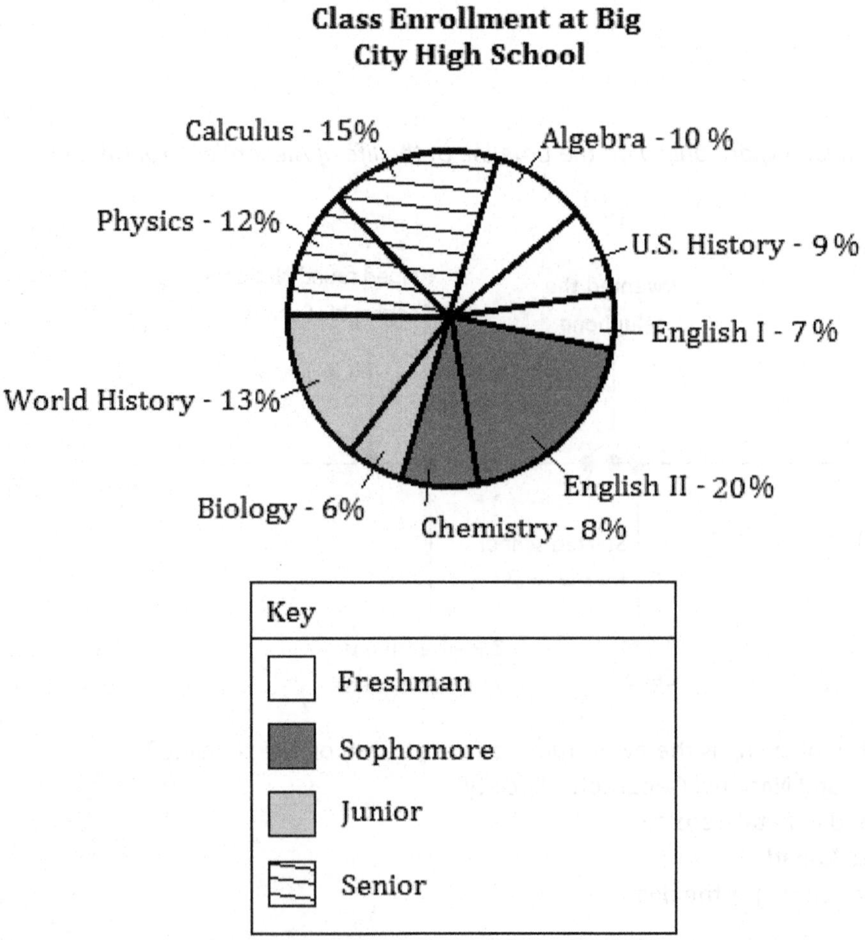

27. Which grade level has the most students in it?
    a. Freshman
    b. Sophomore
    c. Junior
    d. Senior

28. What percent of the school is made up of freshman?
   a. 26%
   b. 27%
   c. 28%
   d. 29%

Questions 29-34 are based on the following passage:

When researchers and engineers undertake a large-scale scientific proje discoveries and developing technologies that have far wider uses than c especially true in NASA, one of the most influential and innovative scientific organiza NASA *spinoff technology* refers to innovations originally developed for NASA space projects that are now used in a wide range of different commercial fields. Many consumers are unaware that products they are buying are based on NASA research! Spinoff technology proves that it is worthwhile to invest in science research because it could enrich people's lives in unexpected ways.

The first spinoff technology worth mentioning is baby food. In space, where astronauts have limited access to fresh food and fewer options about their daily meals, malnutrition is a serious concern. Consequently, NASA researchers were looking for ways to enhance the nutritional value of astronauts' food. Scientists found that a certain type of algae could be added to food, improving the food's neurological benefits. When experts in the commercial food industry learned of this algae's potential to boost brain health, they were quick to begin their own research. The nutritional substance from algae then developed into a product called life's DHA, which can be found in over 90% of infant food sold in America.

Another intriguing example of a spinoff technology can be found in fashion. People who are always dropping their sunglasses may have invested in a pair of sunglasses with scratch resistant lenses—that is, it's impossible to scratch the glass, even if the glasses are dropped on an abrasive surface. This innovation is incredibly advantageous for people who are clumsy, but most shoppers don't know that this technology was originally developed by NASA. Scientists first created scratch resistant glass to help protect costly and crucial equipment from getting scratched in space, especially the helmet visors in space suits. However, sunglasses companies later realized that this technology could be profitable for their products, and they licensed the technology from NASA.

29. What is the main purpose of this article?
   a. To advise consumers to do more research before making a purchase
   b. To persuade readers to support NASA research
   c. To tell a narrative about the history of space technology
   d. To define and describe instances of spinoff technology

30. What is the organizational structure of this article?
   a. A general definition followed by more specific examples
   b. A general opinion followed by supporting arguments
   c. An important moment in history followed by chronological details
   d. A popular misconception followed by counterevidence

[illegible] NASA scientists research algae?
[illegible]ey already knew algae was healthy for babies.
[illegible]hey were interested in how to grow food in space.
c. They were looking for ways to add health benefits to food.
d. They hoped to use it to protect expensive research equipment.

32. What does the word "neurological" mean in the second paragraph?
    a. Related to the body
    b. Related to the brain
    c. Related to vitamins
    d. Related to technology

33. Why does the author mention space suit helmets?
    a. To give an example of astronaut fashion
    b. To explain where sunglasses got their shape
    c. To explain how astronauts protect their eyes
    d. To give an example of valuable space equipment

34. Which statement would the author probably NOT agree with?
    a. Consumers don't always know the history of the products they are buying.
    b. Sometimes new innovations have unexpected applications.
    c. It is difficult to make money from scientific research.
    d. Space equipment is often very expensive.

Questions 35-40 are based on the following passage.

This excerpt is an adaptation from The Immortal Cells of Henrietta Lacks by Rebecca Skloot.

Henrietta Lacks is an African American woman who died from an aggressive strain of cervical cancer. The word HeLa is used to refer to the cells grown from Henrietta Lacks's cervix. HeLa is known as the first immortal human cell line ever grown in culture.

The Cloning of HeLa

Today, when we hear the word clone, we imagine scientists creating entire living animals—like Dolly the famous cloned sheep—using DNA from one parent. But before the cloning of whole animals, there was the cloning of individual cells—Henrietta's cells.

To understand why cellular cloning was important, you need to know two things: First, HeLa didn't grow from one of Henrietta's cells. It grew from a sliver of her tumor, which was a cluster of cells. Second, cells often behave differently, even if they're all from the same sample, which means some grow faster than others, some produce more poliovirus, and some are resistant to certain antibiotics. Scientists wanted to grow cellular clones—lines of cells descended from individual cells—so they could harness those unique traits. With HeLa, a group of scientists in Colorado succeeded, and soon the world of science had not only HeLa but also its hundreds, then thousands, of clones.

The early cell culture and cloning technology developed using HeLa helped lead to many later advances that required the ability to grow single cells in culture, including isolating stem cells, cloning whole animals, and in vitro fertilization. Meanwhile, as the standard human cell in most labs, HeLa was also being used in research that would advance the new field of human genetics.

Researchers had long believed that human cells contained forty-eight chromosomes, the threads of DNA inside cells that contain all of our genetic information. But chromosomes clumped together, making it impossible to get an accurate count. Then, in 1953, a geneticist in Texas accidentally mixed the wrong liquid with HeLa and a few other cells, and it turned out to be a fortunate mistake. The chromosomes inside the cells swelled and spread out, and for the first time, scientists could see each of them clearly. That accidental discovery was the first of several developments that would allow two researchers from Spain and Sweden to discover that normal human cells have forty-six chromosomes.

Once scientists knew how many chromosomes people were supposed to have, they could tell when a person had too many or too few, which made it possible to diagnose genetic diseases. Researchers worldwide would soon begin identifying chromosomal disorders, discovering that patients with Down syndrome had an extra chromosome number 21, patients with Klinefelter syndrome had an extra sex chromosome, and those with Turner syndrome lacked all or part of one.

With all the new developments, demand for HeLa grew, and Tuskegee wasn't big enough to keep up. The owner of Microbiological Associates—a military man named Samuel Reader—knew nothing about science, but his business partner, Monroe Vincent, was a researcher who understood the potential market for cells. Many scientists needed cells, but few had the time or ability to grow them in large enough quantities. They just wanted to buy them. So together, Reader and Vincent used HeLa cells as the springboard to launch the first industrial-scale, for-profit cell distribution center.

35. The author's use of second person pronouns in the following text has all EXCEPT for which of the following effects? *"To understand why cellular cloning was important, you need to know two things…"*

a. It personalizes the experience.
b. It allows the reader to more easily understand the text.
c. It encourages the reader to empathize with Henrietta Lack.
d. It distances the reader from the text by overemphasizing the story.

36. The reference to "Dolly the famous cloned sheep" in the text points to which of the following facts?

a. The HeLa cells research was not the only DNA-based research that has taken place.
b. HeLa cells are the best evidence of cell mutation.
c. HeLa cells provide no known evidence of the existence of immortal cells.
d. Researchers doubt that HeLA cells exist.

37. What is the meaning of the word "harness" in the following sentence? *"Scientists wanted to grow cellular clones—lines of cells descended from individual cells—so they could harness those unique traits."*

a. Duplicate
b. Obtain
c. Couple
d. Leash

38. Where did HeLa cells initially originate?

a. Within Henrietta Lack's heart
b. Through Henrietta Lack's hair follicles
c. Through DNA testing
d. In a sliver of tumor from Henrietta Lack's cancerous cervical tissue

39. The discovery of HeLa cells has helped to further the scientific world through all EXCEPT which of the following?

a. Isolating stem cells
b. Cloning whole animals
c. In vitro fertilization
d. Separating Siamese twins

40. Normally developed humans have how many chromosomes?

a. 48
b. 46
c. 43
d. 41

Answer Explanations

1. B: Narrative, Choice *A*, means a written account of connected events. Think of narrative writing as a story. Choice C, expository writing, generally seeks to explain or describe some phenomena, whereas Choice *D*, technical writing, includes directions, instructions, and/or explanations. Choice *E*, informative writing, may be an appealing choice since this passage is informative in some ways, but informative texts should be very objective in their language. In contrast, this passage is definitely persuasive writing, which hopes to change someone's beliefs based on an appeal to reason or emotion. The author is aiming to convince the reader that smoking is terrible. They use health, price, and beauty in their argument against smoking, so Choice *B*, persuasive, is the correct answer. Persuasive is another term for argumentative.

2. B: The author is clearly opposed to tobacco. He cites disease and deaths associated with smoking. He points to the monetary expense and aesthetic costs. Choices *A* and *C* are wrong because they do not summarize the passage but rather are each just a premise. Choice *D* is wrong because, while these statistics are a premise in the argument, they do not represent a summary of the piece. Choice *B* is the correct answer because it states the three critiques offered against tobacco and expresses the author's conclusion. Choice *E* is wrong because alternatives to smoking are not even addressed in the passage.

3. C: We are looking for something the author would agree with, so it will almost certainly be anti-smoking or an argument in favor of quitting smoking. Choice *A* is wrong because the author does not speak against means of cessation. Choice *B* is wrong because the author does not reference other substances, but does speak of how addictive nicotine, a drug in tobacco, is. Choice *D* is wrong because the author certainly would not encourage reducing taxes to encourage a reduction of smoking costs, thereby helping smokers to continue the habit. Choice *E* is wrong because the author states that according to the National Institute of Drug Abuse, nearly 35 million smokers expressed a desire to quit smoking in 2015. If the author had used the word "only" instead of "nearly" (and perhaps if the number was a lot lower) that would have changed the argument. Choice *C* is correct because the author is definitely attempting to persuade smokers to quit smoking.

4. D: Here, we are looking for an opinion of the author's rather than a fact or statistic. Choice *A* is wrong because quoting statistics from the Centers of Disease Control and Prevention is stating facts, not opinions. Choice *B* is wrong because it expresses the fact that cigarettes sometimes cost more than a few gallons of gas. It would be an opinion if the author said that cigarettes were not affordable. Choice *C* is incorrect because yellow stains are a known possible adverse effect of smoking. Choice *E* is incorrect because decreased life expectancy for smokers is a known fact because of the health problems it can create. Choice *D* is correct as an opinion because smell is subjective. Some people might like the smell of smoke, they might not have working olfactory senses, and/or some people might not find the smell of smoke akin to "pervasive nastiness," so this is the expression of an opinion. Thus, Choice *D* is the correct answer.

5. D: Although Washington is from a wealthy background, the passage does not say that his wealth led to his republican ideals, so Choice *A* is not supported. Choice *B* also does not follow from the passage. Washington's warning against meddling in foreign affairs does not mean that he would oppose wars of every kind, so Choice *B* is wrong. Choice *C* is also unjustified since the author does not indicate that Alexander Hamilton's assistance was absolutely necessary. Choice *E* is incorrect because we don't know which particular presidents Washington would befriend. Choice *D* is correct because the farewell address clearly opposes political parties and partisanship. The author then notes that presidential elections often hit a fever pitch of partisanship. Thus, it is follows that George Washington would not approve of modern political parties and their involvement in presidential elections.

6. C: The author finishes the passage by applying Washington's farewell address to modern politics, so the purpose probably includes this application. Choice *A* does focus on modern politics, but it is incorrect. The passage does not state that it is the election process itself that George Washington would oppose; in fact, it mentions that he was also elected. Choice *B* is wrong because George Washington is already a well-established historical figure; furthermore, the passage does not seek to introduce him. Choice *D* is wrong because the author is not convincing readers. Persuasion does not correspond to the passage. Choice *C* states the primary purpose.

7. D: Choices *A* and *E* are wrong because the last paragraph is not appropriate for a history textbook nor a research journal, both which should be strictly objective and research-based. Choice *B* is false because the piece is not a notice or announcement of Washington's death. Choice *C* is clearly false because it is not fiction, but a historical writing. Choice *D* is correct. The passage is most likely to appear in a newspaper editorial because it cites information relevant and applicable to the present day, a popular format in editorials.

8. D: The passage does not proceed in chronological order since it begins by pointing out Leif Erikson's explorations in America so Choice *A* does not work. Although the author compares and contrasts Erikson with Christopher Columbus, this is not the main way the information is presented; therefore, Choice *B* does not work. Neither does Choice *C* because there is no mention of or reference to cause and effect in the passage. However, the passage does offer a conclusion (Leif Erikson deserves more credit) and premises (first European to set foot in the New World and first to contact the natives) to substantiate Erikson's historical importance. Thus, Choice *D* is correct. Choice *E* is incorrect because spatial order refers to the space and location of something or where things are located in relation to each other.

9. C: Choice *A* is wrong because it describes facts: Leif Erikson was the son of Erik the Red and historians debate Leif's date of birth. These are not opinions. Choice *B* is wrong; that Erikson called the land Vinland is a verifiable fact as is Choice *D* because he did contact the natives almost 500 years before Columbus. Choice *E* is also a fact and the passage mentions that there are several secondhand accounts (evidence) of their meetings. Choice *C* is the correct answer because it is the author's opinion that Erikson deserves more credit. That, in fact, is his conclusion in the piece, but another person could argue that Columbus or another explorer deserves more credit for opening up the New World to exploration. Rather than being an incontrovertible fact, it is a subjective value claim.

10. B: Choice *A* is wrong because the author aims to go beyond describing Erikson as a mere legendary Viking. Choice *C* is wrong because the author does not focus on Erikson's motivations, let alone name the spreading of Christianity as his primary objective. Choice *D* is wrong because it is a premise that Erikson contacted the natives 500 years before Columbus, which is simply a part of supporting the author's conclusion. Choice *E* is incorrect because the author states at the beginning that he or she believes it can't be considered "discovering" if people already lived there. Choice *B* is correct because, as stated in the previous answer, it accurately identifies the author's statement that Erikson deserves more credit than he has received for being the first European to explore the New World.

11. B: Choice *A* is wrong because the author is not in any way trying to entertain the reader. Choice *D* is wrong because he goes beyond a mere suggestion; "suggest" is too vague. Choice *E* is wrong for the same reason. Although the author is certainly trying to alert the readers (make them aware) of Leif Erikson's underappreciated and unheralded accomplishments, the nature of the writing does not indicate the author would be satisfied with the reader merely knowing of Erikson's exploration (Choice *C*). Rather, the author would want the reader to be informed about it, which is more substantial (Choice *B*).

12. D: Choice *A* is wrong because the author never addresses the Vikings' state of mind or emotions. Choice *B* is wrong because the author does not elaborate on Erikson's exile and whether he would have become an explorer if not for his banishment. Choice *C* is wrong because there is not enough information to support this premise. It is unclear whether Erikson informed the King of Norway of his finding. Although it is true that the King did not send a follow-up expedition, he could have simply chosen not to expend the resources after receiving Erikson's news. It is not possible to logically infer whether Erikson told him. Choice *E* is incorrect because the passage does not mention anything about Columbus' awareness of Erikson's travels. Choice *D* is correct because there are two examples—Leif Erikson's date of birth and what happened during the encounter with the natives—of historians having trouble pinning down important dates in Viking history.

13. D: The question asks which of the battles in the chart that are listed in this question had more Confederate casualties than Union casualties. There were more Confederate casualties than Union casualties at the Battles of Gettysburg and Atlanta. Of the two, only Atlanta is listed as an answer choice out of the battles explicitly listed or referred to by their dates. Thus, *D*, Atlanta, is the correct answer.

14. D: The question is asking you to find where the dates are located in the table and to identify the earliest battle. Answer D, Shiloh, occurred in April 1862 and no other battle listed on the table happened until May 1863. Choice *E,* Gettysburg, is listed first but did not occur first.

15. A: Robert E. Lee led the Confederate army in all battles listed on the table, except Shiloh and Atlanta. Looking at the dates and corresponding battles, as well as the battle explicitly listed, Shiloh is not listed as a choice, therefore Atlanta, option *A* is the correct answer.

16. A: This question is asking you to compare the Union and Confederate casualties and find the one listed where the Union casualties most exceeded the Confederate ones. At Cold Harbor, there were approximately 8,142 more Union casualties than Confederate. At Chancellorsville, there were approximately 3,844 more Union casualties. At Atlanta and Gettysburg, the number of Confederate casualties exceeded the Union number, so neither of these can be the correct answer. At Shiloh, there were approximately 2,378 more Union casualties. Thus, the number of Union casualties most greatly exceeding the Confederate number was at Cold Harbor, making *A*, Cold Harbor, the correct answer.

17. D: To calculate the total American casualties, we combine the Union and Confederate casualties since it was a civil war with Americans on both sides, so Choice *E* is incorrect. There were approximately 51,112 (Union + Confederate losses) American casualties at Gettysburg; thus, the correct answer will be a battle with approximately 25,556 casualties, which is half of that number. Shiloh is the closest with a total of 23,716 casualties, making *D* the correct answer.

18. C: The correct answer choice is *C,* 1910. There are two ways to arrive at the correct answer. You could find the five answer choices on the graph, or you could have identified that the population never dips at any point. Thus, the correct answer needs to be the only answer choice that is earlier in time than the others, Choice *C*.

19. D: The population increased the most between 1990 and 2010. The question is asking you to identify the rate of change for each interval. Between 1790 to 1810, the population increased by about 3.3 million. Between 1930 and 1950, the population increased by approximately 28 million. Between 1950 and 1970, the population increased by approximately 52 million. Between 1970 and 1990, the population increased by approximately 45 million. Between 1990 and 2010, the population increased by approximately 60 million. Thus, *D* is the correct answer. The slope is also the steepest in this interval, which represents its higher increase.

20. B: Primary producers make up the base of the food chain, so the correct answer will be in the level just above: a primary consumer. The cobra, wild dog, and aardvark are all secondary consumers. The gazelle is a primary consumer, so ***B*** is the correct answer. Grass *is* a primary producer, making *E* incorrect.

21. A: According to the passage preceding the food chain, the apex predators do not have natural predators. So, the question is really asking which of the answer choices is an apex predator. The cobra, mongoose, and aardvark are all secondary consumers. Grass is a primary producer. The vulture is an apex predator; thus, a vulture has no natural predators, making *Choice A* the correct answer.

22. D: A mongoose is a secondary consumer; thus, the mongoose consumes primary consumers. The shrub is a primary producer. The aardvark is a secondary consumer. The vulture and the lion are apex predators. The mouse is a primary consumer, so Choice *D* is the correct answer.

23. D: This question is testing whether you realize how a timeline illustrates information in chronological order from left to right. "Started school for the deaf" is fourth on the timeline from the left, which means that it is the fourth event on the timeline. Thus, Choice *D* is the correct answer.

24. B: This question is asking you to determine the length of time between the pairs of events listed as answer choices. Events in timelines are arranged proportional to time. To determine the answer to this question, one must find the largest space between two events. Visually, this can be seen between the events of befriending Helen Keller and dying in Canada. Thus, choice *B* is the correct answer.

25. C: This question is testing whether you can discern accurate conclusions from a timeline. Although the incorrect answer choices can seem correct, they cannot be confirmed from the information presented on the timeline. Choice *A* is incorrect; while it may be reasonable to assume that the timeline documents all major life events, we do not know for certain that Bell did not engage in any notable activities after founding the National Geographic Society. Choice *B* is incorrect because the timeline does not confirm that the school was in Canada; Bell actually started it in the United States. Choice *D* is incorrect because nothing on the timeline shows causation between the two events. Choice *E* is incorrect because the timeline states he was born in Scotland and died in Canada. Choice *C* is the only verifiable statement based on the timeline. Thus, *C* is the correct answer.

26. D: The founding of the National Geographic Society is the event listed farthest to the right of the events in the answer choices. This means it occurred most recently. Thus, *B* is the correct answer.

27. B: The sophomore class is made up of English II and Chemistry and encompasses 28% of the students. Freshman only make up 26% of the students, while Seniors make up 27%, and Juniors make up 26%.

28. A: To find this add up the percent of Algebra, US History, and English I. This comes up to 26%.

29. D: To define and describe instances of spinoff technology. This is an example of a purpose question—*why* did the author write this? The article contains facts, definitions, and other objective information without telling a story or arguing an opinion. In this case, the purpose of the article is to inform the reader. The only answer choice that is related to giving information is answer Choice *D*: to define and describe.

30. A: A general definition followed by more specific examples. This organization question asks readers to analyze the structure of the essay. The topic of the essay is about spinoff technology; the first paragraph gives a general definition of the concept, while the following two paragraphs offer more detailed examples to help illustrate this idea.

31. C: They were looking for ways to add health benefits to food. This reading comprehension question can be answered based on the second paragraph—scientists were concerned about astronauts' nutrition and began researching useful nutritional supplements. Choice *A* in particular is not true because it reverses the order of discovery (first NASA identified algae for astronaut use, and then it was further developed for use in baby food).

32. B: Related to the brain. This vocabulary question could be answered based on the reader's prior knowledge; but even for readers who have never encountered the word "neurological" before, the passage does provide context clues. The very next sentence talks about "this algae's potential to boost brain health," which is a paraphrase of "neurological benefits." From this context, readers should be able to infer that "neurological" is related to the brain.

33. D: To give an example of valuable space equipment. This purpose question requires readers to understand the relevance of the given detail. In this case, the author mentions "costly and crucial equipment" before mentioning space suit visors, which are given as an example of something that is very valuable. *A* is not correct because fashion is only related to sunglasses, not to NASA equipment. *B* can be eliminated because it is simply not mentioned in the passage. While *C* seems like it could be a true statement, it is also not relevant to what is being explained by the author. A similar thing could be said about *E*. The passage does not talk about helmet use on Earth.

34. C: It is difficult to make money from scientific research. The article gives several examples of how businesses have been able to capitalize on NASA research, so it is unlikely that the author would agree with this statement. Evidence for the other answer choices can be found in the article: *A*, the author mentions that "many consumers are unaware that products they are buying are based on NASA research"; *B* is a general definition of spinoff technology; *D* is mentioned in the final paragraph, and *E* is mentioned in the opening paragraph and is a theme throughout.

35. D: The use of "you" could have all of the effects for the reader with the Choices *A, B, C,* and *E;* it could serve to personalize the text, make the passage easier to understand, cause the reader to empathize with Henrietta Lack's story, and engage the reader. However, it doesn't distance the reader from Lack's experiences, thus eliminating Choice *D*.

36. A: Choices *C* and *D* are incorrect because they are disproven in the text. Choice *B* is incorrect because there is no mention of what the best evidence of cell mutation is. Choice *E* is not mentioned in the text and does not really make logical sense. The author references Dolly to point the reader to another popular case of DNA research.

37. A: The word "harness" in the text means to duplicate because the scientists' desire is to develop more immortal cells. *Choice B,* "obtain," doesn't logically make sense, because the scientists couldn't obtain traits at this stage in their development. Choice *C,* "couple," is also incorrect, as scientists in this context are more prone to duplicating unique traits than coupling them. Choice *D* is unrelated;

sometimes leashes and harnesses are used to walk dogs or other animals, but this application is incorrect in this context.

38. D: Choice *D* is correct because the text states that HeLa cells came from a sliver of one of the Henrietta Lack's tumor. Choices *A* and *B* are not mentioned in the text. Choice *C* is incorrect, as the HeLa cells did not come through DNA testing, as is *E* because they were not from a healthy individual.

39. D: The discovery of HeLa cells has helped to further the scientific world through *A,* isolating stem cells, *B,* cloning whole animals, *C,* in vitro fertilization, and *E,* our understanding of human genetics. Choice *D,* separating Siamese twins, is not mentioned in the text.

40. B: The text states that normally developed humans have 46 chromosomes. Originally scientists thought that human cells contained 48 chromosomes, but later a geneticist in Texas proved that incorrect.

Essay

Essay Skills

Brainstorming

One of the most important steps in writing an essay is prewriting. Before drafting an essay, it's helpful to think about the topic for a moment or two, in order to gain a more solid understanding of what the task is. Then, spending about five minutes jotting down the immediate ideas that could work for the essay is recommended. It is a way to get some words on the page and offer a reference for ideas for when drafting. Scratch paper is provided for writers to use any prewriting techniques such as webbing, free writing, or listing. The goal is to get ideas out of the mind and onto the page.

Considering Opposing Viewpoints

In the planning stage, it's important to consider all aspects of the topic, including different viewpoints on the subject. There are more than two ways to look at a topic, and a strong argument considers those opposing viewpoints. Considering opposing viewpoints can help writers present a fair, balanced, and informed essay that shows consideration for all readers. This approach can also strengthen an argument by recognizing and potentially refuting the opposing viewpoint(s).

Drawing from personal experience may help to support ideas. For example, if the goal for writing is a personal narrative, then the story should be from the writer's own life. Many writers find it helpful to draw from personal experience, even in an essay that is not strictly narrative. Personal anecdotes or short stories can help to illustrate a point in other types of essays as well.

Moving from Brainstorming to Planning

Once the ideas are on the page, it's time to turn them into a solid plan for the essay. The best ideas from the brainstorming results can then be developed into a more formal outline. An outline typically has one main point (the thesis) and at least three sub-points that support the main point. Here's an example:

> Main Idea
> -Point #1
> -Point #2
> -Point #3

Of course, there will be details under each point, but this approach is the best for dealing with timed writing.

Staying On Track

Basing the essay on the outline aids in both organization and coherence. The goal is to ensure that there is enough time to develop each sub-point in the essay, roughly spending an equal amount of time on each idea. Keeping an eye on the time will help. If there are fifteen minutes left to draft the essay, then it makes sense to spend about 5 minutes on each of the ideas. Staying on task is critical to success, and timing out the parts of the essay can help writers avoid feeling overwhelmed.

Parts of the Essay

The introduction should do a few important things:

- Establish the topic of the essay in original wording (i.e., not just repeating the prompt)
- Clarify the significance/importance of the topic or purpose for writing (not too many details, a brief overview)
- Offer a thesis statement that identifies the writer's own viewpoint on the topic (typically one-two brief sentences as a clear, concise explanation of the main point on the topic)

Body paragraphs reflect the ideas developed in the outline. Three-four points is probably sufficient for a short essay, and they should include the following:

- A topic sentence that identifies the sub-point (e.g., a reason why, a way how, a cause or effect)
- A detailed explanation of the point, explaining why the writer thinks this point is valid
- Illustrative examples, such as personal examples or real world examples, that support and validate the point (i.e., "prove" the point)
- A concluding sentence that connects the examples, reasoning, and analysis to the point being made

The conclusion, or final paragraph, should be brief and should reiterate the focus, clarifying why the discussion is significant or important. It is important to avoid adding specific details or new ideas to this paragraph. The purpose of the conclusion is to sum up what has been said to bring the discussion to a close.

Don't Panic!

Writing an essay can be overwhelming, and performance panic is a natural response. The outline serves as a basis for the writing and helps writers keep focused. Getting stuck can also happen, and it's helpful to remember that brainstorming can be done at any time during the writing process. Following the steps of the writing process is the best defense against writer's block.

Timed essays can be particularly stressful, but assessors are trained to recognize the necessary planning and thinking for these timed efforts. Using the plan above and sticking to it helps with time management. Timing each part of the process helps writers stay on track. Sometimes writers try to cover too much in their essays. If time seems to be running out, this is an opportunity to determine whether all of the ideas in the outline are necessary. Three body paragraphs are sufficient, and more than that is probably too much to cover in a short essay.

More isn't always better in writing. A strong essay will be clear and concise. It will avoid unnecessary or repetitive details. It is better to have a concise, five-paragraph essay that makes a clear point, than a ten-paragraph essay that doesn't. The goal is to write one to two pages of quality writing. Paragraphs should also reflect balance; if the introduction goes to the bottom of the first page, the writing may be going off-track or be repetitive. It's best to fall into the one-two page range, but a complete, well-developed essay is the ultimate goal.

The Final Steps

Leaving a few minutes at the end to revise and proofread offers an opportunity for writers to polish things up. Putting one's self in the reader's shoes and focusing on what the essay actually says helps writers identify problems—it's a movement from the mindset of writer to the mindset of editor. The goal is to have a clean, clear copy of the essay. The following areas should be considered when proofreading:

- Sentence fragments
- Awkward sentence structure
- Run-on sentences
- Incorrect word choice
- Grammatical agreement errors
- Spelling errors
- Punctuation errors
- Capitalization errors

The Short Overview

The essay may seem challenging, but following these steps can help writers focus:

15. 1. Take one or two minutes to think about the topic.
16. 2. Generate some ideas through brainstorming (three-four minutes).
17. 3. Organize ideas into a brief outline, selecting just three-four main points to cover in the essay (eventually the body paragraphs).
18. 4. Develop essay in parts:
19. 5. Introduction paragraph, with intro to topic and main points
20. 6. Viewpoint on the subject at the end of the introduction
21. 7. Body paragraphs, based on outline
22. 8. Each paragraph: makes a main point, explains the viewpoint, uses examples to support the point
23. 9. Brief conclusion highlighting the main points and closing
24. 10. Read over the essay (last five minutes).
25. 11. Look for any obvious errors, making sure that the writing makes sense.

The following sections will provide slightly more specific information to keep in mind when crafting a successful essay. While this information should be used to help assemble a coherent essay on the FTCE, it's use extends beyond the testing date and can be applied to general academic writing. These foundational principles will be helpful in the classroom, while instructing students on the art and science of high-quality writing.

Understanding the Task, Purpose, and Audience

<u>Identifying the Task, Purpose, and Intended Audience</u>
An author's *writing style*—the way in which words, grammar, punctuation, and sentence fluidity are used—is the most influential element in a piece of writing, and it is dependent on the purpose and the audience for whom it is intended. Together, a writing style and mode of writing form the foundation of a written work, and a good writer will choose the most effective mode and style to convey a message to readers.

Writers should first determine what they are trying to say and then choose the most effective mode of writing to communicate that message. Different writing modes and *word choices* will affect the tone of a piece—that is, its underlying attitude, emotion, or character. The argumentative mode may utilize words that are earnest, angry, passionate, or excited whereas an informative piece may have a sterile, germane, or enthusiastic tone. The tones found in narratives vary greatly, depending on the purpose of the writing. *Tone* will also be affected by the audience—teaching science to children or those who may be uninterested would be most effective with enthusiastic language and exclamation points whereas teaching science to college students may take on a more serious and professional tone, with fewer charged words and punctuation choices that are inherent to academia.

Sentence fluidity—whether sentences are long and rhythmic or short and succinct—also affects a piece of writing as it determines the way in which a piece is read. Children or audiences unfamiliar with a subject do better with short, succinct sentence structures as these break difficult concepts up into shorter points. A period, question mark, or exclamation point is literally a signal for the reader to stop and takes more time to process. Thus, longer, more complex sentences are more appropriate for adults or educated audiences as they can fit more information in between processing time.

The amount of *supporting detail* provided is also tailored to the audience. A text that introduces a new subject to its readers will focus more on broad ideas without going into greater detail whereas a text that focuses on a more specific subject is likely to provide greater detail about the ideas discussed.

Writing styles, like modes, are most effective when tailored to their audiences. Having awareness of an audience's demographic is one of the most crucial aspects of properly communicating an argument, a story, or a set of information.

<u>Choosing the Most Appropriate Type of Writing</u>
Before beginning any writing, it is imperative that a writer have a firm grasp on the message he or she wishes to convey and how he or she wants readers to be affected by the writing. For example, does the author want readers to be more informed about the subject? Does the writer want readers to agree with his or her opinion? Does the writer want readers to get caught up in an exciting narrative? The following steps are a guide to determining the appropriate type of writing for a task, purpose, and audience:

1. Identifying the purpose for writing the piece
2. Determining the audience
3. Adapting the writing mode, word choices, tone, and style to fit the audience and the purpose

It is important to distinguish between a work's purpose and its main idea. The essential difference between the two is that the *main idea* is what the author wants to communicate about the topic at hand whereas the *primary purpose* is why the author is writing in the first place. The primary purpose is what will determine the type of writing an author will choose to utilize, not the main idea, though the two are related. For example, if an author writes an article on the mistreatment of animals in factory farms and, at the end, suggests that people should convert to vegetarianism, the main idea is that vegetarianism would reduce the poor treatment of animals. The primary purpose is to convince the reader to stop eating animals. Since the primary purpose is to galvanize an audience into action, the author would choose the argumentative writing mode.

The next step is to consider to whom the author is appealing as this will determine the type of details to be included, the diction to be used, the tone to be employed, and the sentence structure to be used. An audience can be identified by considering the following questions:

What is the purpose for writing the piece?
To whom is it being written?
What is their age range?
Are they familiar with the material being presented, or are they just being newly introduced to it?
Where are they from?
Is the task at hand in a professional or casual setting?
Is the task at hand for monetary gain?

These are just a few of the numerous considerations to keep in mind, but the main idea is to become as familiar with the audience as possible. Once the audience has been understood, the author can then adapt the writing style to align with the readers' education and interests. The audience is what determines the *rhetorical appeal* the author will use—ethos, pathos, or logos. *Ethos* is a rhetorical appeal to an audience's ethics and/or morals. Ethos is most often used in argumentative and informative writing modes. *Pathos* is an appeal to the audience's emotions and sympathies, and it is found in argumentative, descriptive, and narrative writing modes. *Logos* is an appeal to the audience's logic and reason and is used primarily in informative texts as well as in supporting details for argumentative pieces. Rhetorical appeals are discussed in depth in the informational texts and rhetoric section of the test.

If the author is trying to encourage global conversion to vegetarianism, he or she may choose to use all three rhetorical appeals to reach varying personality types. Those who are less interested in the welfare of animals but are interested in facts and science would relate more to logos. Animal lovers would relate better to an emotional appeal. In general, the most effective works utilize all three appeals.

Finally, after determining the writing mode and rhetorical appeal, the author will consider word choice, sentence structure, and tone, depending on the purpose and audience. The author may choose words that convey sadness or anger when speaking about animal welfare if writing to persuade, or he or she will stick to dispassionate and matter-of-fact tones, if informing the public on the treatment of animals in factory farms. If the author is writing to a younger or less-educated audience, he or she may choose to shorten and simplify sentence structures and word choice. If appealing to an audience with more expert knowledge on a particular subject, writers will more likely employ a style of longer sentences and more complex vocabulary.

Depending on the task, the author may choose to use a first person, second person, or third person point of view. First person and second person perspectives are inherently more casual in tone, including the author and the reader in the rhetoric, while third person perspectives are often seen in more professional settings.

<u>Evaluating the Effectiveness of a Piece of Writing</u>

An effective and engaging piece of writing will cause the reader to forget about the author entirely. Readers will become so engrossed in the subject, argument, or story at hand that they will almost identify with it, readily adopting beliefs proposed by the author or accepting all elements of the story as believable. On the contrary, poorly written works will cause the reader to be hyperaware of the author, doubting the writer's knowledge of a subject or questioning the validity of a narrative. Persuasive or expository works that are poorly researched will have this effect, as well as poorly planned stories with significant plot holes. An author must consider the task, purpose, and audience to sculpt a piece of writing effectively.

When evaluating the effectiveness of a piece, the most important thing to consider is how well the purpose is conveyed to the audience through the mode, use of rhetoric, and writing style.

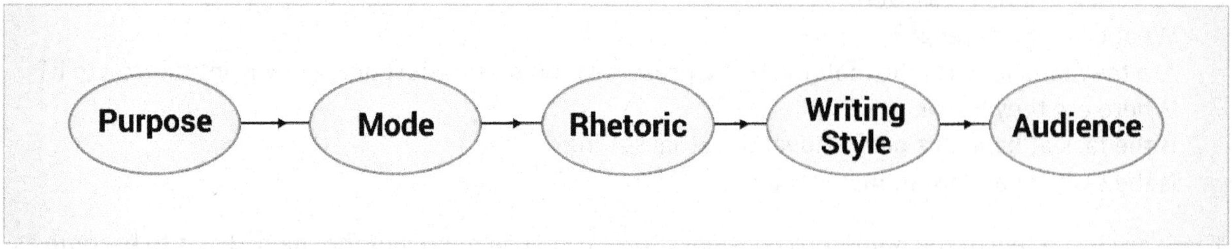

The purpose must pass through these three aspects for effective delivery to the audience. If any elements are not properly considered, the reader will be overly aware of the author, and the message will be lost. The following is a checklist for evaluating the effectiveness of a piece:

- Does the writer choose the appropriate writing mode—argumentative, narrative, descriptive, informative—for his or her purpose?
- Does the writing mode employed contain characteristics inherent to that mode?
- Does the writer consider the personalities/interests/demographics of the intended audience when choosing rhetorical appeals?
- Does the writer use appropriate vocabulary, sentence structure, voice, and tone for the audience demographic?
- Does the author properly establish himself/herself as having authority on the subject, if applicable?
- Does the piece make sense?

Another thing to consider is the medium in which the piece was written. If the medium is a blog, diary, or personal letter, the author may adopt a more casual stance towards the audience. If the piece of writing is a story in a book, a business letter or report, or a published article in a journal or if the task is to gain money or support or to get published, the author may adopt a more formal stance. Ultimately, the writer will want to be very careful in how he or she addresses the reader.

Finally, the effectiveness of a piece can be evaluated by asking how well the purpose was achieved. For example, if students are assigned to read a persuasive essay, instructors can ask whether the author influences students' opinions. Students may be assigned two differing persuasive texts with opposing perspectives and be asked which writer was more convincing. Students can then evaluate what factors contributed to this—for example, whether one author uses more credible supporting facts, appeals more effectively to readers' emotions, presents more believable personal anecdotes, or offers stronger counterargument refutation. Students can then use these evaluations to strengthen their own writing skills.

Organization

Good writing is not merely a random collection of sentences. No matter how well written, sentences must relate and coordinate appropriately with one another. If not, the writing seems random, haphazard, and disorganized. Therefore, good writing must be organized, where each sentence fits a larger context and relates to the sentences around it.

Transition Words

The writer should act as a guide, showing the reader how all the sentences fit together. Consider the seat belt example again:

> Seat belts save more lives than any other automobile safety feature. Many studies show that airbags save lives as well. Not all cars have airbags. Many older cars don't. Air bags aren't entirely reliable. Studies show that in 15% of accidents, airbags don't deploy as designed. Seat belt malfunctions are extremely rare.

There's nothing wrong with any of these sentences individually, but together they're disjointed and difficult to follow. The best way for the writer to communicate information is through the use of transition words. Here are examples of transition words and phrases that tie sentences together, enabling a more natural flow:

> To show causality: as a result, therefore, and consequently
> To compare and contrast: however, but, and on the other hand
> To introduce examples: for instance, namely, and including
> To show order of importance: foremost, primarily, secondly, and lastly

NOTE: This is not a complete list of transitions. There are many more that can be used; however, most fit into these or similar categories. The important point is that the words should clearly show the relationship between sentences, supporting information, and the main idea.

Here is an update to the previous example using transition words. These changes make it easier to read and bring clarity to the writer's points:

> Seat belts save more lives than any other automobile safety feature. Many studies show that airbags save lives as well; however, not all cars have airbags. For instance, some older cars don't. Furthermore, air bags aren't entirely reliable. For example, studies show that in 15% of accidents, airbags don't deploy as designed, but, on the other hand, seat belt malfunctions are extremely rare.

Also, test takers should be prepared to analyze whether the writer is using the best transition word or phrase for the situation. For example, the sentence: "As a result, seat belt malfunctions are extremely rare" doesn't make sense in the context above because the writer is trying to show the contrast between seat belts and airbags, not the causality.

Logical Sequence

Even if the writer includes plenty of information to support their point, the writing is only coherent when the information is in a logical order. First, the writer should introduce the main idea, whether for a paragraph, a section, or the entire piece. Then they should present evidence to support the main idea by using transitional language. This shows the reader how the information relates to the main idea and to the sentences around it. The writer should then take time to interpret the information, making sure necessary connections are obvious to the reader. Finally, the writer can summarize the information in a closing section.

Though most writing follows this pattern, it isn't a set rule. Sometimes writers change the order for effect. For example, the writer can begin with a surprising piece of supporting information to grab the reader's attention, and then transition to the main idea. Thus, if a passage doesn't follow the logical order, don't immediately assume it's wrong. However, most writing usually settles into a logical sequence after a nontraditional beginning.

Introductions and Conclusions

Examining the writer's strategies for introductions and conclusions puts the reader in the right mindset to interpret the rest of the text. Look for methods the writer might use for introductions such as:

> Stating the main point immediately, followed by outlining how the rest of the piece supports this claim.
>
> Establishing important, smaller pieces of the main idea first, and then grouping these points into a case for the main idea.
>
> Opening with a quotation, anecdote, question, seeming paradox, or other piece of interesting information, and then using it to lead to the main point.

Whatever method the writer chooses, the introduction should make their intention clear, establish their voice as a credible one, and encourage a person to continue reading.

Conclusions tend to follow a similar pattern. In them, the writer restates their main idea a final time, often after summarizing the smaller pieces of that idea. If the introduction uses a quote or anecdote to grab the reader's attention, the conclusion often makes reference to it again. Whatever way the writer chooses to arrange the conclusion, the final restatement of the main idea should be clear and simple for the reader to interpret. Finally, conclusions shouldn't introduce any new information.

Precision

People often think of precision in terms of math, but precise word choice is another key to successful writing. Since language itself is imprecise, it's important for the writer to find the exact word or words to convey the full, intended meaning of a given situation. For example:

> The number of deaths has gone down since seat belt laws started.

There are several problems with this sentence. First, the word *deaths* is too general. From the context, it's assumed that the writer is referring only to deaths caused by car accidents. However, without clarification, the sentence lacks impact and is probably untrue. The phrase "gone down" might be accurate, but a more precise word could provide more information and greater accuracy. Did the numbers show a slow and steady decrease of highway fatalities or a sudden drop? If the latter is true, the writer is missing a chance to make their point more dramatically. Instead of "gone down" they could substitute *plummeted*, *fallen drastically*, or *rapidly diminished* to bring the information to life. Also, the phrase "seat belt laws" is unclear. Does it refer to laws requiring cars to include seat belts or to laws requiring drivers and passengers to use them? Finally, *started* is not a strong verb. Words like *enacted* or *adopted* are more direct and make the content more real.

When put together, these changes create a far more powerful sentence:

> The number of highway fatalities has plummeted since laws requiring seat belt usage were enacted.

However, it's important to note that precise word choice can sometimes be taken too far. If the writer of the sentence above takes precision to an extreme, it might result in the following:

The incidence of high-speed, automobile accident related fatalities has decreased 75% and continued to remain at historical lows since the initial set of federal legislations requiring seat belt use were enacted in 1992.

This sentence is extremely precise, but it takes so long to achieve that precision that it suffers from a lack of clarity. Precise writing is about finding the right balance between information and flow. This is also an issue of conciseness (discussed in the next section).

The last thing to consider with precision is a word choice that's not only unclear or uninteresting, but also confusing or misleading. For example:

The number of highway fatalities has become hugely lower since laws requiring seat belt use were enacted.

In this case, the reader might be confused by the word *hugely*. Huge means large, but here the writer uses *hugely* to describe something small. Though most readers can decipher this, doing so disconnects them from the flow of the writing and makes the writer's point less effective.

Conciseness

"Less is more" is a good rule to follow when writing a sentence. Unfortunately, writers often include extra words and phrases that seem necessary at the time, but add nothing to the main idea. This confuses the reader and creates unnecessary repetition. Writing that lacks conciseness is usually guilty of excessive wordiness and redundant phrases. Here's an example containing both of these issues:

> When legislators decided to begin creating legislation making it mandatory for automobile drivers and passengers to make use of seat belts while in cars, a large number of them made those laws for reasons that were political reasons.

There are several empty or "fluff" words here that take up too much space. These can be eliminated while still maintaining the writer's meaning. For example:

> "Decided to begin" could be shortened to "began"
> "Making it mandatory for" could be shortened to "requiring"
> "Make use of" could be shortened to "use"
> "A large number" could be shortened to "many"

In addition, there are several examples of redundancy that can be eliminated:

> "Legislators decided to begin creating legislation" and "made those laws"
> "Automobile drivers and passengers" and "while in cars"
> "Reasons that were political reasons"

These changes are incorporated as follows:

> When legislators began requiring drivers and passengers to use seat belts, many of them did so for political reasons.

There are many general examples of redundant phrases, such as "add an additional," "complete and total," "time schedule," and "transportation vehicle." If asked to identify a redundant phrase on the test, look for words that are close together with the same (or similar) meanings.

Sentence Types

There are four ways in which we can structure sentences: simple, compound, complex, and compound-complex. Sentences can be composed of just one clause or many clauses joined together.

When a sentence is composed of just one clause (an independent clause), we call it a simple sentence. Simple sentences do not necessarily have to be short sentences. They just require one independent clause with a subject and a predicate. For example:

> Thomas marched over to Andrew's house.
>
> Jonah and Mary constructed a simplified version of the Eiffel Tower with Legos.

When a sentence has two or more independent clauses we call it a compound sentence. The clauses are connected by a comma and a coordinating conjunction—*and, but, or, nor, for*—or by a semicolon. Compound sentences do not have dependent clauses. For example:

> We went to the fireworks stand, and we bought enough fireworks to last all night.
>
> The children sat on the grass, and then we lit the fireworks one at a time.

When a sentence has just one independent clause and includes one or more dependent clauses, we call it a complex sentence:

> Because she slept well and drank coffee, Sarah was quite productive at work.
>
> Although Will had coffee, he made mistakes while using the photocopier.

When a sentence has two or more independent clauses and at least one dependent clause, we call it a compound-complex sentence:

> It may come as a surprise, but I found the tickets, and you can go to the show.
>
> Jade is the girl who dove from the high-dive, and she stunned the audience silent.

Sentence Fragments

Remember that a complete sentence must have both a subject and a verb. Complete sentences consist of at least one independent clause. Incomplete sentences are called sentence fragments. A sentence fragment is a common error in writing. Sentence fragments can be independent clauses that start with subordinating words, such as *but, as, so that,* or *because,* or they could simply be missing a subject or verb.

You can correct a fragment error by adding the fragment to a nearby sentence or by adding or removing words to make it an independent clause. For example:

> Dogs are my favorite animals. Because cats are too independent. (Incorrect; the word because creates a sentence fragment)
>
> Dogs are my favorite animals because cats are too independent. (Correct; the fragment becomes a dependent clause.)
>
> Dogs are my favorite animals. Cats are too independent. (Correct; the fragment becomes a simple sentence.)

Run-on Sentences

Another common mistake in writing is the run-on sentence. A run-on is created when two or more independent clauses are joined without the use of a conjunction, a semicolon, a colon, or a dash. We don't want to use commas where periods belong. Here is an example of a run-on sentence:

> Making wedding cakes can take many hours I am very impatient, I want to see them completed right away.

There are a variety of ways to correct a run-on sentence. The method you choose will depend on the context of the sentence and how it fits with neighboring sentences:

> Making wedding cakes can take many hours. I am very impatient. I want to see them completed right away. (Use periods to create more than one sentence.)
>
> Making wedding cakes can take many hours; I am very impatient—I want to see them completed right away. (Correct the sentence using a semicolon, colon, or dash.)
>
> Making wedding cakes can take many hours and I am very impatient, so I want to see them completed right away. (Correct the sentence using coordinating conjunctions.)
>
> I am very impatient because I would rather see completed wedding cakes right away than wait for it to take many hours. (Correct the sentence by revising.)

Dangling and Misplaced Modifiers

A modifier is a word or phrase meant to describe or clarify another word in the sentence. When a sentence has a modifier but is missing the word it describes or clarifies, it's an error called a dangling modifier. We can fix the sentence by revising to include the word that is being modified. Consider the following examples with the modifier italicized:

> *Having walked five miles,* this bench will be the place to rest. (Incorrect; this version of the sentence implies that the bench walked the miles, not the person.)
>
> *Having walked five miles,* Matt will rest on this bench. (Correct; in this version, *having walked five miles* correctly modifies *Matt*, who did the walking.)
>
> *Since midnight,* my dreams have been pleasant and comforting. (Incorrect; in this version, the adverb clause *since midnight* cannot modify the noun *dreams*.)

Since midnight, I have had pleasant and comforting dreams. (Correct; in this version, *since midnight* modifies the verb *have had*, telling us when the dreams occurred.)

Sometimes the modifier is not located close enough to the word it modifies for the sentence to be clearly understood. In this case, we call the error a misplaced modifier. Here is an example with the modifier italicized and the modified word in underlined.

We gave the hot <u>cocoa</u> to the children *that was filled with marshmallows.* (Incorrect; this sentence implies that the children are what are filled with marshmallows.)

We gave the hot <u>*cocoa*</u> *that was filled with marshmallows* to the children. (Correct; here, the cocoa is filled with marshmallows. The modifier is near the word it modifies.)

Parallelism and Subordination

<u>Parallelism</u>
To be grammatically correct we must use articles, prepositions, infinitives, and introductory words for dependent clauses consistently throughout a sentence. This is called parallelism. We use parallelism when we are matching parts of speech, phrases, or clauses with another part of the sentence. Being inconsistent creates confusion. Consider the following example.

Incorrect: Be ready for running and to ride a bike during the triathlon.

Correct: Be ready to run and to ride a bike during the triathlon.

Correct: Be ready for running and for riding a bike during the triathlon.

In the incorrect example, the gerund *running* does not match with the infinitive *to ride*. Either both should be infinitives or both should be gerunds.

<u>Subordination</u>
Sometimes we have unequal pieces of information in a sentence where one piece is more important than the other. We need to show that one piece of information is subordinate to the other. We can make the more important piece an independent clause and connect the other piece by making it a dependent clause. Consider this example:

Central thought: Kittens can always find their mother.

Subordinate: Kittens are blind at birth.

Complex Sentence: Despite being blind at birth, kittens can always find their mother.

The sentence "Kittens are blind at birth" is made subordinate to the sentence "Kittens can always find their mother" by placing the word "Despite" at the beginning and removing the subject, thus turning an independent clause ("kittens are blind at birth") into a subordinate phrase ("Despite being blind at birth").

Clauses

Clauses are groups of words within a sentence that have both a subject and a verb. We can distinguish a clause from a phrase because phrases do not have both a subject and a verb. There are several types of clauses; clauses can be independent or dependent and can serve as a noun, an adjective, or an adverb.

An *independent clause* could stand alone as its own sentence if the rest of the sentence were not there. For example:

The party is on Tuesday after the volleyball game is over.

I am excited to go to the party because my best friend will be there.

A *dependent clause*, or subordinating clause, is the part of the sentence that gives supportive information but cannot create a proper sentence by itself. However, it will still have both a subject and a verb; otherwise, it is a phrase. In the example above, *after the volleyball game is over* and *because my best friend will be there* are dependent because they begin with the conjunctions *after* and *because*, and a proper sentence does not begin with a conjunction.

Noun clauses are groups of words that collectively form a noun. Look for the opening words *whether, which, what, that, who, how,* or *why*. For example:

I had fun cooking *what we had for dinner last night.*

I'm going to track down *whoever ate my sandwich.*

Adjective clauses collectively form an adjective that modifies a noun or pronoun in the sentence. If you can remove the adjective clause and the leftovers create a standalone sentence, then the clause should be set off with commas, parentheses, or dashes. If you can remove the clause it is called nonrestrictive. If it can't be removed without ruining the sentence, then it is called restrictive and does not get set off with commas.

Jenna*, who hates to get wet,* fell into the pool. (Nonrestrictive)

The girl *who hates to get wet* fell into the pool. (Restrictive; the clause tells us which girl, and if removed there is confusion)

Adverbial clauses serve as an adverb in the sentence, modifying a verb, adjective, or other adverb. Look for the opening words *after, before, as, as if, although, because, if, since, so, so that, when, where, while,* or *unless.*

She lost her wallet after she left the theme park.

Her earring fell through the crack before she could catch it.

Phrases

A phrase is a group of words that go together but do not include both a subject and a verb. We use them to add information, explain something, or make the sentence easier for the reader to understand. Unlike clauses, phrases cannot ever stand alone as their own sentence if the rest of the sentence were not there. They do not form complete thoughts. There are noun phrases, prepositional phrases, verbal phrases, appositive phrases, and absolute phrases. Let's look at each of these.

Noun phrases: A noun phrase is a group of words built around a noun or pronoun that serves as a unit to form a noun in the sentence. Consider the following examples. The phrase is built around the underlined word. The entire phrase can be replaced by a noun or pronoun to test whether or not it is a noun phrase.

I like the chocolate chip ice cream. (I like it.)

I know all the shortest routes. (I know them.)

I met the best supporting actress. (I met her.)

Prepositional phrases: These are phrases that begin with a preposition and end with a noun or pronoun. We use them as a unit to form the adjective or adverb in the sentence. Prepositional phrases that introduce a sentence are called introductory prepositional phrases and are set off with commas.

I found the Frisbee *on the roof peak.* (Adverb; where it was found)

The girl *with the bright red hair* was prom queen. (Adjective; which girl)

Before the sequel, we wanted to watch the first movie. (Introductory phrase)

Verbal phrases: Some phrases look like verbs but do not serve as the verb in the sentence. These are called verbal phrases. There are three types: participial phrases, gerund phrases, and infinitive phrases.

Participial phrases start with a participle and modify nouns or pronouns; therefore, they act as the adjective in the sentence.

Beaten by the sun, we searched for shade to sit in. (Modifies the pronoun *we*)

The hikers, *being eaten by mosquitoes,* longed for repellant. (Modifies the noun *hikers*)

Gerund phrases often look like participles because they end in *-ing*, but they serve as the noun, not the adjective, in the sentence. Like any noun, we can use them as the subject or as the object of a verb or preposition in the sentence.

Eating green salad is the best way to lose weight. (Subject)

Sumo wrestlers are famous for *eating large quantities of food.* (Object)

Infinitive phrases often look like verbs because they start with the word *to,* but they serve as an adjective, adverb, or noun.

To survive the chill is the goal of the Polar Bear Plunge. (Noun)

A hot tub is at the scene *to warm up after the jump.* (Adverb)

The jumpers have hot cocoa *to drink right away.* (Adjective)

Appositive phrases: We can use any of the above types of phrases to rename nouns or pronouns, and we call this an appositive phrase. Appositive phrases usually appear either just before or just after the noun or pronoun they are renaming. Appositive phrases are essential when the noun or pronoun is too general, and they are nonessential when they just add information.

The two famous brothers Orville and Wilbur Wright invented the airplane. (Essential)

Sarah Calysta, *my great grandmother,* is my namesake. (Nonessential)

Absolute phrases: When a participle comes after a noun and forms a phrase that is not otherwise part of the sentence, it's called an absolute phrase. Absolute phrases are not complete thoughts and cannot stand alone because they do not have a subject and a verb. They are not essential to the sentence in that they do not explain or add additional meaning to any other part of the sentence.

The engine roaring, Jada closed her eyes and waited for the plane to take off.

The microphone crackling, the flight attendant announced the delayed arrival.

Parts of Speech

<u>Nouns</u>

A noun is a person, place, thing, or idea. All nouns fit into one of two types, common or proper.

A *common noun* is a word that identifies any of a class of people, places, or things. Examples include numbers, objects, animals, feelings, concepts, qualities, and actions. *A, an,* or *the* usually precedes the common noun. These parts of speech are called *articles*. Here are some examples of sentences using nouns preceded by articles.

A building is under construction.
The girl would like to move to *the* city.

A *proper noun* (also called a *proper name*) is used for the specific name of an individual person, place, or organization. The first letter in a proper noun is capitalized. "My name is *Mary*." "I work for *Walmart*."

Nouns sometimes serve as adjectives (which themselves describe nouns), such as "hockey player" and "state government."

- *An abstract noun is an idea, state, or quality. It is something that can't be touched, such as happiness, courage, evil, or humor.*

A concrete noun is something that can be experienced through the senses (touch, taste, hear, smell, see). Examples of concrete nouns are birds, skateboard, pie, and car.

A collective noun refers to a collection of people, places, or things that act as one. Examples of collective nouns are as follows: team, class, jury, family, audience, and flock.

Pronouns

A word used in place of a noun is known as a *pronoun*. Pronouns are words like *I, mine, hers,* and *us.*

Pronouns can be split into different classifications (see below) which make them easier to learn; however, it's not important to memorize the classifications.

- Personal pronouns: refer to people
- first person: we, I, our, mine
- second person: you, yours
- third person: he, them
- Possessive pronouns: demonstrate ownership (mine, my, his, yours)
- Interrogative pronouns: ask questions (what, which, who, whom, whose)
- Relative pronouns: include the five interrogative pronouns and others that are relative (whoever, whomever, that, when, where)
- Demonstrative pronouns: replace something specific (this, that, those, these)
- Reciprocal pronouns: indicate something was done or given in return (each other, one another)
- Indefinite pronouns: have a nonspecific status (anybody, whoever, someone, everybody, somebody)

Indefinite pronouns such as *anybody, whoever, someone, everybody,* and *somebody* command a singular verb form, but others such as *all, none,* and *some* could require a singular or plural verb form.

Antecedents

An *antecedent* is the noun to which a pronoun refers; it needs to be written or spoken before the pronoun is used. For many pronouns, antecedents are imperative for clarity. In particular, many of the personal, possessive, and demonstrative pronouns need antecedents. Otherwise, it would be unclear who or what someone is referring to when they use a pronoun like *he* or *this.*

Pronoun reference means that the pronoun should refer clearly to one, clear, unmistakable noun (the antecedent).

Pronoun-antecedent agreement refers to the need for the antecedent and the corresponding pronoun to agree in gender, person, and number. Here are some examples:

> The *kidneys* (plural antecedent) are part of the urinary system. *They* (plural pronoun) serve several roles."
>
> The kidneys are part of the *urinary system* (singular antecedent). *It* (singular pronoun) is also known as the renal system.

Pronoun Cases

The subjective pronouns —*I, you, he/she/it, we, they,* and *who*—are the subjects of the sentence.

> Example: *They* have a new house.

The objective pronouns—*me, you* (*singular*), *him/her, us, them,* and *whom*—are used when something is being done for or given to someone; they are objects of the action.

> Example: The teacher has an apple for *us.*

The possessive pronouns—*mine, my, your, yours, his, hers, its, their, theirs, our,* and *ours*—are used to denote that something (or someone) belongs to someone (or something).

Example: It's *their* chocolate cake.
Even Better Example: It's *my* chocolate cake!

One of the greatest challenges and worst abuses of pronouns concerns *who* and *whom*. Just knowing the following rule can eliminate confusion. *Who* is a subjective-case pronoun used only as a subject or subject complement. *Whom* is only objective-case and, therefore, the object of the verb or preposition.

Hint: When using *who* or *whom*, think of whether someone would say *he* or *him*. If the answer is *he*, use *who*. If the answer is *him*, use *whom*. This trick is easy to remember because *he* and *who* both end in vowels, and *him* and *whom* both end in the letter *M*.

<u>Verbs</u>
The *verb* is the part of speech that describes an action, state of being, or occurrence.

A *verb* forms the main part of a predicate of a sentence. This means that the verb explains what the noun (which will be discussed shortly) is doing. A simple example is *time <u>flies</u>*. The verb *flies* explains what the action of the noun, *time*, is doing. This example is a *main* verb.

Helping (*auxiliary*) verbs are words like *have, do, be, can, may, should, must,* and *will.* "I *should* go to the store." Helping verbs assist main verbs in expressing tense, ability, possibility, permission, or obligation.

Particles are minor function words like *not, in, out, up,* or *down* that become part of the verb itself. "I might *not*."

Participles are words formed from verbs that are often used to modify a noun, noun phrase, verb, or verb phrase.

The *running* teenager collided with the cyclist.

Participles can also create compound verb forms.

He is *speaking*.

Verbs have five basic forms: the *base* form, the *-s* form, the *-ing* form, the *past* form, and the *past participle* form.

The *past* forms are either *regular* (*love/loved; hate/hated*) or *irregular* because they don't end by adding the common past tense suffix "-ed" (*go/went; fall/fell; set/set*).

<u>Verb Forms</u>
Shifting verb forms entails *conjugation*, which is used to indicate *tense, voice,* or *mood.*

Verb tense is used to show when the action in the sentence took place. There are several different verb tenses, and it is important to know how and when to use them. Some verb tenses can be achieved by changing the form of the verb, while others require the use of helping verbs (e.g., *is, was,* or *has*).

Present tense shows the action is happening currently or is ongoing:

I walk to work every morning.

She is stressed about the deadline.

- *Past tense shows that the action happened in the past or that the state of being is in the past:*

I walked to work yesterday morning.

She was stressed about the deadline.

- *Future tense shows that the action will happen in the future or is a future state of being:*

I will walk to work tomorrow morning.

She will be stressed about the deadline.

- *Present perfect tense shows action that began in the past, but continues into the present:*

I have walked to work all week.

She has been stressed about the deadline.

- *Past perfect tense shows an action was finished before another took place:*

I had walked all week until I sprained my ankle.

She had been stressed about the deadline until we talked about it.

- *Future perfect tense shows an action that will be completed at some point in the future:*

By the time the bus arrives, I will have walked to work already.

Voice

Verbs can be in the active or passive voice. When the subject completes the action, the verb is in *active voice*. When the subject receives the action of the sentence, the verb is in *passive voice*.

Active: Jamie ate the ice cream.

Passive: The ice cream was eaten by Jamie.

In active voice, the subject (*Jamie*) is the "do-er" of the action (*ate*). In passive voice, the subject *ice cream* receives the action of being eaten.

While passive voice can add variety to writing, active voice is the generally preferred sentence structure.

Mood

Mood is used to show the speaker's feelings about the subject matter. In English, there is *indicative mood, imperative mood,* and *subjective mood*.

Indicative mood is used to state facts, ask questions, or state opinions:

Bob will make the trip next week.

When can Bob make the trip?

Imperative mood is used to state a command or make a request:

Wait in the lobby.

Please call me next week.

Subjunctive mood is used to express a wish, an opinion, or a hope that is contrary to fact:

If I were in charge, none of this would have happened.

Allison wished she could take the exam over again when she saw her score.

Adjectives

Adjectives are words used to modify nouns and pronouns. They can be used alone or in a series and are used to further define or describe the nouns they modify.

Mark made us a delicious, four-course meal.

The words *delicious* and *four-course* are adjectives that describe the kind of meal Mark made.

Articles are also considered adjectives because they help to describe nouns. Articles can be general or specific. The three articles in English are: a, an, and the.

Indefinite articles (a, an) are used to refer to nonspecific nouns. The article *a* proceeds words beginning with consonant sounds, and the article *an* proceeds words beginning with vowel sounds.

A car drove by our house.

An alligator was loose at the zoo.

He has always wanted a ukulele. (The first *u* makes a *y* sound.)

Note that *a* and *an* should only proceed nonspecific nouns that are also singular. If a nonspecific noun is plural, it does not need a preceding article.

Alligators were loose at the zoo.

The *definite article (the)* is used to refer to specific nouns:

The car pulled into our driveway.

Note that *the* should proceed all specific nouns regardless of whether they are singular or plural.

The cars pulled into our driveway.

Comparative adjectives are used to compare nouns. When they are used in this way, they take on positive, comparative, or superlative form.

The positive form is the normal form of the adjective:

Alicia is tall.

The *comparative* form shows a comparison between two things:

Alicia is taller than Maria.

Superlative form shows comparison between more than two things:

Alicia is the tallest girl in her class.

Usually, the comparative and superlative can be made by adding *–er* and *–est* to the positive form, but some verbs call for the helping verbs *more* or *most.* Other exceptions to the rule include adjectives like *bad,* which uses the comparative *worse* and the superlative *worst.*

An adjective phrase is not a bunch of adjectives strung together, but a group of words that describes a noun or pronoun and, thus, functions as an adjective. *Very ugly* is an adjective phrase; so are *way too fat* and *faster than a speeding bullet.*

Adverbs

Adverbs have more functions than adjectives because they modify or qualify verbs, adjectives, or other adverbs as well as word groups that express a relation of place, time, circumstance, or cause. Therefore, adverbs answer any of the following questions: *How, when, where, why, in what way, how often, how much, in what condition,* and/or *to what degree. How good looking is he? He is very handsome.*

Here are some examples of adverbs for different situations:

- how: quickly
- when: daily
- where: there
- in what way: easily
- how often: often
- how much: much
- in what condition: badly
- what degree: hardly

As one can see, for some reason, many adverbs end in *-ly.*

Adverbs do things like emphasize (*really, simply,* and *so*), amplify (*heartily, completely,* and *positively*), and tone down (*almost, somewhat,* and *mildly*).

Adverbs also come in phrases.

The dog ran as though his life depended on it.

Prepositions

Prepositions are connecting words and, while there are only about 150 of them, they are used more often than any other individual groups of words. They describe relationships between other words. They are placed before a noun or pronoun, forming a phrase that modifies another word in the sentence.

Prepositional phrases begin with a preposition and end with a noun or pronoun, the *object of the preposition. A pristine lake is <u>near the store</u> and <u>behind the bank</u>.*

Some commonly used prepositions are *about, after, anti, around, as, at, behind, beside, by, for, from, in, into, of, off, on, to,* and *with.*

Complex prepositions, which also come before a noun or pronoun, consist of two or three words such as *according to, in regards to,* and *because of.*

<u>Conjunctions</u>

Conjunctions are vital words that connect words, phrases, thoughts, and ideas. Conjunctions show relationships between components. There are two types:

Coordinating conjunctions are the primary class of conjunctions placed between words, phrases, clauses, and sentences that are of equal grammatical rank; the coordinating conjunctions are *or, and, nor, but, or, yes,* and *so*. A useful memorization trick is to remember that the first letter of these conjunctions collectively spell the word *fanboys*.

> I need to go shopping, *but* I must be careful to leave enough money in the bank.
> She wore a black, red, *and* white shirt.

Subordinating conjunctions are the secondary class of conjunctions. They connect two unequal parts, one *main* (or *independent*) and the other *subordinate* (or *dependent*). I must go to the store *even though* I do not have enough money in the bank.

> *Because* I read the review, I do not want to go to the movie.

Notice that the presence of subordinating conjunctions makes clauses dependent. *I read the movie* is an independent clause, but *because* makes the clause dependent. Thus, it needs an independent clause to complete the sentence.

<u>Interjections</u>

Interjections are words used to express emotion. Examples include *wow*, *ouch*, and *hooray*. Interjections are often separate from sentences; in those cases, the interjection is directly followed by an exclamation point. In other cases, the interjection is included in a sentence and followed by a comma. The punctuation plays a big role in the intensity of the emotion that the interjection is expressing. Using a comma or semicolon indicates less excitement than using an exclamation mark.

Capitalization Rules

Here's a non-exhaustive list of things that should be capitalized.

- the first word of every sentence
- the first word of every line of poetry
- the first letter of proper nouns (World War II)
- holidays (Valentine's Day)
- days of the week and months of the year (Tuesday, March)
- the first word, last word, and all major words in the titles of books, movies, songs, and other creative works (To Kill a Mockingbird, note that a is lowercase since it's not a major word, but to is capitalized since it's the first word of the title.
- titles when preceding a proper noun (President Roberto Gonzales, Aunt Judy)

When simply using a word such as president or secretary, though, the word is not capitalized.

Officers of the new business must include a *president* and *treasurer*.

Seasons—spring, fall, etc.—are not capitalized.

North, *south*, *east*, and *west* are capitalized when referring to regions but are not when being used for directions. In general, if it's preceded by *the* it should be capitalized.

I'm from the South.
I drove south.

End Punctuation

Periods (.) are used to end a sentence that is a statement (*declarative*) or a command (*imperative*). They should not be used in a sentence that asks a question or is an exclamation. Periods are also used in abbreviations, which are shortened versions of words.

- Declarative: The boys refused to go to sleep.
- Imperative: Walk down to the bus stop.
- Abbreviations: Joan Roberts, M.D., Apple Inc., Mrs. Adamson
- If a sentence ends with an abbreviation, it is inappropriate to use two periods. It should end with a single period after the abbreviation.

The chef gathered the ingredients for the pie, which included apples, flour, sugar, etc.

Question marks (?) are used with direct questions (*interrogative*). An *indirect question* can use a period:

Interrogative: When does the next bus arrive?

Indirect Question: I wonder when the next bus arrives.

An *exclamation point (!)* is used to show strong emotion or can be used as an *interjection*. This punctuation should be used sparingly in formal writing situations.

What an amazing shot!

Whoa!

Commas

A *comma* (,) is the punctuation mark that signifies a pause—breath—between parts of a sentence. It denotes a break of flow. Proper comma usage helps readers understand the writer's intended emphasis of ideas.

In a complex sentence—one that contains a subordinate (dependent) clause or clauses—separate the clauses with commas.

I will not pay for the steak, *because I don't have that much money*.

First, see how the purpose of each comma usage is to designate an interruption in flow. Then, notice how the last clause is dependent because it requires the earlier independent clauses to make sense.

Use a comma on both sides of an interrupting phrase.

I will pay for the ice cream, *chocolate and vanilla,* and I will eat it all myself.

The words forming the phrase in italics are nonessential (extra) information. To determine if a phrase is nonessential, try reading the sentence without the phrase and see if it's still coherent.

A comma is not necessary in this next sentence because no interruption—nonessential or extra information—has occurred. Read sentences aloud when uncertain.

I will pay for his chocolate and vanilla ice cream and I will eat it all myself.

If the nonessential phrase comes at the beginning of a sentence, a comma should only go at the end of the phrase. If the phrase comes at the end of a sentence, a comma should only go at the beginning of the phrase.

Other types of interruptions include the following:

- interjections: Oh no, I am not going.
- abbreviations: Barry Potter, M.D., specializes in heart disorders.
- direct addresses: Yes, Claudia, I am tired and going to bed.
- parenthetical phrases: His wife, lovely as she was, was not helpful.
- transitional phrases: Also, it is not possible.

The second comma in the following sentence is called an Oxford comma.

I will pay for ice cream, syrup, and pop.

It is a comma used after the second-to-last item in a series of three or more items. It comes before the word *or* or *and*. Not everyone uses the Oxford comma; it is optional, but many believe it is needed. The comma functions as a tool to reduce confusion in writing. So, if omitting the Oxford comma would cause confusion, then it's best to include it.

Commas are used in math to mark the place of thousands in numerals, breaking them up so they are easier to read. Other uses for commas are in dates (*March 19, 2016*), letter greetings (*Dear Sally,*), and in between cities and states (*Louisville, KY*).

Semicolons

A *semicolon (;)* is used to connect ideas in a sentence in some way. There are three main ways to use semicolons.

Link two independent clauses without the use of a coordinating conjunction:

I was late for work again; I'm definitely going to get fired.

Link two independent clauses with a transitional word:

The songs were all easy to play; therefore, he didn't need to spend too much time practicing.

Between items in a series that are already separated by commas or if necessary to separate lengthy items in a list:

> Starbucks has locations in Media, PA; Swarthmore, PA; and Morton, PA.
>
> Several classroom management issues presented in the study: the advent of a poor teacher persona in the context of voice, dress, and style; teacher follow-through from the beginning of the school year to the end; and the depth of administrative support, including ISS and OSS protocol.

Colons

A *colon* is used after an independent clause to present an explanation or draw attention to what comes next in the sentence. There are several uses.

Explanations of ideas:

> They soon learned the hardest part about having a new baby: sleep deprivation.

Lists of items:

> Shari picked up all the supplies she would need for the party: cups, plates, napkins, balloons, streamers, and party favors.

Time, subtitles, general salutations:

> The time is 7:15.
>
> I read a book entitled *Pluto: A Planet No More*.
>
> To whom it may concern:

Parentheses and Dashes

Parentheses are half-round brackets that look like this: *( )*. They set off a word, phrase, or sentence that is an afterthought, explanation, or side note relevant to the surrounding text but not essential. A pair of commas is often used to set off this sort of information, but parentheses are generally used for information that would not fit well within a sentence or that the writer deems not important enough to be structurally part of the sentence.

> The picture of the heart (see above) shows the major parts you should memorize.
> Mount Everest is one of three mountains in the world that are over 28,000 feet high (K2 and Kanchenjunga are the other two).

See how the sentences above are complete without the parenthetical statements? In the first example, *see above* would not have fit well within the flow of the sentence. The second parenthetical statement could have been a separate sentence, but the writer deemed the information not pertinent to the topic.

The dash (—) is a mark longer than a hyphen used as a punctuation mark in sentences and to set apart a relevant thought. Even after plucking out the line separated by the dash marks, the sentence will be intact and make sense.

> Looking out the airplane window at the landmarks—Lake Clarke, Thompson Community College, and the bridge—she couldn't help but feel excited to be home.

The dashes use is similar to that of parentheses or a pair of commas. So, what's the difference? Many believe that using dashes makes the clause within them stand out while using parentheses is subtler. It's advised to not use dashes when commas could be used instead.

Ellipses

An *ellipsis* (...) consists of three handy little dots that can speak volumes on behalf of irrelevant material. Writers use them in place of a word(s), line, phrase, list contents, or paragraph that might just as easily have been omitted from a passage of writing. This can be done to save space or to focus only on the specifically relevant material.

> Exercise is good for some unexpected reasons. Watkins writes, "Exercise has many benefits such as ...reducing cancer risk."

In the example above, the ellipsis takes the place of the other benefits of exercise that are more expected.

The ellipsis may also be used to show a pause in sentence flow.

> "I'm wondering...how this could happen," Dylan said in a soft voice.

Quotation Marks

Double *quotation marks* are used to at the beginning and end of a direct quote. They are also used with certain titles and to indicate that a term being used is slang or referenced in the sentence. Quotation marks should not be used with an indirect quote. Single quotation marks are used to indicate a quote within a quote.

> Direct quote: "The weather is supposed to be beautiful this week," she said.
>
> Indirect quote: One of the customers asked if the sale prices were still in effect.
>
> Quote within a quote: "My little boy just said 'Mama, I want cookie,'" Maria shared.

Titles: Quotation marks should also be used to indicate titles of short works or sections of larger works, such as chapter titles. Other works that use quotation marks include poems, short stories, newspaper articles, magazine articles, web page titles, and songs.

> "The Road Not Taken" is my favorite poem by Robert Frost.
>
> "What a Wonderful World" is one of my favorite songs.

Specific or emphasized terms: Quotation marks can also be used to indicate a technical term or to set off a word that is being discussed in a sentence. Quotation marks can also indicate sarcasm.

The new step, called "levigation", is a very difficult technique.

He said he was "hungry" multiple times, but he only ate two bites.

Use with other punctuation: The use of quotation marks with other punctuation varies, depending on the role of the ending or separating punctuation.

In American English, *periods* and *commas* always go inside the quotation marks:

"This is the last time you are allowed to leave early," his boss stated.

The newscaster said, "We have some breaking news to report."

Question marks or *exclamation points* go inside the quotation marks when they are part of a direct quote:

The doctor shouted, "Get the crash cart!"

When the question mark or exclamation point is part of the sentence, not the quote, it should be placed outside of the quotation marks:

Was it Jackie that said, "Get some potatoes at the store"?

Apostrophes

This punctuation mark, the apostrophe (') is a versatile mark. It has several different functions:

- Quotes: Apostrophes are used when a second quote is needed within a quote.
- In my letter to my friend, I wrote, "The girl had to get a new purse, and guess what Mary did? She said, 'I'd like to go with you to the store.' I knew Mary would buy it for her."
- Contractions: Another use for an apostrophe in the quote above is a contraction. I'd is used for I would.
- Possession: An apostrophe followed by the letter s shows possession (Mary's purse). If the possessive word is plural, the apostrophe generally just follows the word. Not all possessive pronouns require apostrophes.
- The trees' leaves are all over the ground.

Hyphens

The *hyphen* (-) is a small hash mark that can be used to join words to show that they are linked.

Hyphenate two words that work together as a single adjective (a compound adjective).

honey-covered biscuits

Some words always require hyphens, even if not serving as an adjective.

merry-go-round

Hyphens always go after certain prefixes like *anti-* & *all-*.

Hyphens should also be used when the absence of the hyphen would cause a strange vowel combination (*semi-engineer*) or confusion. For example, *re-collect* should be used to describe something being gathered twice rather than being written as *recollect*, which means to remember.

Subjects

Every sentence must include a subject and a verb. The *subject* of a sentence is who or what the sentence is about. It's often directly stated and can be determined by asking "Who?" or "What?" did the action:

Most sentences contain a direct subject, in which the subject is mentioned in the sentence.

> *Kelly mowed the lawn.*
>
> Who mowed the lawn? *Kelly*
>
> *The air-conditioner ran all night*
>
> What ran all night? *the air-conditioner*

The subject of imperative sentences is *you*, because imperative subjects are commands. the subject is implied because it is a command:

> *Go home after the meeting.*
>
> Who should go home after the meeting? *you* (implied)

In *expletive sentences* that start with "there are" or "there is," the subject is found after the predicate. The subject cannot be "there," so it must be another word in the sentence:

> *There is a cup sitting on the coffee table.*
>
> What is sitting on the coffee table? *a cup*

Simple and Complete Subjects

A *complete subject* includes the simple subject and all the words modifying it, including articles and adjectives. A *simple subject* is the single noun without its modifiers.

> A warm, chocolate-chip cookie sat on the kitchen table.
>
> Complete subject: *a warm, chocolate-chip cookie*
>
> Simple subject: *cookie*

The words *a, warm, chocolate,* and *chip* all modify the simple subject *cookie*.

There might also be a *compound subject*, which would be two or more nouns without the modifiers.

> A little girl and her mother walked into the shop.
>
> Complete subject: *A little girl and her mother*

Compound subject: *girl, mother*

In this case, *the girl and her mother* are both completing the action of walking into the shop, so this is a *compound subject*.

Predicates

In addition to the subject, a sentence must also have a predicate. The *predicate* contains a verb and tells something about the subject. In addition to the verb, a predicate can also contain a direct or indirect object, object of a preposition, and other phrases.

The cats napped on the front porch.

In this sentence, *cats* are the subject because they are who or what the sentence is about.

The *complete predicate* is everything else in the sentence: *napped on the front porch.* This phrase is the predicate because it tells us what the cats did.

This sentence can be broken down into a simple subject and predicate:

Cats napped.

In this sentence, *cats* are the simple subject, and *napped* is the *simple predicate*.

Although the sentence is very short and doesn't offer much information, it's still considered a complete sentence because it contains a subject and predicate.

Like a compound subject, a sentence can also have a ***compound predicate***. This is when the subject is or does two or more things in the sentence.

This easy chair reclines and swivels.

In this sentence, *this easy chair* is the complete subject. *Reclines and swivels* shows two actions of the chair, so this is the compound predicate.

Subject-Verb Agreement

The subject of a sentence and its verb must agree. The cornerstone rule of subject-verb agreement is that subject and verb must agree in number. Whether the subject is singular or plural, the verb must follow suit.

Incorrect: The houses is new.
Correct: The houses are new.
Also Correct: The house is new.

In other words, a singular subject requires a singular verb; a plural subject requires a plural verb. The words or phrases that come between the subject and verb do not alter this rule.

Incorrect: The houses built of brick is new.
Correct: The houses built of brick are new.

Incorrect: The houses with the sturdy porches is new.
Correct: The houses with the sturdy porches are new.

The subject will always follow the verb when a sentence begins with *here* or *there.* Identify these with care.

Incorrect: Here *is* the *houses* with sturdy porches.
Correct: Here *are* the *houses* with sturdy porches.

The subject in the sentences above is not *here*, it is *houses*. Remember, *here* and *there* are never subjects. Be careful that contractions such as *here's* or *there're* do not cause confusion!

Two subjects joined by *and* require a plural verb form, except when the two combine to make one thing:

Incorrect: Garrett and Jonathan is over there.
Correct: Garrett and Jonathan are over there.

Incorrect: Spaghetti and meatballs are a delicious meal!
Correct: Spaghetti and meatballs is a delicious meal!

In the example above, *spaghetti and meatballs* is a compound noun. However, *Garrett and Jonathan* is not a compound noun.

Two singular subjects joined by *or, either/or,* or *neither/nor* call for a singular verb form.

Incorrect: Butter or syrup are acceptable.
Correct: Butter or syrup is acceptable.

Plural subjects joined by *or, either/or,* or *neither/nor* are, indeed, plural.

The chairs or the boxes are being moved next.

If one subject is singular and the other is plural, the verb should agree with the closest noun.

Correct: The chair or the boxes are being moved next.
Correct: The chairs or the box is being moved next.

Some plurals of money, distance, and time call for a singular verb.

Incorrect: Three dollars *are* enough to buy that.
Correct: Three dollars *is* enough to buy that.

For words declaring degrees of quantity such as *many of, some of,* or *most of,* let the noun that follows *of* be the guide.

Incorrect: Many of the books is in the shelf.
Correct: Many of the books are in the shelf.

Incorrect: Most of the pie *are* on the table.
Correct: Most of the pie *is* on the table.

For indefinite pronouns like anybody or everybody, use singular verbs.

Everybody *is* going to the store.

However, the pronouns *few, many, several, all, some,* and *both* have their own rules and use plural forms.

Some *are* ready.

Some nouns like *crowd* and *congress* are called *collective nouns* and they require a singular verb form.

Congress *is* in session.
The news *is* over.

Books and movie titles, though, including plural nouns such as *Great Expectations*, also require a singular verb. Remember that only the subject affects the verb. While writing tricky subject-verb arrangements, say them aloud. Listen to them. Once the rules have been learned, one's ear will become sensitive to them, making it easier to pick out what's right and what's wrong.

Direct Objects

The *direct object* is the part of the sentence that receives the action of the verb. It is a noun and can usually be found after the verb. To find the direct object, first find the verb, and then ask the question *who* or *what* after it.

The bear climbed the tree.

What did the bear climb? *the tree*

Indirect Objects

An *indirect object* receives the direct object. It is usually found between the verb and the direct object. A strategy for identifying the indirect object is to find the verb and ask the questions *to whom/for whom* or *to what/ for what.*

Jane made her daughter a cake.

For whom did Jane make the cake? *her daughter*

Cake is the direct object because it is what Jane made, and *daughter* is the indirect object because she receives the cake.

Complements

A *complement* completes the meaning of an expression. A complement can be a pronoun, noun, or adjective. A verb complement refers to the direct object or indirect object in the sentence. An object complement gives more information about the direct object:

The magician got the kids excited.

Kids is the direct object, and *excited* is the object complement.

A *subject complement* comes after a linking verb. It is typically an adjective or noun that gives more information about the subject:

The king was noble and spared the thief's life.

Noble describes the *king* and follows the linking verb *was*.

Predicate Nouns

A *predicate noun* renames the subject:

John is a carpenter.

The subject is *John,* and the predicate noun is *carpenter*.

Predicate Adjectives

A *predicate adjective* describes the subject:

Margaret is beautiful.

The subject is *Margaret,* and the predicate adjective is *beautiful.*

Practice Prompt

Prepare an essay of about 300-600 words on the topic below.

Some people feel that sharing their lives on social media sites such as Facebook, Instagram, and Snapchat is fine. They share every aspect of their lives, including pictures of themselves and their families, what they ate for lunch, who they are dating, and when they are going on vacation. They even say that if it's not on social media, it didn't happen. Other people believe that sharing so much personal information is an invasion of privacy and could prove dangerous. They think sharing personal pictures and details invites predators, cyberbullying, and identity theft.

Write an essay to someone who is considering whether to participate in social media. Take a side on the issue and argue whether or not he/she should join a social media network. Use specific examples to support your argument.

CPSIA information can be obtained
at www.ICGtesting.com
Printed in the USA
LVOW04s1321201117
557016LV00019B/482/P

9 781628 454178